Jurisprudence

Themes and Concepts

Jurisprudence: Themes and Concepts takes an innovative approach to the study of jurisprudence. Drawing together a range of specialists making original contributions, it provides a summary, analysis and critique of basic themes in, and major contributions to, the study of jurisprudence.

The book explores issues and ideas in jurisprudence in a way that integrates them with legal study more broadly, avoiding the tendency in recent years for the subject to become overly inward-looking, specialist and technical. Since the approach taken is an interdisciplinary one, it also makes connections with contemporary issues in political and social theory – such as changing conceptions of sovereignty, globalisation, the role of rights, and the relationship of other forms of power to the legal realm – in order to situate current jurisprudential debates.

The book is divided into three parts: Law and Politics, Legal Reasoning, and Law and Modernity. Its coverage is therefore broad and links legal, political, philosophical and social analysis to wider contemporary concerns with which the study of jurisprudence should be engaged.

Scott Veitch, **Emilios Christodoulidis** and **Lindsay Farmer** teach jurisprudence at the University of Glasgow.

Jurisprudence

Themes and Concepts

Scott Veitch, Emilios Christodoulidis and Lindsay Farmer

With contributions from:

Gavin Anderson
Zenon Bankowski
Kay Goodall
Neil MacCormick

Routledge·Cavendish
Taylor & Francis Group
LONDON AND NEW YORK

First published 2007
by Routledge-Cavendish
2 Park Square, Milton Park, Abingdon, Oxon OX14 4RN, UK

Simultaneously published in the USA and Canada
by Routledge-Cavendish
270 Madison Ave, New York, NY 10016

*Routledge-Cavendish is an imprint of the Taylor & Francis Group,
an informa business*

© 2007 Scott Veitch, Emilios Christodoulidis and Lindsay Farmer
Transferred to Digital Printing 2008

Typeset in Times and Gill Sans by
RefineCatch Limited, Bungay, Suffolk
Printed and bound in Great Britain by
Cpod, Trowbridge, Wiltshire

British Library Cataloguing in Publication Data
A catalogue record for this book is available from the British Library

Library of Congress Cataloging-in-Publication Data
Jurisprudence : themes and concepts / edited by Scott Veitch,
Emilios Christodoulidis and Lindsay Farmer.
   p. cm.
   Includes index.
   ISBN 978-1-84568-070-1 (hardback : alk. paper) – ISBN 978-1-85941-815-4
(pbk. : alk. paper) 1. Jurisprudence. 2. Law–Philosophy. 3. Law–Political
aspects. 4. Rule of law I. Veitch, Scott. II. Christodoulidis, Emilios A. III. Farmer,
Lindsay, 1963-
   K237.J87 2007
   340–dc22   2007005432

ISBN10: 1-85941-815-5 (pbk)
ISBN10: 1-84568-070-7 (hbk)

ISBN13: 978-1-85941-815-4 (pbk)
ISBN13: 978-1-84568-070-1 (hbk)

Contents

Introduction

In a series of lectures delivered at the University of Glasgow beginning in 1762, Adam Smith, the Professor of Moral Philosophy, delineated the province of jurisprudence. He defined it in general terms as 'the theory of the rules by which civil governments ought to be directed', otherwise, 'the theory of the general principles of law and government' (Smith 1978, pp 5 and 398). This he saw as comprising four main objects: the maintenance of justice, the provision of police, the raising of revenue and the establishment of arms. What immediately strikes the modern reader of this definition is its breadth. He includes subjects such as taxation or police and security that obviously concern relations between state and citizen, but which are all too often viewed as purely technical areas of government. Just as importantly a theory of law and government for Smith requires that we attend not merely to matters of the definition or application of law, but also of how these relate to politics and the practice of governing. His approach to these questions is striking, for he approaches the topic with a method that is (in contemporary terms) both historical and sociological: that is to say that he is concerned with both the question of understanding the historical development of forms of law and government, and that of how it relates to stages of social and economic development of the society to be governed.

The contemporary study of jurisprudence rarely aspires to a comparable breadth in either subject matter or method. Anglo-American jurisprudence, indeed, has for a long time been more interested in law than government, has focused more on abstract rules than institutions, and has paid patchy attention to the historical or sociological context within which law and legal and political institutions develop. While we do not have the space here to address the question of why it has come about that the scope of province of jurisprudence has narrowed so dramatically, we would argue that the contemporary approach is too narrow and too technical. Thus it not only risks losing the interest of students, but more importantly risks undermining the relevance of the subject itself. The aim of this book, then, is to restore some of the breadth of subject matter and method that animated the studies of our illustrious predecessor here in the University of Glasgow.

Our starting point in this enterprise is that jurisprudence is the study of law and legal institutions in their historical, philosophical and political contexts. The study of law in this sense cannot be abstracted from the questions of the nature and theory of government; indeed, the two must necessarily be considered in their relation to each other. This book offers a range of competing interpretations of how the role of law is best understood, considering among other things the relation between law and politics, law and the economy, law and moral values, the role of judges in a democracy, and the virtues of the rule of law and threats to its realisation in practice. The book provides students with an introduction to and overview of the historical and philosophical development of understandings of a range of profoundly important social concerns, with the aim of enabling them to analyse and reflect on the role of law and legal practice more broadly.

These are complex issues that invite complex answers. We have attempted to navigate through the complexity by organising the material around three broad thematic axes: law and politics, legal reasoning, and law and modernity. The first seeks to locate the place of law within the study of institutions of government; the second examines the application of law in particular cases, with specific reference to the relation with other disciplines or rationalities; and the third attempts to place the study of law within the specific historical context of the development of modernity. We shall have more to say about each of these themes shortly, but before doing so, we want to say a little more about our 'thematic' approach to this subject.

All too often, in our experience, jurisprudence is taught in one of two ways. Either it is presented as a series of imaginary debates between positions or approaches that might at first glance seem to have little in common (natural law v positivism, conceptualism v realism, and so on), or it is taught as a stately progression from one great thinker to another (Bentham to Austin to Hart to Dworkin, and so on). The problem with the first approach is that it presents the debates in a rather abstract way, wrenching them out of any sort of context in which the debate might be considered meaningful. It is difficult (especially for a student encountering jurisprudence for the first time) to care much about the relative merits of natural law and positivism in the abstract, but when considered in the context of what they can say about different theories of sovereignty, of the relation between legal power and political power, or the day-to-day realities of judicial interpretation, the debates can become much more meaningful. Likewise, presenting ideas through the theories of thinkers who advanced them, can make the study of jurisprudence seem a hermetically sealed world, developing with reference only to its own history and where jurists engage only with other jurists. Against this we would argue that it is important to understand something of the historical context in which particular theories were developed, or of the problems of state and law that the theorists were addressing. Jurisprudence, in other words, should neither be understood nor taught as a purely abstract or philosophical subject. The most important jurists, and the major juris-prudential theories have much to say about the pressing legal and political issues of their, and our own, time.

The way in which we have sought to address these shortcomings in this book is to address theoretical debates and issues through the three broad themes and a series of 'sub-themes' and concepts. The themes lay out certain broad contexts within which questions of law and government should be considered; and sub-themes develop issues and debates, showing how particular debates, far from being abstract or distant from the 'real world' are often addressing matters of central political or legal concern. Our aim in doing this is to try and make the subject of jurisprudence easier to understand by relating it to the kind of subjects that are already being studied in the curriculum of the LLB. Thus, for example, we take concepts such as sovereignty or discrimination that already have an established place within the law curriculum, but address them in a way that seeks to broaden and deepen the issues around them, so that the student can see that they are not just matters of technical, positive law, but are also related to contemporary social and political issues.

This has three other consequence that we should note. We have, so far as possible, eschewed an approach that looks at the 'complete' theory of a particular philosopher, or indeed (within limits) an approach that looks at discrete thinkers at all. Instead, our thematic approach means that we focus primarily on issues, and thus what particular thinkers had to say about these issues, rather than addressing a corpus of thought. This means that the work of certain theorists, such as HLA Hart or Max Weber appear at different places in the book, where we might address different aspects of their overall theoretical positions in order to illuminate the topic under discussion. What is lost in the failure to cover the 'complete' theory, is hopefully made up for by the fact that we are able to present a range of positions in relation to the issue. This also has consequences for the way that certain concepts are addressed, as the thematic approach means that certain issues will appear more than once, in different sections of the book, and will be addressed differently in the light of the context established by the overall theme. Thus, for example, the issue of globalisation is discussed in relation to theories of sovereignty and the rule of law in Part I, but is then discussed again from the different perspective of theories of legal modernity in Part III. This should underline the point that there is not necessarily a single correct approach to an issue, but that the approach or understanding might depend on the context or perspective from which it is addressed. The third consequence relates to the range of issues covered. The book misses out certain issues that might normally be covered in a jurisprudence course – such as theories of punishment or responsibility – while also including others that are not, perhaps, part of the conventional course. This is not because we do not think that these things are important – far from it. However, in seeking to present a relatively short introduction to the subject we have preferred to focus on the issues that we take to be related to our three central themes – and which are also related to our own research and writing in the area. We are not so much setting out to define the scope of the subject, as to set out a method and themes that will whet the appetite of the student and hopefully lead them on to the fuller study of the subject.

In doing so we are thus moving away from what has become in recent decades an unfortunate tendency to channel jurisprudence through the distorting lens of analytical jurisprudence. This tendency has resulted both in an increasingly narrow specialisation which separates the study of jurisprudence from other disciplines, and its marginalisation from other parts of the law curriculum. By seeking to challenge these unhappy exclusions we hope to engage students' curiosity about the role and worth of law, its promises and its drawbacks, its history and the challenges it faces now and in the future.

The themes

As we have suggested above, each of the themes is intended to set out a broad framework or context within which we can address more specific issues about the role and function of law. Each broad theme thus sets out a general problematic – the relation between law and politics; the nature of legal reasoning or argumentation; law and modernity – and discusses a range of theoretical issues and perspectives. There is a certain logic to this approach for it is our starting point (with Smith) that a central aim of jurisprudence must be a theory of the general principles of law and government. Thus we begin by looking at the relationship between law and politics.

The articulation of law and politics is one of legal and political theory's most perplexing questions. On the one hand, law is an expression of political sovereignty, the product of political processes of will-formation and entrusted to the political apparatus of the state for its administration and enforcement. And yet at the same time it claims autonomy from politics, an objective meaning of its own, an expression of principle, even justice, somehow above and beyond the 'messy' world of politics. Moreover, in recent decades, legal organisation and society generally have seen massive shifts in the political landscape through the emergence of regional institutions such as the European Union, as well as the pressures that are associated with processes of globalisation. How law is involved in, and responds to, these developments requires scrutiny if we are to understand more fully the nature of the contemporary relationship between law and politics.

Under the second category we collect theories and issues that surround legal reasoning. The questions here are often more technical, but arguably no less political or controversial. The question is whether law invites and deploys a mode of reasoning that is peculiarly its own, characteristically involving the application of rules to cases, or whether and to what extent ethical and political concerns, perspectives and imperatives impact on legal reasoning. Again, the stakes are high, particularly given that there is a common expectation that legal rules, once instituted, are to be largely insulated from disagreements that we might call political or ethical, which might be thought to be more properly debated in the political rather than the legal domain. But if that is the case is a *politics of legal reasoning* feasible, and if yes, is it also desirable?

Finally, in the category of 'law and modernity' we take a step back into the sphere commonly referred to as the sociology of law, to ask more general questions about the role that law plays in society, its function in maintaining social structures and its role in realising the project of modernity. Here we attempt to place some of the issues that have been addressed in the first two sections of the book in a social and historical context. How, for example, has the relationship between law and politics, or the modern state, developed? How is this conception of the state related to the social and economic structures of society, and how might it change in the context of developments such as globalisation? The aim here is to question whether the projects and ends of modern law continue to be adequate in contemporary social conditions.

How to use this book

This book is introductory. We expect it to work as a point of departure rather than an end point in itself, particularly since not all that can wisely be covered in such a course of study is covered here. Rather our aim is to engage students new to the subject by providing some initial coverage of themes and concepts we think important, and by provoking them into pursuing further reflections and research on topics raised here, among others. We have, for that reason, not attempted to be comprehensive in our coverage, but to focus on issues and debates, and to connect these to more general themes.

Each part is divided into general themes and advanced topics. It is intended that the general themes provide an overview of central aspects of the subject under consideration. The advanced topics focus on more specific sets of problems, which develop in some detail aspects of the main themes. They are also pitched at a more advanced level and presuppose that the 'general themes' have already been covered.

Throughout all three parts we have provided readings that we see as indispensable to the comprehension of the text: these are set in 'boxes' in the 'general themes' and come at the end of each 'advanced' theme, along with further reading, which is aimed mainly for purposes of further research on the topic. Each part also contains a series of tutorials that might be used as the basis for discussion of issues covered in that part of the book. There are three types of tutorial, each of which is designed to encourage different types of skill in the student. The first type are problem-solving. These describe a scenario, often based on actual cases, and ask the student to think through certain issues as they are dramatised in the factual situation. The second type are aimed at developing skills in the critical reading of texts. We have either provided extracts from a text, such as a judgment, or have directed the student to a journal article or section from a book, and provided a series of questions that should assist the student in reading and analysing the text. The third type are more open-ended 'essay'-style questions, in response to suggested readings either from this book or other texts. These can provide the basis for classroom discussion, or alternatively students might be asked to prepare presentations on the basis of the questions. Finally we should note that there are two levels of tutorials. The first type are introductory in scope and are related only to issues covered in the general section of each part; the second type are identified as advanced level tutorials and are better suited to those courses which are exploring issues in greater depth and complexity. These might relate to the advanced topics, or offer a more advanced engagement with issues covered in the general topics.

The book can thus be used in a number of different ways. It is intended primarily as a textbook for a basic course on jurisprudence, which could focus on the three themes, allowing the teacher either to address the tutorials and advanced topics included in the book or to introduce their own according to their own interests. The purpose of the book here is thus to provide the student with a basic introduction to some central issues in jurisprudence and to encourage them to tackle some of the primary texts in the area. Alternatively, the book may be used in a more advanced course, focusing primarily on the advanced topics, where we have given both an overview of the issues and sufficient guidance that they can go on and read some of the primary texts.

There is of course no correct way to use the book; our main hope is that students find it lively and interesting and that it stimulates them to read more widely in the subject.

Reference

Smith, A, 1978, *Lectures on Jurisprudence*, RL Meek, DD Raphael and PG Stein (eds) Oxford: Oxford University Press.

Acknowledgements and attributions

Many people have contributed to and assisted in the writing of this book, often unwittingly. These include the Jurisprudence classes in the Universities of Glasgow and Edinburgh where the themes have been tried out over a period of several years, and where some of the materials were first prepared for students. We are grateful to both students and colleagues on these courses for their forbearance and understanding. The more substantial contributions of certain colleagues are recognised in the attributions below.

Our greatest debt, however, is to Beverley Brown. As a teacher she instilled in each of us both an interest in the topic of jurisprudence and a questioning attitude. Subsequently, as an editor at Cavendish, she was instrumental in commissioning this book and in encouraging us to work out its distinctive approach. We would like to thank her here for her support and friendship over many years

SV/EC/LF
February 2007
Glasgow

In Part I, sections 1.1–1.3 and 2.5 were written by Neil MacCormick. Sections 1.4 and 2.1 were written by Zenon Bankowski. Sections 1.5 and 2.3 were written by Gavin Anderson.

In Part II, section 2.4 was written by Kay Goodall, who also contributed to the writing of 1.1.

In Part III, sections 1.4 and 2.1 were written by Gavin Anderson.

All remaining parts were written by the editors. They too are alone responsible for the organisation of the book.

Contributors

Gavin Anderson is Senior Lecturer in Law at the University of Glasgow.

Zenon Bankowski is Professor of Legal Theory at the University of Edinburgh.

Emilios Christodoulidis is Professor of Legal Theory at the University of Glasgow.

Lindsay Farmer is Professor of Law at the University of Glasgow.

Kay Goodall is Senior Lecturer in Law at the University of Stirling.

Neil MacCormick is Regius Professor of Public Law and the Law of Nature and Nations at the University of Edinburgh.

Scott Veitch is Reader in Law at the University of Glasgow.

Abbreviations

Part I
Chapter 1

EC	European Community (or Commission)
ECHR	European Convention on Human Rights
ECJ	European Court of Justice
EEC	European Economic Community
EU	European Union
MP	Member of Parliament
UDHR	Universal Declaration of Human Rights
UK	United Kingdom
UN	United Nations
US	United States

Chapter 2

ECHR	European Convention on Human Rights
EU	European Union
GDP	gross domestic product
ICC	International Criminal Court
MEP	Member of European Parliament
NGO	nongovernmental organisation
TRC	Truth and Reconciliation Commission (S Africa)
UK	United Kingdom
US	United States
WTO	World Trade Organization

Part II
Chapter 1

CLS	Critical legal studies
UK	United Kingdom
US	United States

Chapter 2

BNP	British National Party
EAT	Employment Appeals Tribunal
EOC	Equal Opportunities Commission
EU	European Union
PVS	persistent vegetative state
UK	United Kingdom

Part III
Chapter 1

EU	European Union
NGO	nongovernmental organisation
WTO	World Trade Organization

Chapter 2

ADR	alternative dispute resolution
EU	European Union
IMF	International Monetary Fund
ISA	Ideological State Apparatuses
PFI	private finance initiatives
PPP	public private partnerships
UK	United Kingdom
UNIDROIT	International Institute for the Unification of Private Law (Fr)
US	United States
WB	World Bank
WTO	World Trade Organization

Part I

Law and politics

Chapter 1

General themes

1.1 Introduction to the relationship between law and politics

1.1.1 On power – political power and legal power

Law and politics both concern power – power relations and the exercise of power. They interact in many important ways. Yet, they are distinct. They differ because they involve different kinds of power. All power is relational, so the task is first to identify the element common to all kinds of power relation, and next to identify the elements.

Common is the idea of a relationship such that one person, group or corporate entity is able to affect some other persons, groups or entities in their reasons for acting and indeed in how they act. To have interpersonal power is to be able to get somebody to act in ways s/he would not otherwise choose to do. This is done by manipulating in some way the reasons in response to which other people govern their actions. If I care for my bodily safety, and you credibly threaten me with physical violence unless I act in a certain way, you give me reason to act in that way, though it is perhaps an action I would not otherwise consider performing. That is a case of coercive physical power. If you have control of economic resources to which I need to have access, and you grant me access to them only on condition of my acting in a certain way, you exercise economic power. Your decisions materially affect my reasons for acting and thus my possible decisions and courses of action. In as many ways as one person can, by virtue of general features of their position, affect the reasons others have for acting, and can thus affect the way they act, so many are the kinds or forms of power. Yet all those we have considered so far concern one's ability in fact to change reasons for acting because of physical or economic or other relations actually existing between people.

A different case is where some 'ought propositions' or 'norms', apply to a person, and these include norms according to which one person or set of persons ought to act in accordance with decisions of another person. The latter can then, by announcing appropriate decisions, give the former new reasons for acting, namely, reasons to act in accordance with the announced decision. Such is a case of power that is normative in character. Where some person has a standing or position that enables him or her under a certain normative conception to govern others' reasons for acting over a determined range of issues, that person has normative power or 'authority', over those others in respect of those issues. The biblical commandment to 'honour thy father and mother' can be interpreted as implying that children ought to be governed by the commands, requests and guidance given to them by their parents. So understood, it implies a normative power of parents over children, as a matter of God's law, or of the moral law, or whatever one takes to be the character of the commandments. A constitution that grants competence to a legislature to make laws concerning the peace, order and good government of a country, similarly confers normative power on the legislature over everyone who is subject to that constitution.

In some settings, interest in power relations focuses primarily on the question of how far and by what means one person or group can in fact bring about certain courses of conduct by others, by virtue of some standing feature of the persons involved and the relations between them. Political power is an idea best explicated along those lines. Political power consists in being able in fact to exercise effective governance within a defined territory, through manipulating the reasons other people have for acting, and thus affecting their action so as to bring about desired rather than undesired behaviour within the subject group.

In other perspectives, the question is not so much who can in fact do certain things, but who has the right to do so. The latter question amounts to asking whose rules or commands ought to be obeyed if issued on certain subjects and following prescribed procedures. Such a person has a position defined by some normative order empowering them in this normative, rather than factual, sense to lay down what others must receive as, for them, valid or binding norms or reasons for action. Here, what is in issue is authority; power in its normative form. Legal power, that is, legal authority is normative in character, for laws are essentially normative in character.

Of course, any separation between legal and political power is purely conceptual. If no one pays any attention to the acts and decisions of a person claiming to exercise ultimate legal authority on some matter, the claim becomes an empty one. There can be no real legal authority without some political power. Conversely, the prospects of exercising political power over any extensive territory are highly dependent on some sense of legitimacy, and legitimacy is largely, though not exclusively, a matter of holding a legal-constitutional position of authority. So there is rarely real political power without some legal authority. This is mutual interdependence, not conceptual identity.

For a development of these themes see MacCormick (1999) ch 8.

1.1.2 Making power safe: the separation of powers and the constitutional state

In contemporary constitutional states, political activity concerns competition for and, for successful competitors, exercise of, elective office, which in turn involves the exercise of power. Election may be either to membership of a legislature or to executive office. In parliamentary systems such as that of Germany, the United Kingdom (UK), Italy or Ireland, executive office is achieved through the securing of a majority in the legislature and is held by the leaders of the largest party. In presidential systems, such as in France or the United States (US), election to the highest executive office is by direct election, and the legislature with its elected members is more clearly separated from the executive than in parliamentary systems. In parliamentary systems, the headship of state is a mainly ceremonial office, whether held by an elected president or by a hereditary monarch. Kings or queens and presidents may, however, have considerable influence by virtue of their public standing, and sometimes have particular duties in respect of safeguarding the constitution itself.

The legislature and the executive are two of the great branches of government in constitutional states. The third is the judiciary. Maintaining some form of separation between these three branches has long been understood to be a necessity for the sake of free (rather than tyrannical) government. The tasks of the three branches are those of:

- making law and keeping the executive under scrutiny – the legislature;
- executive government concerned with the pursuit of public policy in implementation of the law or otherwise within a legal framework – the executive;
- adjudication aimed at upholding the law, both in disputes between private persons and in matters involving private persons and public authorities – the judiciary.

Some, not necessarily perfect or complete, separation of these powers among different persons and institutions is a defining feature of the constitutional state. Democratic forms of election to public office as a member of the legislature or as the chief or a member of the executive government, though not (with a few exceptions) to judicial office, have also come to be a feature of these states. Fully democratic electoral systems, based on 'one person one vote', emerged later than the separation of powers, and would be all but impossible to achieve or sustain in other circumstances.

All states, whether or not conforming to this constitutional pattern, have five essential characteristics: (a) they have a *territory*, over which they claim to exercise effective control by the use, if necessary, of coercive force against external and internal threats; (b) they claim that this territorial control is *legitimate*, in that their governing authorities exercise it as of right on some moral-cum-political ground; (c) they claim universal *jurisdiction* within the territory, involving authority to make laws and to try all allegations of crime and legal disputes arising within it; (d) they claim *independence*, on the ground that the people of the state are entitled to a form of government free from external interference by other states; (e) *recognition* of these claims to territoriality, legitimacy and independence is accorded by other states. In international law, indeed, a state is defined as a territory with a *recognised and effective government*, and each state is entitled to respect under the principle of mutual non-interference.

Government concerns the maintenance of order and the pursuit of some conception of a common good or of the public interest of the state and its citizens. Where the separation of powers is maintained in any of its possible versions, the activities of the executive branch of government and of law-enforcement agencies such as the police are carried out under general rules that are the responsibility of the legislature. The legislature can also hold the executive to account politically. So far as concerns the legality of all exercises of governmental power, the judiciary has a final say upon what are the limits of the law laid down by the legislature or contained in a constitution itself. In short, there are rules that permit official use of force in reasonably defined circumstances, and these rules also prohibit non-official uses of force save in exceptional cases of self-defence. By this means, the state acquires a monopoly of the legitimate use of coercive force in its territory – not that such a legal monopoly is ever fully effective in real life. States can thus be identified primarily in territorial and political terms, but the idea of legitimacy and of mutual recognition has a basis in international law as this emerged in the period subsequent to the Peace of Westphalia of 1648, and came to be expressed by theorists of international law starting with De Vattel in 1758 (see Vattel 1883). (In a slightly anachronistic way, it has become common to describe states in the form they had acquired by the twentieth century as 'Westphalian' states.)

The 'Rule of Law' is the ideal according to which all political and governmental power is in fact exercised under rules of law. Yet obviously effective government cannot just be a matter of 'rule following' – it calls for statesmanship and political commitment, and its ends are expressed in political programmes, not legal codes. A constitution, whether a formally adopted constitutional text, or a mixed body of law and custom such as makes up UK constitutional law, has to designate the functions of various office holders and the method of their election or appointment to office. It must leave considerable scope to the discretion and judgement of those exercising the various offices of state. Yet at the same time it must enable them to exercise effective checks and balances to prevent the holder of any one of the powers of state from coming, in fact, to enjoy unlimited power rather than the defined, but extensive, power the constitution confers. This means that the legislature, in further empowering the executive or in regulating its powers must never grant unlimited discretion, and the courts must exercise scrutiny of governmental conduct to ensure that limits are respected. When that is so, it is possible for the conduct of the affairs of state to be genuinely carried on under law.

In this context, citizens – and indeed everyone within the jurisdiction – can have confidence that their activities will be judged in accordance only with established rules and principles of law. Thus their personal liberty and liberty to conduct business affairs is subject to restraint, only by virtue of legal powers clearly vested in persons acting with the authority of the state under the constitution or under legislation as interpreted by the judges in courts of law. Civil liberty in a free society depends on respect for the rule of law. Citizenship is above all concerned with the right to participate in the political processes of a state, at least by the exercise of the vote, and by the opportunity to participate in political and non-political organisations within the 'civil society' which the state sustains.

On the idea of 'making politics safe' see MacCormick (1989) and (2007) chs 10 and 11. For a fuller treatment of citizenship see below (Part I 2.2).

1.1.3 Jurisdiction, state and legal system

All this presupposes that law can be considered as a kind of normative order – that is, it is concerned with providing or maintaining a basis for order in human conduct and affairs, through reference to standards of conduct that lay down how people ought to or must behave. Law is also (in several senses) *institutional*, for it is made or reformed by legislatures, implemented by executive agencies and law-enforcement officials, subjected to adjudication by courts, and practised by separate bodies of professionals such as solicitors and advocates. When a court finally reaches judgment, that judgment is coercively enforceable by relevant processes using specialised agencies, depending on whether criminal penalties or civil remedies are in issue.

The law of modern states is thus also coercive in character, with the executive and enforcement agencies of the state exercising physical force (and claiming a monopoly on the legitimate exercise of such force) to ensure implementation of judgments by the courts, based on laws laid down by legislatures or developed through judicial precedent. State law is thus normative (concerning what ought to be or must be done or omitted) and institutional, as well as coercive – implemented by physical force used along with a claim that this is a monopoly of legitimate force.

The *system* element depends on the way in which the activities and practices of the institutions and agencies hang together in a relatively coherent way. This depends on the institutions acknowledging a common body of constitutional or sub-constitutional rules and principles that empower each of them to act as they do and that seek to co-ordinate their activity, as well as regulating and empowering conduct of citizens. Where the 'separation of powers' exists the 'Rule of Law' is possible, in that each of the institutions keeps or is kept to carrying out functions only in accordance with established law, taking action against citizens only when empowered by law and only in case of violation of the law by citizens. In this context a vital role falls to the courts as the final interpreters of the rules that confer legal power and authority on all the institutions, including the courts themselves.

All the relevant rules and principles of conduct can be seen as systematically interrelated because the courts, especially the highest courts, accept it as obligatory to implement only rules that satisfy common criteria concerning their origin or content. They do so in accordance with a shared interpretation of the relevant criteria. This view of 'system' is thus dependent on a court-centered view of law (other views are possible, for example, those focusing on legislatures, or the democratic underpinnings of a legislature's position). But the court-centered view is appropriate to those who study legal systems as such. This branch of study is essentially court-oriented, though legal systems are also dependent on the legislature for its output of enacted rules. Otherwise, activity within the legislature, and the interaction of legislature and executive, belong more to the political system than to the legal, though they do have to work within the given legal–constitutional framework.

Since states are territorial in character, their legal systems have also a geographical or territorial extent (what Hans Kelsen called a 'spatial sphere' of validity). This can be quite complex and layered, as one can illustrate by reference, for example, to the UK. There are three internal jurisdictions, namely England and Wales, Scotland and Northern Ireland. The legal system applicable in each internal jurisdiction (English law, Scots law, or Northern Irish law) comprises all those rules that the relevant courts are obligated to apply in trials and lawsuits arising within their jurisdiction. Some of these rules are peculiar to one region alone, deriving from institutional writings, from precedents of regional courts, or laws passed by the regional legislature. Others derive from legislation of the central legislature – the UK Parliament – expressed as having specific regional application. There are also rules laid down by that Parliament, which establish common rules applicable generally throughout the whole UK, or derived from precedents of courts exercising a similarly comprehensive jurisdiction.

As a Member State of the European Union (EU), which is a form of supra-national legal order, the UK is bound to observe the treaties establishing the

European Community and EU and any regulations or directives validly made under these treaties. Hence, the rules that UK courts must recognise as binding include those laid down in the treaties or in the exercise of legislative powers that they confer. Such rules are, in principle, EU-wide in their application, so laws binding in the UK are also binding in the same terms on all other member states (though EU directives normally have to be incorporated into national law by specific legislative acts, and these may tailor general provisions to local conditions).

Most European states have also agreed to be bound by the rules laid down in the Council of Europe's European Convention for the Protection of Human Rights and Fundamental Freedoms, which is a binding treaty under international law. It applies even more widely throughout Europe than just in the EC/EU. This is not 'supranational law' in the same sense as the law of the EU and Community. Since the Convention is an international treaty, its rules about fundamental rights do not have automatic direct applicability in states that are parties to it. This comes about only to the extent that a country's national constitutional law (as in the Netherlands) makes them so applicable, or to the extent that this is achieved by specific national legislation (as in the UK's Human Rights Act 1998, together with the Scotland Act 1998). In the contemporary world, states (especially in Europe) tend to have a complex and layered form of legal geography. The illustration of this given here in respect of the UK and its several internal jurisdictions, applies to all other member states of the EU in respect of the nesting of the national legal system within Community law and Convention law on human rights. In all the larger states with forms of federation or internal autonomies or schemes of devolution there is an internal geographical complexity analogous to that of the UK. Everywhere, a specific set of courts with a hierarchical structure of appeals lies at the heart of the legal system or subsystem, which is both the framework of their work and yet also its output.

> On institutional normative orders see MacCormick (1999) ch 1 and (2007) chs 1–3. For a concise statement of Kelsen's thought on these matters see Kelsen (1992), chs V and VIII.

1.2 Sovereignty

1.2.1 Sovereignty: a contested concept

Sovereignty, like so many terms that straddle the boundary between law and politics, is a concept denoting a cluster of related ideas rather than one single clearly defined one. Moreover, in nearly all its clustered elements, it is a contested concept, in the sense that different theoretical approaches dispute over its correct explanation or definition, usually also disagreeing about its practical relevance. Sometimes it is used mainly in a political sense, to denote a kind of untrammelled power of rulers over those they rule. Sometimes it is conceived of in legal terms, as a kind of supreme normative power or highest possible legal authority. It is not even agreed what kind of entity it primarily applies to. Some treat it as an attribute of a person, or entity or agency within a state, such as an emperor, a king, a dictator, or a parliament. Some treat it as an attribute primarily of the state itself – a 'sovereign state' being one that is fully self-governing and independent of external control. Some treat it as mainly belonging to the people of a territory, on the ground that they are ultimate and self-governing masters of the institutions of the state established there. 'We the people' adopt a constitution and establish a state with constituted organs of government, limited by the terms of our grant of power to them. Thereafter, 'we' can exercise our sovereignty only through the constitutionally established organs of government, with their powers divided and limited according to the constitution whereby 'we' established them. Alternatively, but only in accordance with constitutionally prescribed procedures, we can exercise the constitutional power of constitutional amendment. In the moment of its exercise, absolute popular sovereignty transforms itself into limited constitutional sovereignty.

1.2.2 Attributing sovereignty – to whom or what?

However that may be, there could be other possible points of attribution of sovereignty apart from 'the people'. One starting point that seems useful towards figuring out some features of the clusters of related-but-contested concepts is the English common lawyers' view of the sovereignty of the UK Parliament. This affords one striking instance of the ascription of sovereignty to an entity within a state. Strictly, this is sovereignty of a composite body, namely, 'the Queen in Parliament', which is the monarch acting in procedurally fixed ways along with the two Houses of Parliament – the Lords and the Commons. With the growth and eventual triumph of democracy as the underlying ideology of governance, however, the House of Commons has become the predominant element in this composite sovereign. At the same time, the electoral power of political parties in a system of representative democracy gives party whips and party leaders in normal circumstances a tight grip on the voting behaviour of individual Members of Parliament (MPs). Hence, when a party has a comfortable majority in the House of Commons, its leader, as Prime Minister, can, with the support of a Cabinet, each of whose members is appointed and can be dismissed by that same Prime Minister, acquire a personally predominant position.

Parliamentary sovereignty becomes a highly concentrated form of power at the disposal, temporarily at least, of a single political leader.

One of the most sophisticated and influential jurisprudential accounts of the sovereignty of the 'Queen in Parliament' in the United Kingdom remains Hart (1961); see especially chs IV–VI. cf. MacCormick (1999) ch 4.

Legal parliamentary sovereignty may thus have developed almost to the point of placing the political powers of an 'elective dictatorship' in the hands of a Prime Minister. (The term 'elective dictatorship' was coined by Lord Hailsham of St Marylebone as a way of characterising the real working of the contemporary constitution as early as in the 1970s.) If so, this represents the partial recurrence of an idea to its earlier origins, when the personal dominance of a single ruler was at stake, though doubtless at a time prior to the emergence of anything exactly like sovereignty or the state in their modern usages. After the Norman Conquest of 1066 and the imposition of a feudal form of government on England, a sovereign monarchy came into existence. It was grounded on the military power and formidable organisation of king and feudal tenants-in-chief, who were, however, circumvented through the device of oaths of fealty to the king demanded of subordinate feudal tenants. The sovereign dominion exercised by feudal monarchs who achieved their position by conquest of a territory and its inhabitants finds a paradigm example in the English case. Government, though appealing to underlying ideas of right, was secured by force so far as necessary. Over time, ideas of underlying right became more explicit, and were expressed as being the law and custom of the realm, the 'common law'. Successor monarchs came to occupy a position that was in some measure conditional on the common law. Kings and queens became dependent to some extent on what remained a largely aristocratic Parliament.

After many struggles – the Revolution of 1688–89, the Treaty and Acts of Union of 1706–07, and the practices of governance that became accepted under the Hanoverian monarchs starting with George I in 1714 – it was brought about that monarchs finally became constitutionally subordinate, for most purposes, to Parliament. Sovereignty thereby shifted from the monarch-in-parliament to Parliament itself, then to the democratically elected house of the Parliament, and finally, in a conditional way, to the political leader of the majority party in that house so long as s/he commanded the loyalty of the majority party. Parliamentary sovereignty meant the legally unlimited power of Parliament to enact any law it chooses, except one that would have the effect of binding later parliaments; but what the law ascribed to Parliament was politically exercisable in a much more autocratic way.

The jurisprudential reflection of all this is found in the legal positivism of Jeremy Bentham and John Austin, which exercised so powerful a hold on the British juristic imagination during much of the nineteenth and twentieth centuries. They were building to a great extent on ideas originally advanced by Thomas Hobbes in the context of a very minimalist view about natural law – law in a state of nature. In such a state, he contended, people would effectively face a war of all against all with no binding rules among them, and the only way out would be to agree on having a sovereign with absolute power to make and enforce rules establishing and protecting rights and property. While Bentham and Austin rejected the fiction of the state of nature and the social contract as a way out of it, they nonetheless argued for the thesis that law always depends on some sovereign person or assembly of persons whom others in a certain territory do in fact habitually obey, for whatever reason. Laws then are whatever the sovereign issues by way of general commands.

Hobbes's argument is famously made in Hobbes (1996), especially chs XIII–XXI. For Austin's account see Austin (1954). On the 'Benthamite Constitution' see MacCormick (1999) ch 5.

Not all countries under monarchical rule acknowledged their monarchy as dependent on conquest. Scotland, before the Union of 1707, was home to the idea (never uncontested, as one must acknowledge) of kingship by consent, developing out of older tribal or clan-based forms of rule. Here, we can discern in primitive form the idea of a monarchy that was in a genuine, if somewhat crude sense, covenant-based or social-contractual. Leaders of clans or communities could in a sense agree on behalf of the whole to the exercise of limited but essential powers of governance by members of a traditionally acknowledged ruling family. This originally even involved some form of restricted election from within the royal kin-group, and only subsequently became strictly hereditary by primogeniture. In such a conception of kingship, the position of a king is not even in principle that of a holder of untrammelled sovereign power. A misruling king or queen who becomes in effect a tyrant is deemed to be lawfully removable, and is subject to lawful resistance by the people. Power is by delegation from the 'community of the realm', or the people as a whole. Hence it may be considered that sovereignty finally belongs to the people themselves, rather than the rulers they acknowledge as their governors in peace and leaders in war.

Such views of the Scottish kingdom, advanced by theorists like George Buchanan with reference to Queen Mary's deposition from the Scottish throne in 1566, were taken up in the following century by English opponents of royal absolutism and of the 'divine right of kings'. (The latter, incidentally, was enthusiastically propounded by the Scottish king, James VI, in refutation of the views of his erstwhile tutor Buchanan, and on his becoming King James I of England in 1603, he applied it with a firm brush to the broader canvas of his new southern kingdom. This must be accounted one among the causes of the civil wars that broke out against his son and successor, Charles I, who acted on more or less the same theory of divine right, but without his father's subtlety, and outraged powerful sections of opinion in both kingdoms.) English thinkers anxious to establish what was the condition of England before the imposition of the 'Norman yoke' took the Buchananite view of Scotland as a model for what went before the Conquest, and argued for a reversion to kingship by consent, or to republican rule, on that foundation. Philosophers of outstanding distinction, such as John Locke and then, half a century later, Jean-Jacques Rousseau, developed contractual theories of political society in a way that generalised the idea. Such approaches depict all rule as ultimately derivable from some actual or ideal common consent of the governed, which sets limits to the rightful powers of those who are in government over others.

These arguments are elaborated in MacCormick (1982).

Abstract theory was in due course transformed into concrete reality (inevitably, in messy and imperfect replication of neat theoretical pictures) in the revolutions of the eighteenth century. First the Americans and then the French threw off kingly rule in revolutionary upheavals that established republican forms of self-government, permanently in the American case, but not conclusively in France until nearly a century later. Sovereignty was claimed by (and for) the people in the United States, and the nation in France. These adopted the constitution that determined the way they were to be governed, indeed were to exercise their self-government. Always, of course, there was a vanguard of 'founding fathers', but the constitutions they drafted required, by their own terms, ratification by the people through what were considered appropriate forms of popular legitimation. As democratic ideas have extended their scope and become the dominant ideology of governmental legitimacy throughout the whole world in the closing years of the twentieth century, so has the idea of the sovereignty of the people extended its sway. A widely prevailing model of constitutional legitimacy is that whereby representative authors prepare constitutional drafts that are to take effect when, and only when, approved by the people they represent, through a referendum under conditions of universal adult suffrage. This model is already actualised fairly generally in most mainland European countries of the EU, and indeed in Ireland as well. In such a context, the attribution of sovereignty cannot credibly be to any single organ of government within the state, and the concept of the people as itself the sovereign, for all the paradoxical quality we have already noted in this idea, may again come into its own.

An alternative, which may escape the paradox, is to attribute sovereignty to 'the state' itself. The existence of a sovereign in the Austinian sense of the term, where sovereignty is attributed to a person or institution, implies effective governance of some territory and of the people living in it. Where sovereigns of this kind exist, they are holders of a power that is logically independent of any higher power of the same kind. There can, of course, be different sovereigns in different territories. Logically, they must be mutually independent, for if one ruler were in effect the overlord of another, that other would cease to have sovereignty. Mutual independence is a necessary attribute of sovereigns, as is territorial separation.

However, where constitutional government has developed in ways expressive of some conception of popular sovereignty, it is most likely that the constitution does not allow for or constitute any sovereign official or institution – indeed, a constitution such as that of France expressly prohibits this. In polities of this kind, the constitutional framework typically establishes some version of the classical 'separation of powers' discussed above. At a minimum, executive, legislative and judicial powers are assigned to distinct agencies, with some form of checks and balances among the agencies. In large polities, federal or quasi-federal forms of government may further complicate the constitutional picture, insofar as there are separate states, each with its own internal separation of powers, and a division of competences between the authorities of each state and those of the federal government. In such contexts, there is no single person or institution that exercises an unfettered supreme power; that is, there is no 'sovereign' in the Austinian sense.

But a country under such a constitution – whether it be a unitary state or a federal state – may enjoy as complete legal and political independence from power exercisable by other like entities as a state ruled by a sovereign monarch or dictator or a sovereign parliament. The state or federation may, in that sense, enjoy sovereignty. It is often, indeed usually, the case that the constitution of the state or federation was established by some method of popular approval, expressed through a referendum, a constitutional convention, or the like. It is also normal that the constitution provides for its own amendment by similar processes. Where all this is so, popular sovereignty connects in an obvious way with state sovereignty. The state is sovereign in its external relations with other states. Internally, the power to determine or alter the legal frameworks in which government is carried on belongs to the people acting in constitutionally stipulated ways. Democratic forms of government also involve the will of the people, usually expressed through political parties, to determine or at least strongly influence the course of legislation and the policies pursued by the executive.

The idea of the state as itself the repository of sovereignty is implicated in the idea, introduced earlier, of the 'Westphalian state'. Each such state is conceived as independent of every other and the rule of mutual non-intervention applies equally to all. This naturally entails the absence of any superior authority above the state level, though it does not preclude voluntary associations of states agreeing on common treaties or conventions that establish criteria of right conduct among them – like the Hague Convention on prisoners of war, or the Vienna Convention on Diplomatic Immunity, or even the United Nations Covenant on Civil and Political Rights or on Economic and Social Rights. From the viewpoint of sovereignty theory, however, the truly legal character of such solemn international undertakings can be problematic. Austinian theories that make the existence of genuine law conditional on the existence of a common sovereign with political power to enforce sanctions in case of breaches imply that 'international law' is not true law, but some kind of solemnly announced 'positive morality' among states.

These arguments are analysed further in the British context, making particular reference to the work of HLA Hart, in MacCormick (1999) ch 6.

For a historical analysis with reference to the theological-political context see Buijs (2003).

For a reading of the French perspective see Ziller (2003).

1.2.3 Post-sovereignty?

The very fact that Austinian sovereignty theory leads to such an insipid characterisation of solemn undertakings among states may itself weaken the case for favouring sovereignty in that sense. But one of the things that may then also be weakened is the doctrine of 'parliamentary sovereignty', so fundamental to the British constitutional tradition, especially according to those who interpret it from the standpoint of English law. This is a sense of sovereignty that might plausibly have become redundant under the developments of the last three decades of the twentieth century. For a start, most modern polities, and all democratic law-states, simply do not fit the Austinian picture, even when this is re-expressed in terms of common-law principles. Among European states, including the UK, the development of the EU has had decisive significance, along with other developments such as the (European) Convention for the Protection of Human Rights and Fundamental Freedoms, especially as this has come to be policed by the European Court of Human Rights.

Of course, it may be argued that the positivistic conception was based all along on a conceptual mistake, and that sovereignty was never anything like the positivists' imaginings of it. Sovereignty was always something quite different, for example, 'an expression of a political relationship [that is, a political rather than an economic or a narrowly legal relationship, or one based on pure brute force or on property interests] between the people and the state' (Loughlin 2003, pp 82–3). Thus sovereignty has both political and legal implications, depending on whether one focuses on power in fact or on normative power, as discussed earlier (1.1.1). It remains doubtful how far either sense has full application in an EU that is increasingly pluralistic in its legal structures.

Since its inception in 1958, the European Economic Community (EEC), along with related Communities, and subsequently the 'European Union' (since the Treaty of Maastricht of 1992) has undergone a process of 'constitutionalisation'. The foundational Treaties, especially the Treaties of Paris (1950) and Rome (1957), came to be interpreted as a kind of 'constitutional charter' for the Communities and then the Union. This was tied up with decisions by the European Court of Justice (ECJ) that the Treaties and Regulations or Directives made under them enjoyed both supremacy over the laws of the Member States, to the extent of any conflict between them, and direct effect on and in favour of citizens of the states, not only the states themselves. This involved characterising EC law as being a new kind of law '*sui generis*' (of its own kind, neither national law nor international law, but something quite novel). One implication of this for the UK became clear in 1991 with the case of *Factortame v Minister of Transport*, which held as a matter of law that the UK must 'disapply' as against EU citizens involved in fisheries the material provisions of the Merchant Shipping Act enacted by the Queen in Parliament in 1988.

In this light, one can no longer adhere to the traditional doctrine of parliamentary sovereignty. It must be radically re-interpreted or even abandoned. Yet this is not because a new European Sovereign has come into existence. The EU is a 'sui generic' legal order, but certainly not one characterised by sovereignty in the Austinian sense.

What about other senses? It is instructive to reflect on constitutional developments in the period 2001–2005. The European Council at Laeken in December 2001, called into being the Convention on the Future of Europe under the Presidency of Valéry Giscard D'Estaing. Over a period of 18 months, this Convention produced a 'Draft Treaty establishing a Constitution for Europe'. In October 2004, the representatives of the Member States at an Intergovernmental Conference signed a revised version of this draft, and made it open to ratification by each state according to its own constitutional processes within the two following years. It is controversial how far a 'constitution', thus adopted state-by-state, with resort to a referendum in some countries but not others, would satisfy purist theories of popular sovereignty.

In any event, substantial negative referendum votes in France and the Netherlands in May/June 2005 derailed the project of adopting this constitution, probably permanently. But even if the Constitution had been – or were to be – ratified in every Member State, and even if every state eventually held an affirmative referendum, there would remain a problem about the location of sovereignty. Would it be vested in the total population of the Union, or in the peoples of the states, or in some way shared? Or would it have been, indeed is it, a collective possession of the states, which remain in the last resort collectively masters of the Treaties? Can sovereignty be divided or shared, and can it exist in the absence of a single European people or nation self-constituted by the very act of adopting a constitution? These are questions it would be difficult to answer with confidence. What they suggest is, strongly, that sovereignty is currently a concept in transition in Europe, and that our understanding of law should be used to cast light on difficult questions about sovereignty. Explanations of law in terms of sovereignty would amount to explaining a difficult idea in terms of a complex, contested and obscure one.

For MacCormick's account of 'post-sovereignty' see, generally, Mac-Cormick (1999) and especially ch 8. For a very useful overview see N Walker, 'Late Sovereignty in the European Union' in Walker (2003).

For a defence of modern sovereignty see M Loughlin, 'Ten Tenets of Sovereignty' in Walker (2003).

1.3 The rule of law

1.3.1 The rule of law – meaning and value

We have made reference to the 'Rule of Law' earlier, but we should now consider it in greater depth. Only where officials faithfully observe the constraints laid down in laws and constitutions does the rule of law obtain. It is commonplace that societies that live under the rule of law enjoy great benefits by comparison with those that do not. The rule of law is a possible condition to be achieved under human governments. Among the values that it can secure, none is more important than legal certainty, except perhaps its stablemate – security of legal expectations and safety of the citizen from arbitrary interference by governments and their agents.

Where the rule of law is observed, people can have reasonable certainty, in advance, concerning the rules and standards by which their conduct will be judged, and the requirements they must satisfy to give legal validity to their transactions. They can then have reasonable security in their expectations of the conduct of others, and in particular of those holding official positions under law. They can challenge governmental actions that affect their interest by demanding a clear legal warrant for official action, or nullification of unwarrantable acts through review by an independent judiciary. This is possible, it is often said, provided there is a legal system composed principally of quite clearly enunciated rules that normally operate only in a prospective manner, that are expressed in terms of general categories, not particular, indexical, commands to individuals or small groups singled out for special attention. The rules should set realistically achievable requirements for conduct, and should form overall some coherent pattern, not a chaos of arbitrarily conflicting demands. (see 1.4 below)

This is attractive in itself, yet it must not blind us to the extent to which in a free society law necessarily also has an argumentative quality. Any legal text may be open to several interpretations in the light of contested principles and values that are taken to underlie this or that rule of law or branch of law. People are entitled to argue for one favoured interpretation against another, and in disputes between citizen and citizen, or citizen and state, each side may seek interpretations favourable to their own view of the matter (and hoped-for outcome). It is indeed right to look at every side of every important question, and not come down at once on the side of prejudice or apparent certainty.

> For a helpful elaboration of the tension between certainty and the arguable character of the rule of law, see MacCormick (2005) ch 2.
>
> Compare also Raz's important essay, 'The Rule of Law and its Virtue', in Raz (1979).

1.3.2 Challenges to the rule of law

This can, however, lead to a degree of scepticism concerning the possibility of a genuine 'rule of law' that does uphold tolerable certainty in human affairs. If everything is arguable (or even if rather many points are arguable) and open to a decision either way, the decision is a matter for the discretion of judges. How the judges decide, on whatever grounds they favour, determines legal outcomes both for individuals and, through the system of judicial precedent, for society at large. A 'rule of laws, not men' becomes no better than a rule by one set of men (the judiciary) rather than another (the legislature). Moreover, the prized 'separation of powers' is revealed as something of a sham, and with it the distinction laboriously drawn earlier between law and politics.

There are two possible manifestations of this scepticism. One is a scholarly one, concerning the false consciousness implicit in (and generated by) theorising about the rule of law and the separation of powers. People may be taught to believe in the virtue of legal certainty and its possible achievement under the rule of law or in a *Rechtsstaat*, a 'law-state'; but the belief is an illusion. They may be comforted by the thought that it is actually achieved in their own state, but the thought is false. It is not true that even when substantive results in lawsuits go against one's own individual interest or class interest, at least formal justice is achieved, or that we all live under the same rules, and they are fairly enforced. Enforcement is capricious and biased, and cannot be otherwise. Legal uncertainty is pervasive and legal decision making is done in response to ideology under cover of rule-of-law talk.

The other response is political, expressed, for example, in conflict between the executive and the judiciary. In the UK in 2004–2005, Prime Minister Blair's Government was greatly concerned with terrorist threats coming from militant Islamists allied to the Al-Qaida network. Indeed, since the '9/11' attack on New York's Trade Towers, the British and all Western governments had active concerns about this, and the terrorist bombings in Madrid in May 2004 and in London in July 2005, showed how serious were the grounds for concern. At the same time, however, the courts have had to adjudicate on the lawfulness of certain counter-measures involving, for example, detention without trial of terrorist suspects or the contestable character of evidence obtained, or allegedly obtained, through torture. Litigation on this has raised issues both about long-standing principles of the common law and about human rights, in the context of the UK's Human Rights Act 1998, which imported into domestic law a very substantial part of the European Convention on Human Rights. The judiciary have reached decisions against the government in some very salient cases, and ministers have responded that the judges are crossing the boundary of judicial deference to law and have invaded the role of the executive. The judges have responded that they are only giving effect to the clear meaning of the law. Can this be true? Are the judges or the politicians more in the right in this matter? Do they really have different grounds and methods of deciding or are the 'legal' decisions just political ones through and through?

To respond fully to these points would call for a fairly thorough-going account of legal reasoning and of the extent to which, and grounds on which, one can ascribe objective rightness or wrongness to decisions about contested matters of law (see Part II). It is sufficient here to note that 'rule of law' theory may tend to exaggerate the possibility of legal determinacy and certainty, and the possibility to settle everything in advance by well-drafted and clearly conceptualised rules of statute law (far less, case law) meshing coherently across a whole legal system. (Indeed, as commentators like F A Hayek point out, excessively detailed regulatory interventions actually undermine the kinds of freedom the rule of law ought to serve, which is achieved best under broad principles of common law – evolved law rather than designed law.) Nevertheless, law is less radically indeterminate than critical theorists suggest, and the canons of good legal reasoning, fortified by a sense of reasonableness can in fact settle quite clear bases for discriminating between sound and unsound, or better and worse, legal arguments in disputed cases. Certainly judges from time to time make mistakes – but the very fact that they can be seen as mistakes indicates there really is a possibility that on other occasions they make no mistake, that is, reach an objectively correct decision.

The kinds of liberty supposedly upheld by respecting the rule of law are thus genuinely, albeit never perfectly, achievable, and are of real value.

But such 'liberal liberty' may itself be insufficient. Anatole France famously remarked that the law in its majestic equality forbids the rich and the poor alike to sleep under the bridges of Paris. Equality before the law and liberty under the rule of law are compatible with very great economic and social inequalities and indeed injustices. Where law produces what seems substantively unsatisfactory outcomes for people, why should they accept that there is any value at all in the 'majestic equality' of the impartial administration of rules that affect very differently the interests of different individuals and different classes?

The possibilities implicit in democratic institutions may afford one answer to this. One reason to put up with bad laws and indeed to demand that they be fairly and regularly administered is because they can be changed, and the same logic will then demand fair and regular administration of reformed laws. Those who want laws changed only have to mobilise politically and secure a majority in the legislature to enact suitable reforms. These, if fairly administered, will generate different outcomes for the interest groups affected. Whether this is a reasonable hope or yet another illusion in the conditions of post-industrial global capitalism is another question, and for present purposes must be left as an open question.

On the question of objectivity in decision making, see MacCormick (2005), ch 13.

For Hayek's defence of the Rule of Law and the challenges to it in practice, see Hayek (1944) ch 6.

Craig offers a survey in the context of public law in Craig (1997), and see also, Dyzenhaus (2000).

For a helpful overview of a range of critiques, see Sypnowich (2000) 178–91.

1.4 The 'inner morality of law'

In our society, democratic liberty is best expressed by the rule of law or government under law. What does this mean? According to Neil MacCormick, 'It is that stance in legal politics according to which matters of legal regulation or controversy ought to, so far as possible, be conducted in accordance with predetermined rules of considerable generality and clarity in which legal relations comprise rights, duties, powers and immunities reasonably clearly defined by reference to such rules and in which acts of government however desirable teleologically must be subordinated to respect for such rules and rights.' (1989, p 184)

> For the full account of MacCormick's treatment of legalism and its ethical value, read MacCormick (1989).

What are the values that stem from the rule of law? There appear to be two general sorts of reasons that seem to show why the law might be desirable.

1.4.1 Justice reasons

The legal regulation of social relations is to take place through general rules applied in an impartial fashion to all persons alike and known in advance. The rules are to be applied by impartial specialists in law according to the internal logic and validity of the system and excluding any personal or non-legal considerations. Hence generality and reference to formal sources guarantee certain fundamental notions of fairness. The rule of law means (1) equality of legal subjects before the law in that individual cases are dealt with in terms of their facts alone and no one may be exempt; (2) government accountability and hence control of arbitrary action (including the actions of judges) – the doctrine of separation of powers means that judges should merely apply rules, not create them; (3) since legal systems involve coercion and stigmatisation, the rule of law attempts to make coercion 'the friend of freedom' by regulating its use. Is it not a good thing if private persons (pursuers or plaintiffs) and public officials (procurators fiscal, police) can call upon courts to do such coercing/stigmatising only by offering to prove – and to prove that there is some legal warrant for this – some 'major premise' which is a legal rule and that some relevant facts or 'minor premises' hold good? We can consider all these as aspects of the phrase 'government of law not men'.

1.4.2 Instrumental reasons

The rule of law offers an efficient technique of social management in governing a pluralist market society where no underlying consensus of values can be presumed and there are conflicts of interests. The uniformity and predictability of law facilitates personal and commercial planning, entrepreneurial initiative in the market and in private spheres of action. Clear and technically authorised general rules are the perfect instrument for pursuing social and individual goals, whatever they may be. Weber thought of the rule of law, in the shape of general formal and abstract rules as being instrumental in the rise of capitalism and Marxist writers, who also saw it as inextricably connected with capitalist society, and criticised it in its role in legitimating an unjust social order (see, further, Part III 2.3).

For a brief and nuanced account from a Marxist perspective assessing whether the rule of law in capitalist societies is an 'unqualified human good', see EP Thompson's classic statement in Thompson (1977), pp 265–9.

In one of the most interesting and influential jurisprudential accounts of these problems, Lon Fuller elevates the core features of the rule of law to nothing less than what he calls the 'inner morality of law'. Legality, for Fuller, is the 'enterprise of subjecting human conduct to the governance of rules' (Fuller 1969, p 106). As such, its tendency is to minimise irrationality in human affairs. Its purpose is to prevent our being governed by arbitrary will. What this means is that law is an essential element in the governance of civil power through the rational principles of civic order. It is there in order to prevent our domination by the arbitrary will of officials and others who claim to know what is best for us – there being no curb on their power. It is there to open up, and to preserve, free communication between people. For Fuller, the proper way of 'putting ourselves under the governance of rules' is through legality, that complex ideal embracing standards for assessing and criticising decisions that purport to be legal. Where this ideal exists, according to Fuller, official action is enmeshed in and restrained by the web of rules, and no power is immune from criticism or completely free to follow its own bent, however well intentioned. Law is to be seen as intrinsically involving a procedural 'inner morality'. This inner morality offers some fundamental constraints simply through law's formal features.

What are the features of this inner morality? What are the characteristics of legality? Fuller sets out the eight necessary features. These eight features are not to be applied in every situation – legality is an art and we must balance them against each other so that we get the best mix. But they must, in some degree, all be present in a legal system as a whole. The condition of something being called a legal system is that this mix is present.

1. There must be rules: This is interpreted as the demand for generality. There must be rules of some kind and their essential feature is that they must be general in scope.
2. Promulgation: The demand that the law be made public, not kept secret. Citizens are not likely to know the content of all the laws, but they must be able to find them out.
3. No retroactivity: Rules must be prospective. That is, in order to govern

human behaviour they must be set out in advance in order that citizens be able to decide whether to conform to them or not. The basic human right of no punishment without a law expresses this principle.

4. Clarity: Rules must so far as possible be clear in order that they may be understood and followed. While some interpretative leeway is inevitable, and some flexibility of standards desirable, rules that are deliberately unclear contradict the possibility of ordering human conduct according to them.

5. No contradiction in laws: Rules that demand competing actions give no clear guidance as to what behaviour is expected by the law.

6. Laws must not require the impossible: Laws that demand behaviour over which citizens have no possible control cannot allow the fulfilment of subjecting their conduct to rules.

7. Constancy: Laws must not keep changing rapidly if they are to produce stable expectations of what the law requires of its citizens, though of course this does not mean that they cannot change in order to meet the needs of a changing society.

8. Congruence between official action and declared rules: What officials do must be in accordance with the laws set out in advance, otherwise what the rules required and their application would differ in such a way as to leave citizens subject to the arbitrary powers of those in authority.

> Read chapter 2 – 'The Morality that makes Law possible' – of Fuller (1969).

In defining the conditions under which the ideal of the rule of law can be realised, Fuller borrows from the German sociologist Simmel the idea that 'there is a kind of reciprocity between government and the citizen with the respect to the observance of rules. Government says to the citizen in effect, 'These are the rules we expect you to follow. If you follow them, you have our assurance that they are the rules that will be applied to your conduct.' When this bond of reciprocity is finally and completely ruptured by government, nothing is left on which to ground the citizen's duty to observe the rules (Fuller 1969, pp 39–40).

While the ideal of reciprocity requires a firm commitment to the fulfilment of all eight principles of legality, this does not mean – with the exception of publicity – that they can all equally be fully realised on all occasions. For example, clarity is always an aspiration rather than something that can easily be achieved in the writing of all laws; laws do require change over time; principles of strict liability do in some sense demand the impossible where they hold actors liable for consequences that they may have done everything in their power to prevent; and sometimes in the case of common-law judgments, which change or 'develop' the law, the principle of non-retroactivity may appear to be compromised (see, for example, the 'marital rape' cases, *Stallard v HMA* in Scotland or *R v R* in England).

For Fuller the instantiation of each principle is required in a legal order in order that law's fundamental purpose, namely the subjection of human conduct to the governance of rules, be fulfilled. These principles constitute an 'inner morality of law', that is, they are intrinsic to what it means to have law at all. They are the necessary and sufficient condition for the possibility of bringing about the framework of 'reciprocity', which is law's achievement, in that law is distinct from merely instituted power and acquires a 'moral' dimension. Let us have a closer look at why.

One prominent objection to this has been that it is a purely formal account of the rule of law that has no necessary moral dimension as such. After all, couldn't even a fascist, or racist, or communist totalitarian government meet these ideals without sacrificing its programme? For HLA Hart this 'inner morality' is perfectly compatible with the pursuit of immoral ends and he gives the example of the 'morality of poisoning'. Fuller's principles ensure the effectiveness or efficiency of a particular practice – even one such as 'poisoning' – regardless of moral judgements about that activity. Fuller correctly replies that before you make that argument about law you have to know the point of law. If you see law as a social technique for the ordering of society then the objection may have some bite. For then, law is seen as nothing more than a neutral technique for managing a society, and with the separation of means and ends, perhaps the question of effectiveness becomes something distinct from moral value. But if, like Fuller, you see law as something more than a neutral technique, with a moral purpose of its own – that of bringing about reciprocity – then the means of achieving it (clarity, prospectivity, etc) acquire a moral dimension of their own, as making possible that reciprocity. Following Aristotle, the conditions of excellence of a practice are internally derived. Fuller argues then that law is not just a technique and that it has a moral purpose of its own, and this is encapsulated in the 'enterprise of subjecting oneself to rules' and eliminating the arbitrary from everyday life.

The classic post-Second World War jurisprudential debate between HLA Hart and Lon Fuller can be found at *Harvard Law Review* 71 (1958), pp 593 and 630, respectively. See also Fuller's 'Reply to Critics' in Fuller (1969), and his discussion of the 'grudge informer', pp 245–53.

Is Fuller right to argue that law has a moral purpose? Isn't it merely a *means* of getting at goals, even if these goals are sometimes morally worthy, like justice? A robust defence of the morality of law has come more recently from

John Finnis who moves away from the idea that law is, in any sense, a 'necessary' evil, and a view consonant with the instrumentalist approach. One thing, he claims, which any healthy community requires, is some common authority. Unless we all in common accede to the authority of some common code of conduct we cannot live together in community at all. And the implementation of any common code of conduct requires the institutionalisation of some agency or agencies, which adjudicate upon breaches of the common code. The more complex a political society becomes, the more rich and varied are the opportunities it presents for diverse manifestations of the good. But the more that is so, the more we face problems of co-ordination with each other. Hence the more sophisticated are the common public agencies we need for adjudication, administration, enforcement and amendment or enrichment of our common and authoritative code of social conduct. The achievement of co-ordination, which is the achievement of law, becomes in this way of thinking a means of human flourishing – the achievement of moral good.

We can see how form and substance coalesce if, adapting from Finnis, we look at how community develops. Let us take a university seminar as an analogy. Different stages can be seen in the progress of a seminar. At the first stage of the seminar we have a strictly utilitarian version of community. The student is only interested in the seminar insofar as s/he gets the knowledge to pass the exam that s/he desires from it. Their attitude to the teachers and the fellow students (if any) is one of indifference. All s/he is interested in is that s/he gains the knowledge s/he needs from the teacher. Their fellow students count for nothing and s/he is only interested in them insofar as they can contribute to this knowledge. So s/he doesn't care if they come or if in fact they have knowledge of the subject of the seminar – in fact sometimes it is to their advantage that they do not know and do not come. Her/his attitude to the seminar changes when we come to the next stage. There, the student begins to like the exchange in the seminar itself. S/he still wants it for the knowledge, but now s/he is also wanting it for the cut and thrust of debate for the talk in the seminar itself. S/he actually gains a sense of good from the interaction in the seminar as well. Their attitude to the seminar participants alters because of this. S/he now needs them to be there because without them s/he cannot get the good of the debate that s/he wants, as well as the knowledge. S/he is still indifferent to them but knows s/he cares that they turn up and take part, though s/he does not care if they learn anything, or indeed enjoy it, because it is only her/his own good that s/he is interested in. But it means some change in the structuring of the seminar itself. For s/he now wants the teacher to take a more active role to force the other students to talk so that debate can get going. Also it now becomes more important for the seminar to be organised to fit in with a timetable so that everyone is able to come and fit it in with their timetables. Co-ordination now becomes important. Finally the student's attitude to her/his fellow students might change even further. Now s/he wants them to enjoy the seminar, but not because it will make the exchange better for her/him, but because s/he wants them to enjoy it in the way that s/he does. This does not mean s/he wants them to have the same experiences and to learn exactly what s/he does, but it is rather something like the following: s/he is getting a lot out of this and s/he wants them to have the pleasure s/he is experiencing from getting the good of the seminar. And this of course has the result of enhancing her/his good. This again entails a change in organisational policy, for what becomes important now is not merely that everyone comes on time and that they take part (the second stage), but that they are in a state to get the good out of it. This entails not only clear organisation and co-ordination, but also enhancing their ability to participate through remedial classes and other forms of help.

This for Finnis is the state of community as friendship, which is the fullest value of community – where you want something for the friend's sake and also where exchange is valuable per se. If we see this as a metaphor for community then we can see that this stage would entail all sorts of social welfare measures to get people to realise the good. But we can also see that law is important, not only because it provides the conditions that enable us to get that, but that it is also part of the good itself. Law is both part of the procedure for arriving at things and part of the good itself. It is a substantive thing, which becomes a moral good itself.

It is this then that lends further credence to Fuller's view that law requires reciprocity and connection. It is more than a neutral means of organising a society; rather, it is something that is a moral enterprise in itself. That way of living is *in itself* morally good for us. It is in this way that the rule of law becomes something more than a one-way street of norms standing above, to be a shared interaction that both protects and enriches us. And it is thus part of a democratic arrangement even though it appears to stand above us – insulated from us.

To make this clearer, let us use another example, or metaphor, of conversation. A life spent in good conversation would indeed be a fulfilling one. But to have conversation we need something more than words. For we can only make words intelligible as pieces of interaction if we have a grammar to structure them by. The relation of language to grammar might however work in two different ways. Grammar can be both normative, because it tells you how to write, and descriptive, because it merely describes people's practices. If we view it as mainly and wholly normative it could be like a fixed and inflexible force that determines without our say-so, everything we say. If we view it as mainly and wholly descriptive it is hard to see how it can have any purchase on our language at all. We can write and say anything we like as long as we (vaguely) communicate. But we do not have to draw the opposition out like that. It could be also something flexible that both determines our language and also interacts with it; it refreshes and is refreshed by it. If we transfer this analogy to politics then we can see that the rule of law can be seen in the manner of a flexible grammar: something that partly determines our language and thus helps us to write, but also something that, because of its flexible interaction, is embedded in it and thus is part of the enrichment and good of our lives and not just a means to an end.

For the important modern restatement of natural law, see Finnis (1980); for a valuable engagement in response, see MacCormick (1992).

1.5 Rights

Rights represent a particular way of talking about law and politics. Historically, rights were associated with revolution: for example, the 1789 French Declaration of the Rights of Man, in defiance of the old aristocratic order, asserted that 'men are born and remain free and equal in rights'. Today, many people regard society as being in 'the age of rights', which reflects the extent to which rights have come not only to predominate legal and political argument, but to provide the basic standards to which those exercising power must conform. But opinion divides now, particularly in the context of contemporary globalisation, over whether rights can and do still retain their radical character, as a weapon for the powerless in the struggle against oppression.

Rights are a special type of political claim, grounded in a distinctive form of argument. A distinction is often drawn between rights-based and utilitarian arguments in political and legal theory. The former employs what is called a deontological form of reasoning, that is that we should follow a certain course of action because it is the morally correct thing to do; the latter employs consequentialist reasoning, that is that our actions should be guided by results, in particular what will produce the greatest happiness for the greatest number.

We can trace the origins of rights claims to the development of natural law doctrines in the seventeenth century, and in particular, the writings of John Locke. Locke suggested that humans originally lived in a state of nature in which they were free and equal, and possessed certain natural rights, particularly the right to property. The purpose of agreeing to organised rule through government was that these natural freedoms could be better protected by the state – accordingly, with the formation of political society natural rights do not disappear, but are now guaranteed by positive law through a process of instituting government by consent. At the time, this was a revolutionary way of thinking, marking a sharp break with classical political thought. Previously, individuals had been regarded as subjects under a duty of obedience to their rulers. They were now to be considered as the holders of inalienable rights, that is these rights cannot be given or taken away. On this account, natural rights enjoy priority – both in chronological terms, and against laws that might interfere with them. They also have finality in the sense that they provide closure to political disputes – to adopt contemporary language, they are trumps which prevail over political claims framed in consequentialist terms.

This framework gives rise to the important distinction between the right and the good in liberal political philosophy. In advancing their conception of the good society, it is open to governments to pursue a variety of goals, and choose, for example, between laissez-faire and interventionist forms of economic management. However, the idea of the right states that there are certain limits, in the name of individual freedom, to what governments can do, no matter what conception of the good is being implemented. These limits may concern both the substantive content of rights – Locke, for example, argued that 'the great and chief end . . . [of] government is the preservation of their property' (Locke 1988, pp 350–1) – as well as the form of their protection, namely through processes established according to the rule of law.

We can get a sense of the main issues involved in delineating the scope of rights claims by considering Martin Loughlin's argument that the rights movement should be understood as 'an evolutionary process' marked by four trends:

> '*generalization*' (as greater numbers of political claims are expressed in the language of rights), *institutionalization* (as such claims increasingly acquire recognition in positive law), *collectivization* (as claims extend beyond the abstract individual to embrace social groups), and *internationalization* (as rights discourse enters the domain of international relations).
>
> (Loughlin 2000, p 208, emphasis in original)

Loughlin further suggests that each trend promotes an increasing '*politicization*' of rights, which has had a major impact on our understanding of law.

For the development of natural rights theories, and a discussion of some of its principal critiques, see Waldron (1987) chs 1 and 6.

For John Locke's account of the state of nature and its relation to the idea of natural rights, see Locke (1988) chs II, VIII and XI.

One of the most famous and influential defences of natural rights is Tom Paine's *The Rights of Man*: see Paine (1961), especially pp 349–85 and 420–45.

See also MacCormick (2007) chs 7 and 11.

1.5.1 Civil, political and social rights

The last fifty or so years have witnessed a significant colonisation of political argument by rights discourse, whether by oppressed minorities (and majorities) seeking the right to equal treatment, campaigners seeking to vindicate either the rights of women to choose an abortion or the rights of foetuses to life, or the starving and poor seeking the right to basic subsistence and shelter. From the vantage point of history, this latter day ascendancy of rights was by no means guaranteed. Natural rights had been subject to sustained critique, which downgraded their standing in political thought. Bentham famously denounced rights as 'nonsense upon stilts', while Marx saw rights as tools of bourgeois legitimation, each contrasting the rhetoric of rights with the material lack of freedom on the part of many. However, there was a revival in natural rights thinking in response to the atrocities of the Second World War. Leading Nazis were tried at Nuremberg for crimes against peace and humanity, and in 1948, the UN set out in the Universal Declaration of Human Rights (UDHR) a list of basic human rights that should never again be violated on such a massive scale.

According to TH Marshall, the modern growth of rights is related to the demands of three different, but related, elements of citizenship: civil, political and social. Civil rights provide the basic requirements of individual freedom, such as freedom of expression and religion, and personal liberty. The formative period for civil rights was the eighteenth century, when, reflecting their radical roots, they were deployed in the fight against authoritarian rule. Civil rights thus understood are closest to the freedoms Locke envisaged in the state of nature, particularly if we include the right to private property. In the nineteenth century however, these rights, while necessary, were seen by some as insufficient in ensuring equal citizenship, and attention turned to the realisation of political rights, enabling individuals to participate in decisions where political power is exercised. For groups such as the Chartists and Suffragettes, restricting the right to vote on the basis of property or gender rendered it defective, and so the main objective of the movement for political rights was the universal franchise, finally achieved in the UK in 1948. In the twentieth century, it has been argued that full citizenship also requires the protection of social rights. Campaigners contrasted the formal equality granted by civil and political rights with the substantive inequality which these rights seemed unable to remedy, and contended that to enjoy freedom in material terms, it was necessary to guarantee rights such as education, adequate housing and minimum levels of subsistence.

Marshall's analysis underscores the breadth of claims now made in the name of rights. However, highlighting the diversity of rights also reveals that they are potentially in conflict. Whichever type of rights has priority will affect the scope for governmental action by drawing the line between the right and the good in a different place. For example, a strong conception of civil rights could restrict interference with private property, whereas an emphasis on social rights may require the redistribution of existing patterns of wealth and ownership, which may require the state to take private property or at least restrict enjoyment of it. Accordingly, one of the consequences of expanding rights discourse has been fierce political debate over the requirements of freedom: is this better satisfied in negative terms, that is freedom from external constraints, or in positive terms, that is freedom to exercise one's autonomy.

> For Marshall's account of the historical development of rights, see Marshall (1992), pp 8–17 and 27–43.
>
> For discussion of the distinction of positive and negative freedom, see Berlin (1969) pp 121–34.

1.5.2 Politicising law–legalising politics

For much of their existence, rights were part of political struggle and debate directed towards criticising and changing the existing ruling order. Even where enshrined in constitutional texts, they were largely dormant as legal instruments; for example, although the US Bill of Rights dates from 1791, it was only in the twentieth century that the courts began to play a more active role in upholding constitutional rights. However, the recent history of rights has seen a general move towards greater legal protection. This is manifested in two developments: first, the adoption of international and regional treaties following the Second World War such as the ECHR, and second, the spread of liberal democratic ideas and practices after the fall of the Berlin Wall in 1989, for example, the adoption of constitutional charters of rights throughout Central and Eastern Europe.

That the institutionalisation of rights has primarily taken legal form rests on certain ideas about the separation of powers, which justify treating courts as the guardians of fundamental rights. In part, this is an argument about judges' institutional status, that as they are not elected to serve the wishes of the majority, they are less prone to popular pressures which might seek to restrict the rights of minorities. It is also in part an argument from democracy, that rights provide the infrastructure of the political process, and so there needs to be some external check on elected politicians to ensure rights are not abused.

This emphasis on legal institutional forms tends to promote a particular conception of rights. Stronger international machinery exists for the protection of civil and political rights, and these are more readily enforced under national constitutions than social rights, which are often instead seen in more aspirational terms. This is linked to a number of perceptions about the nature of rights and adjudication. First, that we can draw a distinction between negative rights, which prevent the state from doing something, and positive rights, which may require the state to act. Second, that the good constitution promotes freedom by entrenching negative rights to prevent state encroachment on individuals' private spheres. Third, that this is best achieved through the judicial enforcement of civil and political rights. According to Ronald Dworkin, the foundational constitutional principle is that everyone be treated with equal concern and respect, and so it is the duty of the courts in upholding the rule of law to ensure minimal non-interference with individual autonomy. Moreover, cases involving negative rights are suited to courts as they determine the rights and duties of two parties, to which Dworkin argues there is always a legally right answer. Positive rights, on the other hand, raise questions involving the allocation of resources that affect the whole population, to which there can only be politically preferable answers.

These arguments are not uncontroversial. Whether a claim should be framed as a positive or negative right is often open to discussion. For example, does freedom of expression simply require the state to refrain from censorship, or does it impose a duty on the state, say to provide access to the media? Also, while the priority of negative rights is asserted, it is generally accepted that only some rights are absolute (for example, the right not to be tortured), and most texts permit rights to be limited, either in general terms, such as when necessary in a democratic society, or on specific grounds, such as the interests of national security or the protection of health and morals. Resolving these questions involves courts in difficult line-drawing exercises, and there are often sharp differences of judicial opinion within and between cases over what the right answer is. For some critics, the political nature of rights claims does not disappear when they are discussed in a court of law, and in deciding these cases judges inevitably draw on contentious political assumptions over which there can be reasonable disagreement. The extent to which such questions are now the mainstay of legal discourse leads Loughlin to conclude that greater institutional protection of rights inevitably leads to the politicisation of law.

The other side of this story is the legalisation of politics as more disputes over matters of public policy are resolved in the courts. One consequence of advancing rights claims in legal guise is to change the form of argument: for example, rather than debating whether aircraft should be able to land during antisocial hours on grounds of health and safety, this now becomes an aspect of the right to privacy. If those affected by the aircraft passing over their homes can convince the courts that this disproportionately affects their right to privacy and family life then the aircraft will not be able to take off and land, no matter how strong the interest of society in allowing this to happen. Following the lead of the US, there has, comparatively speaking, been an upsurge in rights litigation, which some see as beneficial in correcting basic flaws in the democratic process, particularly in protecting minorities. For others though, the filtering of political claims through the courts leads to a thinning out of democracy, as it reduces the range of political argument by privileging an individualistic outlook, while limiting the participants to those who can afford the cost of legal action.

Dworkin's account of the proper scope of the judicial role in rights adjudication is elaborated in Dworkin (1985) chs 1 and 8.

For further discussion of the difference between negative and positive rights, see Laws (1996) pp 627–35.

For the argument that the resolution of rights cases is inevitably political, see Griffith (1979) pp 7–18.

The question of 'juridification' is analysed in more depth in Part III, 2.2.

1.5.3 The indivisibility of rights?

The historical priority accorded to civil and political rights has recently been challenged, and instead there have been calls for a different, more collective, approach. Some writers speak in terms of generations of rights: first-generation civil and political rights focus on the abstract individual; second-generation social and economic rights are enjoyed by particular groups (for example, the right to healthcare addresses the needs of the sick); and third-generation solidarity rights are claims that affect humankind as a whole, such as the right to a clean environment. There has been a gradual move towards giving these rights greater international and constitutional recognition, although often with weaker enforcement machinery. We should be careful though not to equate the institutionalisation of rights solely with their enumeration in formal texts – for example, with the establishment of the welfare state, it could be said that social rights in practice predominated in postwar Britain, even if they were not called rights.

The argument that second- and third-generation rights should have equal status to first-generation rights seeks to minimise the supposed differences between them. For example, against the claim that social rights distinctively require expenditure and state intervention, it is said that civil and political rights also have financial implications and entail positive action, such as the maintenance of a system of courts. On the other hand, it is said that giving full constitutional protection to social rights would embroil courts in political controversy. But, as we have seen, the charge of politicisation of law arises with respect to civil and political rights. However, while both sets of rights involve decisions over potentially irresolvable conflicts of values, social rights are seen as being more overtly concerned with questions of distributive justice. Thus to the extent that social rights can be perceived as more political than legal, this often works to enhance the higher institutional standing of civil and political rights.

The case for the second and third generations is based on ideas of the indivisibility of rights. In particular, it is argued that a basic standard of living is a prerequisite to being able to enjoy civil and political rights: for example, the right to a fair trial or freedom of speech may be quite useless to someone dying of starvation. Moreover, some see prioritising the first generation as promoting a partial vision of rights that seeks to universalise Western values. It is suggested that regarding rights as claims by individuals made against the state fosters an atomistic view of society, and obscures the systematic widespread abuse of rights often visited on groups, for example, the millions of humans who are denied the basic right to food. Arguments in favour of collective rights seek to recover neglected, including non-Western traditions of rights, which reflect more organic notions of society. This approach again changes the focus of rights discourse. Upendra Baxi argues that in the dominant tradition, the privileged bearer of rights was the white European male. Accordingly, Western notions of rights made human suffering invisible, particularly in the context of colonisation, as they did not treat non-Europeans as fully human and so their rights were not imperilled by genocidal practices. In contrast, regarding all peoples as bearers of rights brings to the fore violations of their ultimate collective right to self-determination, and so has as its principal focus taken suffering seriously.

For a political statement in favour of the indivisibility of human rights, see the Bangkok Declaration (1993).

For an overview of some of the conceptual issues relating to social and economic rights, see Craven (1995) pp 6–16.

For the argument as to the foundational nature of basic subsistence rights, see Thomas Pogge (2002), General Introduction and ch 1.

For a critique of the tendency to regard human rights as exclusively Western, see Baxi (2002) pp 24–35.

1.5.4 Rights in international and global context

Reference to the right to self-determination highlights the role human rights have played in international politics. While self-determination itself first came to prominence at the 1919 Versailles Conference, the main impetus for the internationalisation of rights was the UN's adoption of the UDHR in 1948. There is now a raft of international treaties dealing with a range of subjects such as the abolition of torture or combating discrimination. These developments have two important consequences. First, rights are now genuinely human rights, possessed by everyone by reason of their humanity and without distinctions based on geographical origin. Second, and related, as these human rights are universal, they potentially challenge the principle of state sovereignty and can justify humanitarian intervention by the international community, for example, to prevent the genocide of one ethnic group by another within the same state.

While internationalisation can in many ways be seen as providing a step change in the career of human rights, this is not without its dangers. Rights can become pawns in the power play of international diplomacy. During the Cold War, rights became an ideological tool, as the West argued that lack of respect for civil and political rights undermined the legitimacy of state communist regimes, while the east countered that capitalist societies failed to protect social and economic rights. Throughout this period, each side was prepared to overlook gaps between their own rhetoric and practice in client states, enabling dictatorial regimes to escape scrutiny for rights violations. The fall of the Berlin Wall dramatically changed this context, and ushered in a new consensus on human rights. Today, some international lawyers suggest the right to democratic governance has become the norm, supported by the record number of countries now living under some form of parliamentary rule. Combined with the spread of charters of rights and judicial review, some commentators speak of the globalisation of human rights.

However, while some see this as a cause for celebration, others suggest that the key challenge for human rights concerns how these developments relate to broader patterns of globalisation. In particular, can rights operate as a check on new forms of power associated with the global economy, such as that wielded by multinational corporations, which may now present the strongest threat to individual autonomy? And should they be expected to? Some commentators suggest such an outcome is not envisaged, and that the institutional form of rights that are being globalised reflects a pared down vision of democracy satisfied by fair procedures at elections. Others argue that the spread of rights and global capitalism reflect the same values, as each seeks to carve out an area of private activity free from state interference.

Baxi captures these concerns by juxtaposing two ways of thinking about human rights – one is the universal paradigm, grounded in the 1948 Declaration; the other is of what he calls the 'trade-related market-friendly paradigm' of human rights. The latter reflects the extent to which corporations have been able to advance their interests through rights – for example, by arguing that restrictions on tobacco advertising limit their freedom of expression – and also how rights claims are being reframed in the language of the market – for example, the right to shelter is translated into profit opportunities for construction companies. He suggests that these paradigms reflect an ongoing clash between the politics *of*, and the politics *for*, human rights. The politics *of* human rights uses rights as a means to promote established patterns of power, as happened during the height of the cold war. By contrast, the politics *for* human rights views rights as a way of disturbing oppressive power relations, as when colonised peoples asserted self-determination against imperial rule. Baxi argues that the relative ascendancy of the 'trade-related market-friendly paradigm' shows the extent to which the politics *of* human rights has been appropriated for global capital. He warns that the future of human rights depends on developing a more thorough-going politics *for* human rights at the global level, which has as its object 'that order of progress which makes the state more ethical, governance progressively just, and power increasingly accountable.'

For discussion of human rights and contemporary international politics, see Henkin (1999) pp 1–15.

The spread of the right to democracy, and various critiques thereof, are discussed in Marks (2000) ch 4.

For Baxi's account of the politics of and for human rights, and the extent of the trade-related market-friendly paradigm of human rights, see Baxi (2002) pp 41 and 144–56.

References

Austin, J, 1954, *The Province of Jurisprudence Determined*, London: Weidenfeld and Nicolson.

Bangkok Declaration, 1993, 'Final Declaration of the Regional Meeting for Asia of the World Conference on Human Rights', available at http://law.hku.hk/lawgovtsociety/Bangkok%20Declaration.htm

Baxi, U, 2002, *The Future of Human* Rights, New Delhi: Oxford University Press.

Berlin, I, 1969, *Four Essays on Liberty*, Oxford and New York: Oxford University Press.

Buijs, G, 2003, '*Que les Latins appelland maiestatem*': An exploration into the theological background of the concept of sovereignty', in N Walker (ed).

Craig, P, 1997, 'Formal and Substantive Conceptions of the Rule of Law', *Public Law* 466–487.

Craven, M, 1995, *The International Covenant on Economic, Social and Cultural Rights: A Perspective on its Development*, Oxford: Oxford University Press.

Dworkin, R, 1985, *A Matter of Principle*, Cambridge, MA: Harvard University Press.

Dyzenhaus, D, 2000, 'Form and substance in the Rule of Law', in C Forsyth (ed), *Judicial Review and the Constitution*, Oxford: Hart.

Finnis, J, 1980, *Natural Law and Natural Rights*, Oxford: Clarendon.

Fuller, L, 1969, *The Morality of Law*, New Haven: Yale University Press.

Griffith, JAG, 1979, 'The Political Constitution', 42 *Modern Law Review* 1.

Hart, HLA, 1961, *The Concept of Law*, Oxford: Clarendon.

Hayek, F, 1944, *The Road to Serfdom*, London: Routledge.

Henkin, L, 1999, 'The "S" Word: Sovereignty, and Globalization, and Human Rights Et Cetera', 68 *Fordham Law Review* 1–14.

Hobbes, T, 1996, *Leviathan*, Cambridge: Cambridge University Press.

Kelsen, H, 1992, *Introduction to the problems of Legal Theory*, Oxford: Clarendon.

Laws, J, 1996, 'The Constitution: Morals and Rights', *Public Law* 622–635.

Locke, J, 1988, The Second Treatise of Government, in P Haslett (ed), *Two Treatises of Government*, Cambridge: Cambridge University Press.

Loughlin, M, 2000, *Sword and Scales*, Oxford: Hart.

Loughlin, M, 2003, 'Ten Tenets of Sovereignty', in N Walker.

MacCormick, N, 1982, 'Law, Obligation and Consent: Reflections on Stair and Locke', in N MacCormick, *Legal Right and Social Democracy*, Oxford: Clarendon.

MacCormick, N, 1989, 'The Ethics of Legalism', 2 *Ratio Juris* 184–93.

MacCormick, N, 1992, 'Law and the Separation of Law and Morals', in RP George (ed), *Natural Law Theory*, Oxford: Clarendon.

MacCormick, N, 1999, *Questioning Sovereignty*, Oxford: Oxford University Press.

MacCormick, N, 2005, *Rhetoric and the Rule of Law*, Oxford: Oxford University Press.

MacCormick, N, 2007, *Institutions of Law*, Oxford: Oxford University Press.

Marks, S, 2000, *The Riddle of All Constitutions: International Law, Democracy and the Critique of Ideology*, Oxford: Oxford University Press.

Marshall, TH, 1992, *Citizenship and Social Class*, London: Pluto Press.

Paine, T, 1961, *The Rights of Man*, Garden City: Dolphin Books.

Pogge, T, 2002, *World Poverty and Human Rights: Cosmopolitan Responsibilities and Reforms*, Cambridge: Polity.

Raz, J, 1979, 'The Rule of Law and its Virtue', in J Raz, *The Authority of Law*, Oxford: Clarendon Press.

Sypnowich, C, 2000, 'Utopia and the Rule of Law, in D Dyzenhaus (ed), *Recrafting the Rule of Law*, Oxford: Hart, 2000.

Thompson, EP, 1977, *Whigs and Hunters*, Harmondsworth: Penguin.

Vattel, E, 1883, *The Law of Nations or Principles of the Law of Nature Applied to the Conduct and Affairs of Nations and Sovereigns* (ed J Chitty) Philadelphia Pa: T & J W Johnson & Co.

Waldron, J, 1987, *Nonsense upon Stilts*, London and New York: Methuen.

Walker, N (ed), 2003, *Sovereignty in Transition*, Oxford: Hart.

Ziller, J, 2003, 'Sovereignty in France', in N Walker.

Cases

R v R (Rape: marital exemption) [1991] 4 All ER 481.

Stallard v HMA (1989) SCCR 248.

Advanced topics

2.1 Legalism and legality

2.1.1 Shklar and the meaning of legalism

Judith Shklar (1986) describes the legalistic attitude well. It is a moral attitude that wants to insulate law from politics, preferences and the like. Though it is something that specifically originates in lawyers' thoughts about the world, it seeps through a wide spectrum of opinion and people.

In the law all this is expressed, for Shklar, in what she calls formalism. It is in that way that the law gets the requisite degree of impartiality. It is viewed as a system of perfectly clear and consistent rules. These contain precise and 'scientifically' analysed terms, elaborated out of perfectly analysed and synthesised concepts, the concepts being unvaryingly used in the same sense throughout the whole body of law. Law is treated as a self-contained and autogenerative system that needs to be kept distinct from politics in order to organise our lives. Legalism is uncompromising because rules are, according to Shklar, binary. They either exist and apply or they do not.

Though legalism's ideal of objectivity through formalism depends upon some sort of agreement, it is not the only thing involved. Legalism prescribes agreement through rule following. Though the theory uses rules to create agreement, rules also presuppose that agreement.

This is not to say that law is amoral or severed from morality; laws do in fact encompass the values of the particular culture that they find themselves in. Legalists and lawyers admit that. The claim here is rather that no matter where the rules come from, the effect of legalism is to make them appear objective and unchangeable. Legalism does not so much deny the connection between law and values as hide it from view. Since it concentrates on the rules to the exclusion of everything else, the rules lose their sense of contingency. They dominate the entire moral universe. They are the islands of stability in a chaotic universe. This concentration on law and the rules has made us forget that it is we who make the rules and we that can change them. We see ourselves instead as the technicians of rules that we do not and cannot challenge. The morality of law (or of legality) becomes one of legalism – of the technical rational application of rules. The rules have a life of their own, which cannot be challenged. They control us rather than us controlling them. What we concentrate on is the rules themselves – rather than to look at their instantiation in the social context. And it is in this way that the predictability and certainty of the rules legitimises an escape from personal responsibility.

2.1.2 Legalism and society

It is arguable that a rule-based way of looking at things is closely tied to capitalism. As we will explore more fully in Part III of the book, Max Weber saw a close connection between the development of a highly rationalised form of legal administration and the development of large industrialised capitalist economies. The predictability and order of the law helped secure property and the predictability of economic transactions. At the same time, according to Weber, bureaucracies were increasingly used as institutions for administering work. Here, abstract rules are very important since it is they that enable there to be accountability and adequate supervision of staff at the bottom of the pyramid. The 'red tape' of bureaucracy was there, in the first instance anyway, to protect rather than obfuscate. For Weber, this was all part of a movement, which he called 'rationalisation'. Most attention is paid to maximising efficiency since the most pervasive value is control over the environment and prediction of the future.

Bureaucracies and legal institutions are not committed to any particular set of values and can serve any political system. Thus these three factors – abstract formal rules, bureaucracies, and the division of means and ends – promote both efficiency and the values required for capitalism. We can thus see why legalism has such a strong hold in the sort of societies that Weber describes: people can think that the rules ought to be obeyed – right or wrong – because they are the rules. Shklar, we have seen, shows how many lawyers think this to be the case and think it to be no bad thing. But the opposite way out of this – a celebration of the plasticity and infinite change in human life – does not seem appropriate either. Following the rules blindly might have some negatives attached to it, but it does have its pluses! But there is a middle ground in-between. In looking at what this might involve we need to draw a distinction between legalism and legality. In changing two letters we move a vast distance.

What counts as the middle ground here? The inspiration here will be the distinction Lon Fuller draws between the morality of aspiration and the morality of duty (Fuller 1969). The best way to explain this is to tell a story. Suppose someone asks how he can be a good husband and love his wife. One reply might be something to the effect that they have to be gentle and kind. But this might not satisfy our legalistic interlocutor. He thinks this is too vague and wants some more specific rules that he can follow. I reply that he should give his wife flowers every week; go to a good restaurant once a fortnight; and agree to at least 75 per cent of her requests. This satisfies him and he goes off and duly follows these rules. When he comes to me some time later, aggrieved because his wife has left him, what do I say? He thinks he has done what is necessary – he followed the rules that I gave him. But his mistake would have been to think that that was enough. More was necessary and he would only have learnt what that was if he had not ignored my fine but vague phrases.

One might say that following my rules was the morality of duty – a *sine qua non* of being a good husband. But being a good husband demanded something more than that – he had to look to the morality of aspiration that the rules demanded. The parable of the Good Samaritan makes this clearer. The lesson of that parable is that one should love one's neighbour, a category that, as Jesus implies, is rather wide. But look what happens in the law. In the case of *Donoghue v Stevenson* [1932 AC 599] Lord Atkin said:

> The rule that you are to love your neighbour becomes in law: You must not injure your neighbour, and the lawyer's question: Who is my neighbour? receives a restricted reply. You must take reasonable care to avoid acts or omissions which you can reasonably foresee would be likely to injure your neighbour. Who then, in law, is my neighbour? The answer seems to me to be persons who are so closely and directly affected by my act that I ought reasonably to have them in contemplation as being so affected when I am directing my mind to the acts or omissions which are called in question.

What the law lays down as one's duty is the *sine qua non* without which loving thy neighbour would be impossible. But this clearly does not exhaust the possibility of love nor does it mean that the person who merely does not injure his neighbour, so defined, really loves his neighbour. For that, you need a morality of aspiration, which is given in the parable Jesus told. Loving your neighbour means more than following the duty of the law and you will not even understand what that duty is unless you look to the aspiration guided by the story.

What legalism does is to mistake the rule that expresses the duty as all there is to it. It forgets that it is merely a point on an aspirational scale. The Pharisee who thinks of himself as better than his fellows because he follows the law is damned by Christ. He is not just damned for pride. He is damned because he thinks that following the law in the sense of the morality of duty is all there is to it. We have to look at the rule of duty within the context of the practice of aspiration of which it is a part. Though we have duties for which one might say that legalism is appropriate, this does not mean that they are written in stone. For aspiration will sometimes mean that the *sine qua non* of duty might have to be changed. At other times, duties that seem set in stone can be seen as an imprecise way of helping us to get to the aspiration which will also change those duties. An example of the former case can be seen when the duty is seen as more aspirational. It imposes too heavy a charge and breaking it would not be hypocritical as long as one held to the aspiration of which it is part. The latter case would be when the detailed rules enable one to come to an understanding of the aspiration for which they stand. This would enable one to break the rules, the better to follow the aspiration. Thus when the enlightened Christian moralist tells his perplexed student who finds it almost impossible to follow the church's complex and detailed moral teaching, 'All you need is love', he could mean both of these. He does not mean the love of the flower power days, rather that the rules are to some extent aspirational and should not be read as imposing impossible demands. That is why failing to follow the rules need not be hypocritical. To call it so would be to mistake aspiration for duty. And this is how legality differs from legalism in that sometimes the rules have to be changed or even broken to fulfil the aspiration. This is the true meaning of Hamlet's well-known claim that some customs are 'more honoured in the breach than in the observance': he does not mean, as it is commonly taken, that the customs are more normally breached than followed; rather that they are in fact honoured better by breaching them than by following them.

So we need both the rigidity of duty and of following the rules because they are there, and also the plasticity of being able to move beyond to re-evaluate what we have to do in light of the aspiration to excellence. So rule following is important. But knowing when to go beyond and not be in thrall to the rules in the context of by and large following the rules is what converts legalism into legality. So, in following the rules I must act heteronomously; that is follow them because they are the rules and not think about it, but must also know when it is appropriate to act autonomously – to act not because the rules say so, but because I think that it is appropriate for me to be flexible and go beyond the rules.

2.1.3 Norms and machines

Legalism and formality then, however much it might appear distasteful to Shklar, is necessary. We might think of legality as being a system where by and large people act in a machine-like way, following the rules blindly, precisely because they are the rules. However, they are always ready when appropriate, to move from that machine-like mode and act from careful examination of what to do. So we do not think about the law until, and when, we have to.

How might this look in the actual law? Atiyah (1986) lays the arguments out clearly in his article on 'Form and Substance in Legal Reasoning'. We treat the law as conclusive because it is there; we do not need to inquire behind it and 'think about it'. He uses the example of marriage to show the point behind formal reasoning. He confronts the argument proposed by certain legal scholars, that we do not need marriage as a formal status in the law, for everything that turns on it could be considered ad hoc in the context of a two-person relationship. We could then abolish marriage as a legal institution. We would solve the problems of what, for example, counts as cohabitation for various purposes such as inheritance or social security law, by looking at it case by case and making substantive moral decisions. But this would be ineffective and time consuming. We can see this in the difficulties courts have been having with such concepts as palimony. The introduction of the status of marriage insulates us from many of these problems and gives us clear definitions by tying cohabitation to marriage. But the question still remains – what is the guarantee that the decision made this way is morally acceptable? We seem to be back where we started.

Atiyah says that the reason we feel that our formal decision is right is, in the end, because we are satisfied and certain in our substantive decisions. The implication is that at some time the substantive problems were solved rationally and thus we can now afford to use formal reasoning. The institution comes about because gradually a practice grows up where, for example, we do something we say we will, not merely for the substantive reasons we had in saying we would do it, but also because of the reason that we said we would do it. At first that is one among all the reasons, but gradually it excludes the other and so we might say the convention of promising grows up. We do it because we promised and the other reasons are excluded. Thus the institution grows up on the back of the substantive reasons since the reason that it is a promise can be seen as a universalisation of the substantive reasons. This gives us a democratic, autonomous, input and machine-like heteronomy.

What I am trying to show is that 'not thinking about it' and thus behaving like an automaton is in some situations appropriate and acceptable. Take an example from the work of Jones and Sergot (1992). Here are some simple library regulations:

1. A separate form must be completed by the borrower for each volume borrowed.
2. Books should be returned by the due date.
3. Borrowers must not exceed their allowance of books on loan at any one time.
4. No books will be issued to borrowers who have books overdue for return to the library.

Book allowances:

Undergraduate – 6
Postgraduate – 10
Academic Staff – 20

We can design a system that operates according to these specifications in such a way that we can, as Sergot and Jones say, 'force actuality and ideality to coincide'. How do we do this? First, we produce a database of who has borrowed what and when. Second, the system for borrowing books is now automated in the following way. To borrow a book a library card is inserted and the machine sees, from the information in the card and its database, whether the person is in good standing in respect of the regulations. If not, then the card is ejected and they are not let through. If things are acceptable, then an electronic version of the book is given for the appropriate amount of time after which it self-destructs. We see here that regulations 1 and 4 become obsolete and 2 and 3 are merely statements of what is the case. What we see then is how the normative has become descriptive. This gives us an example of rule following, which has the machine-like quality of heteronomy – we 'don't think about it'.

We can also see something like this working in payroll computers where tax is automatically deducted in accordance with a calculation of the employee's tax liability. Here again, normative laws become descriptive because machines provide for what 'ought to be' through defining what can happen. That is not to say that there may not be an override function that enables a return to the normative modality, for example, through provision of a system of appeals. It is rather to say that in machine-like applications of norms, what ought to happen becomes what does happen, without interpretation, discretion or any flexibility intervening.

In conclusion, our social organisations are faced with the task of having to act both in a machine-like way and in a spontaneous manner. There are times when we need to 'think about it' and times when we do not, and these should be complementary. Legality, properly understood, is this combination. Legalism is connected with legality; it is the rule-bound attitude, implicit in it, as one of its parts. But the kind of legalism that Shklar attacks is where that attitude is taken for the whole of legality. This can have drastic consequences. This is because 'not thinking about it', if left to its own devices, tends to take over the entire social world. The world becomes a place peopled by automata, who act like automata, hurtling to destruction because the only thing that determined their action was the rules.

Legality prevents this happening by introducing a difficult balance in the middle ground. It allows us to think of the law- and rule-governed institutions as linking heteronomy and autonomy together without destroying one or the other. This will create a mode of organisation where both heteronomy and autonomy operate in a way that is complementary, one to the other and, which, in its total operation, can be called legality.

Reading

Shklar (1986) is the best starting point for further research on this topic. She defines 'legalism' as the 'ethical attitude that holds moral conduct to be a matter of rule-following' (p 1), but such morality, she emphasises, can only properly be understood in its concrete manifestations. Her analysis of the function of law in international politics (1986: 123–42) and landmark political trials (Nuremberg and Tokyo, 1986: 143–90) are exemplary manifestations of legalism in practice, and remain as pertinent as ever.

Given the importance of Fuller's work, as referred to in 1.4 above, you should also return to Fuller (1969). Bankowski (2001) develops in greater detail several of the themes and examples outlined here.

References

Atiyah, PS, 1986, 'Form and Substance in Legal Reasoning', in DN MacCormick and P Birks (eds), *The Legal Mind*, Oxford: Oxford University Press.

Bankowski, Z, 2001, *Living Lawfully: Love in Law and Law in Love*, Dordrecht: Kluwer.

Fuller, L, 1969, *The Morality of Law*, New Haven: Yale University Press.

Jones, A and Sergot, M, 1992, 'Deontic logic in the representation of law: towards a methodology', *Artificial Intelligence and Law* 1:1 45–64.

Shklar, J, 1986, *Legalism: Law, Morals, and Political Trials*, Cambridge, MA: Harvard University Press.

2.2 Citizenship: competing conceptions

2.2.1 Citizenship between membership and participation

The last couple of decades have witnessed a remarkable renewal of interest in citizenship. At one level the reasons for this are obvious. Citizenship talk invokes active political participation, self-determination and values of community. It shifts the emphasis from 'rights' and individualism to duty and care; from 'myopic' bargaining to disinterested public deliberation; from self-interest to 'empathy'; from passivity and compromise to the active pursuit of common collective values. The theory professes to fulfil the promise of what Jurgen Habermas calls a 'constitutional patriotism' or even the more elusive one of social solidarity, which, as Michael Walzer once put it, is the patriotism of the Left.

Citizenship, with its roots in both the ideas of *state membership* and *political participation*, stands, in an important way, witness to a tension between the two. For a long time 'citizenship', 'citoyenneté' or 'Staatsbürgerschaft' meant political membership, where membership was conferred from above and established the legal link with a State that exercised effective power over a given territory. Membership was established through a network of duties and rights that connected citizen and State. While the element of membership did not change, as a result of the dramatic events of the late eighteenth century, sovereignty was effectively transferred from the king to 'the people'. The transferral enriched the liberal moment of civil liberties (liberties from the State) with rights of (political) participation in the formation of the people's sovereign will. With it came a shift of emphasis from membership to participation.

One of the main preoccupations in recent legal and political theory has been the relative demise of the Nation-State in the face of the globalisation of the economy and the relative inability of national economies to contain the flow of capital (see 2.3 below). This has led to the need to rethink many assumptions underlying political community and the very concepts we used to describe its sovereignty, its politics and its law. Yet it is of paramount importance to stress that despite these developments the link with the State – 'membership' – is crucial to citizenship and cannot be severed. A double connection underlies citizenship. On the one hand there is the connection to political participation: citizenship is the status or office that can operationalise political rights. On the other hand, there is the connection with the State that defines the contours of the relevant political community and in effect the circumference of political space. Citizenship not only involves a common membership, but relies on that membership to initiate and direct participatory undertakings.

So how is the tension between membership and participation expressed, and what does it entail? Here is how the oppositional understandings are described by Jurgen Habermas and Charles Taylor, respectively:

> From the first perspective, citizenship is conceived in analogy to the model of received membership in an organisation which secures a legal status. From the second, it is conceived in analogy to the model of achieved membership in a self-determining ethical community. In the one interpretation, the individuals remain external to the State, contributing only in a certain manner to its reproduction in return for the benefits of organisational membership. In the other, the citizens are integrated into the political community like parts into a whole.
>
> (Habermas 1992, pp 8–9)

> One model focuses mainly on individual rights and equal treatment, as well as on government performance which takes account of citizen preferences. This is what has to be secured. Citizen capacity consists mainly in the power to retrieve these rights and ensure equal treatment, as well as to influence the effective decision-makers. These institutions have an entirely instrumental significance . . . No value is put on participation in rule for its own sake. The other model by contrast, defines participation in self-rule as of the essence of freedom, as part of what must be secured. This is an essential component of citizen capacity. Full participation in self-rule is seen as being able . . . to have some part in the forming of a ruling consensus, with which one can identify along with others.
>
> (Taylor 1989, p 178ff)

The opposition between the two models is usually assumed to correlate to a *liberal/republican* divide.

2.2.2 Liberal and republican citizenship

It needs to be emphasised that the labels themselves – 'liberal' and 'republican' – are contested, variably understood, often seen as overinclusive. Let us therefore attempt to clarify, in this context of competing conceptions of citizenship, what positions exactly they denote. The 'liberal' conception, largely interchangeable with the term 'pluralist', is linked with a conception of the public democratic sphere as an association, and associational democracy views the State as the 'significant other' of civil society. Theorists of associational democracy focus on social groups and voluntary associations as embodiments of partisan solidarities, ideological and interest group affiliations, partisan beliefs and interests, competing, overlapping, even mutually undercutting. This commitment to a pluralist democratic culture unites theorists as diverse as those who warn against subsuming the heterogeneity of civil society under State political institutions and processes to those writers from the 'old' Eastern Europe, whose obvious target is still the nightmare of collective harmony under the watchful State. What is significant to this position is that it does not view dissonance and fragmentation as undermining civil society's self-discovery and therefore assigns no integrative function to State-sanctioned processes; in fact the latter would prove erosive to that heterogeneity that is constitutive of civil society. In this view, associations are conceived of, primarily, as countervailing forces to the State.

So what is wrong with political pluralism? Nancy Rosenblum summarises it like this: 'Individuals bring interests ready-formed to groups, which simply amplify them; interests are partial and contingent and thus without significance to moral identity; liberal pluralism is based on scepticism about our ability to communicate needs and values in a fashion that moves others towards consensus.' (1994, p 74) If the republicans are sceptical of the pluralist commitment to the sovereignty of associations and their superiority over State sovereignty, it is because this would erode the fundamentally *integrative* role of the democratic deliberative process and the production of authoritative public norms.

The civil society that republicans have in mind is instead one that conceives of the State and civil society on a continuum. Michael Walzer writes characteristically: 'Only a democratic state can create a democratic civil society; only a democratic civil society can sustain a democratic state.' Far from being the 'significant other' of civil society, the State is its presupposition in this formulation. Walzer's argument here is reminiscent of that powerful current in communitarian theory, most evident in Charles Taylor's work, which understands deep allegiance to the State and commitment to one's community as interchangeable. The 'atomism' of liberalism and pluralism – rather than the State – become what threatens civil society with erosion. The individualist underpinning of both liberalism and pluralism, claim the republicans, with the consequent emphasis on issue-based memberships and prepolitical interests, misunderstands the value of the integrative function of political participation itself. As benign guarantor of the democratic process, thus, the State is not rejected but endorsed. No resonances here of the 'bourgeois state' to 'be seized', 'occupied' or to 'wither away'. The empowerment of civil society gains its leverage from the State and its law.

Let us pause here to look at the connection with law that underlies each model. In both cases, though in radically different ways, constitutionalism is the institutional expression of the Public Sphere; constitutionalism provides the institutional form (and guarantee) of political communication through freedom of speech and the press, assembly, association and petition, suffrage and the right to form and join political parties. Within the contours of this constitutionalism, liberal and republican accounts of citizenship can be accommodated. The existence of the constitutional framework underpins both competing positions, because neither transcends the language of citizenship and rights and both seek their anchorage, ultimately, in law.

Citizenship is a status that confers a set of rights upon individuals. Citizenship, in other words, is the right to have those rights. The ascription of the legal status grants the capacity to exercise rights. Special mention needs to be made in this context to the special place of the right to free speech. In terms of political participation in public life it is particularly significant. Sovereignty means self-government and freedom of speech underpins it in this sense: the speech of the individual citizen is the input into the formation of public opinion that gears self-government. The right to speak, as input into the collective self-determination, is the vessel of citizenship; only in that process is citizenship realised. The intimate connection between speech and citizenship is essential if the argument from citizenship is to be understood properly: *speech is the mode of existence of the citizen; free speech makes the citizen sovereign.* Freedom of speech is integral to, rather than a result or a condition of, democracy; it defines the democratic conception of politics.

If liberals and republicans share certain assumptions about the importance of constitutionalism, it is also because the latter in an important sense centres the opposition. Where the liberal sees accommodation of interest the republican sees the grounds for an intersubjectively shared action. Where the liberal sees a one-way process of feeding his/her contribution into the collective Public Opinion, the republican sees also a feedback; in that participation in debate turns back to situate the lone political actor in shared intersubjectivity. But underpinning both positions is a shared legal/constitutional premise, seen in the one case (liberal) as a guarantee from the collective will, in the other (republican) as a springboard for collective praxis.

2.2.3 The paradox of constitutionalism

Let us look more concretely at how the differences play out by turning to a dilemma or paradox so central to constitutional law to have sometimes been identified as the essence of constitutionalism itself in American jurisprudence and in constitutional orders of the European continent, but which also has had a massive impact in the discourse in the UK over the constitutional status of human rights.

The contradiction is generally referred to, as Alexander Bickel famously put it in 1962, as the *counter-majoritarian paradox*. In a nutshell, the problem is that the constitution at once proclaims popular sovereignty and at the same time establishes limits – rights – and a mechanism – judicial review – that may override what the populace may wish at a particular time. The problem currently finds its most urgent expression in the suspect legitimacy of judicial review or, as Bickel put it, in the fact that judicial review remains a 'deviant institution' in democratic thinking (1962, p 18). Because how can it be consistent with basic democratic principle that the Court should be able to invalidate decisions of 'We the People' as expressed through their representatives?

It is instructive for our purposes that liberals and republicans follow different lines of argument out of the quandary. Let us call the liberal solution 'dualist', though it is arguably more a blatant admission of the tension rather than an attempt to overcome it. This solution is to claim rights as 'fundamental' or 'trumps'. This line of argument subordinates democracy to rights and maintains that individual rights should always outweigh – or 'trump' – democratic choices when the two compete. But this does not automatically translate as a privileging of law over politics because, as fundamental rights theorists argue, our very political culture incorporates both rights and democracy as of fundamental value. Western democracy has developed a commitment to upholding fundamental rights as inherent and constitutive feature; therefore, no externality, and therefore, no paradox.

It is precisely here, at the constitutional junction of law and politics, that public lawyers locate republicanism as a theory about the empowerment of civil society. It is a theory that draws on a number of disciplines and integrates the insights into constitutional theory to suggest a thorough rethinking of the premises of constitutionalism.

Where in liberal constitutionalism the Constitution is primarily a framework of constraint for politics, in the republican variant the Constitution becomes the springboard for politics. Republicanism is a theory about how political sovereignty finds expression in law. Law, claim the republicans, substantiates popular sovereignty by lending it constitutional provisions as a vehicle or 'home' of political deliberation. Of course in an important, if limited way, liberal and republican constitutionalism are at one: both seek a home for political deliberation in the Constitution. But the republicans attribute far more decisive functions to constitutional political deliberation, and the aspiration of 'community' is central to their theory. Republicanism's aspiration is for an intimate, mutually nurturing relationship between law and politics. But that is not all. Republicanism is not simply a theory about how law and politics emerge in a new synthesis – it is also a theory about retrieving the self in the process. The citizen actively participates in forming the political future and this active involvement, in turn, feeds back and situates the self-in-community.

The complex interrelationship is established by the republicans in stages (and there are of course variations between the major exponents as to how the interrelationship is to be understood precisely) of which two are significant.

The *first stage* involves them in arguing against a view of the interrelationship between law, politics and community, which they oppose. More accurately, the view they oppose cannot sustain their preferred interrelationship at all. This is an argument very much on communitarian lines, in which the target is the liberal 'thin' theory of the self. The most eloquent account draws its inspiration from Michael Sandel. The liberal image of the individual, says Sandel, is one of the 'unencumbered self' (Sandel 1984), whose values and convictions – as attributes of the self – become relegated to the external and the contingent as features of one's condition rather than as constituents of the person. In this way liberal theory misconstrues communities that generate value and commitment because it remains blind to the intricate ways in which these values and beliefs impinge upon the very constitution of the self. For liberals, already constituted selves 'enter' the community they inhabit in the same way that they would enter a voluntary association. Sandel contrasts this with his 'constitutive' conception of community whose members understand it as describing 'not only what they *have* as fellow citizens but also what they *are*, not a relationship they choose but an attachment they discover, not merely an attribute but a constituent of their identity' (1982, p 150). The recourse to communitarian theory allows republicanism to confront liberalism first and foremost on an epistemological basis. This in turn allows them to argue the fundamental importance of participation in politics as constitutive of both communities and selves.

Linked to this conception of the embedded self are two other central tenets of republicanism: those of *civic virtue* and *the common good*. To establish their importance the republicans will (again) confront the tradition of political pluralism.

What needs to be resisted, say the republicans, is the *pluralist* assumption that politics is a bargaining process where interests battle for recognition and superiority. According to the republicans, the pluralists view the public sphere as a political market that functions on the lines of the economic market. (Typically associated with OW Holmes, the 'marketplace of ideas' is conceived as the medium of competition of ideas and the mechanism of striking a balance.) Here, individual preferences and interests seek a mechanism to best accommodate their competition. Groups are nothing more than organisational forms through which individuals pursue their individual interests more effectively. What wins the competition is conceived as approximating public interest, and the market logic underpinning the political process guarantees democracy's self-correcting capacity. What the republicans most oppose is this conception of the political actor projected from within the logic of the *homo economicus*, which pulls away the ground from any possibility of conceiving an objective public interest in politics that transcends individual and group interests.

Having established their opposition to the theory of political pluralism in the broader framework, the republicans then direct the debate to constitutional theory. The republicans oppose an understanding of constitutional provisions as simply placing limits on political bargaining. Politics is the site where communities strive for self-determination, and the Constitution, claim the republicans, hosts the political process. In this context the republican rebuttal of pluralism is a rebuttal of a misconception that understands law as external to politics and community. The Constitution is misconstrued as a mechanism of checks and balances for, but external to, the bargaining process that is politics. It is in fact constitutively tied to politics. Let us return to the 'counter-majoritarian paradox' to see why this is so.

For the republican 'monist' solution, judicial review is not inimical to but in fact part of how we understand democracy. John Ely is usually hailed as the first major exponent of this argument, but many variations on it have since appeared. Judicial review exists, according to Ely, to 'unblock stoppages in the democratic process' and maintain open the channels of political change by, for example, facilitating the representation of minority interests. By securing political freedoms, judicial review secures what is integral to the function of an 'open and effective democratic process'. Ely's path-breaking work could thus more broadly be seen as suggesting that democracy provides a kind of master narrative that gives content and meaning to provisions about rights and lends the perspective through which rights may be interpreted. As MacCormick puts it:

> the advantage of insisting on rights as constitutionally derivative is, as we now see, that this leaves them in the end subject to democratic processes . . . It is to the people as a whole that belongs the decision about the exact specification of those rights, and about the other essential elements of constitutional structure and distribution of constitutional authority. In this way democracy acquires a self-referential character.
>
> (MacCormick 1993, p 143)

This line of argument is renewed in Dworkin's *Law's Empire* and Habermas's 'co-originality thesis' between democracy and rights, in *Between Facts and Norms*. It is by claiming this special role for law in the democratic deliberative process that the republicans 'dissolve' the constitutional paradox and disprove the externality of law to politics.

Having argued against conceiving law and politics as mutually opposing forces (as the pluralists would have it), the republicans proceed to the *second stage* of their argument, which in line with the 'monist thesis' outlined above, suggests a different function for law. They claim that the constitution provides for the possibility of politics and the substantiation of community. By inserting law into the picture they add a new and decisive variable to the 'communitarian' interconnection we saw them putting forward earlier. For the republicans it is the Constitution that underpins the community's politics, thus in one and the same stroke, promoting 'participation, capacitation and emancipation' (Michelman 1986, p 43). The communitarian connection lingers here not only in the argument about the social construction of the 'embedded' self, but also in the argument that although citizenship is a universal category the dialogue into which it facilitates entry is specific to the historical community. The background to new republican theory is a tradition of political thought with roots in Aristotle's *Politics*, Cicero's *Res Publica*, Macchiavelli, Hegel, Harrington, a tradition renewed by Hannah Arendt and Leo Strauss, all of whom conceive society as a politically constituted system. This tradition envisages man as a 'political being', who could only realise his telos in a *vivere civile*, a republic. The debt to these theorists runs deep. Arendt's own definition of politics sounds very apposite: 'The realm of politics', she says in *On Revolution*, 'is the organisation of the people as it arises out of acting and speaking together, and its true space lies between people living together for this purpose'. The most important element here – and in the new republicanism – is that membership in the political community is not seen – as the liberals and pluralists would have it – as a means to an end, the pursuit of partisan choice, but instead it is in the very process of participation as its own end that perspectives engage with one another and conceptions of a good that is common are shaped. Whereas in the liberal/pluralist worldview, politics is about promoting diverse goods, and thus relies on bargaining within a framework of rules neutral to the bargaining parties, the republican picture of politics is one of the pursuit of the *common good*. In their account, the heterogeneity of interest associated with liberalism gives way to the heterogeneity of perspective. Bargaining gives way to arguing, and this shift allows the republicans to claim 'civic virtue' for their politics, a tenet so central as to be characterised as the 'animating principle' of republicanism.

This is a restatement of popular sovereignty in no uncertain terms. Having argued the meaning and significance of their three key notions – *participation, common good and civic virtue* – the republicans can now celebrate having established a connection between the embedded *self*, where the form of that embeddedness is participation in *dialogue*, that at once both constitutes the realm of politics and substantiates *community*, and finally *law* as enabling the dialogue in the constitutional forum, their recourse to constitutional legal discourse as communal, political discourse.

Reading

For further discussion of the perspectives in terms of national versus European identity see Habermas (1992); Habermas (1999) ch 4; and his much discussed paper, Habermas (2001). For elaboration of the question of the demos in Europe see Weiler (1999) ch 10. For further reading on these issues in the context of the EU, see Bankowski and Christodoulidis (1998); N MacCormick (1999) and Lindahl (1998).

See Michael Sandel's 'The Unencumbered Self' in Sandel (1984) for the classic statement of the communitarian attack on liberalism's conception if the person. See, also, Taylor, 'Cross-Purposes: The Liberal-Communitarian Debate'.

For the theories that see democracy and constitutional rights as complementary or co-original, see Ely (1981), and Habermas (1996), *Between Facts and Norms*, especially the Postscript, which provides a good summary.

For a republican reading of constitutionalism in the UK the classic text is Griffith (1979), and for a recent restatement Tomkins (2005), ch 1. In the US context see especially Michelman (1986), Sunstein (1986) and Michelman (1988) for one of the most interesting republican accounts of constitutional interpretation that engages questions of democracy, community and self-determination.

References

Bankowski, Z and Christodoulidis, E, 1998, 'The European Union as an Essentially Contested Project', *European Law Journal* 341–54.

Bickel, A, 1962, *The Least Dangerous Branch: The Supreme Court as the Bar of Politics*, Cambridge, MA: Harvard University Press.

Ely, JH, 1981, *Democracy and Distrust*, Cambridge, MA: Harvard University Press.

Griffith, JAG, 1979, 'The Political Constitution', 42 *Modern Law Review*, 1.

Habermas, J, 1992, 'Citizenship and National Identity: Some Reflections on the Future of Europe', 12 *Praxis International* 1–19.

Habermas, J, 1996, *Between Facts and Norms*, Cambridge, MA: MIT Press.

Habermas, J, 1999, *The Inclusion of the Other*, Cambridge: Polity.

Habermas, J, 2001, 'Why Europe needs a constitution', 11 *New Left Review* 5–26.

Lindahl, H, 1998, 'The purposiveness of law: two concepts of representation in the European Union', 17 *Law & Philosophy* 481–507.

MacCormick, N, 1993, 'Constitutionalism and democracy' in R Bellamy (ed), *Theories and Concepts of Politics*, Manchester: Manchester University Press, 124–47.

MacCormick, N, 1999, *Questioning Sovereignty*, Oxford: Oxford University Press.

MacCormick, N, 2007, *Institutions of Law*, Oxford: Oxford University Press.

Michelman, F, 1986, 'Foreword: Traces of Self-Government', 100 *Harvard L R* 4.

Michelman, F, 1988, 'Law's Republic', 97 *Yale L.J.* 1493.

Rosenblum, N, 1994, 'Democratic Character and Community', 1, *The Journal of Political Philosophy*, 67.

Sandel, M (ed), 1984, *Liberalism and Its Critics*, Oxford: Blackwell.

Sunstein, C, 1986, 'Legal Interferences with Naked Preferences', *U Chicago L R* 1129.

Taylor, C, 1989, 'Cross-Purposes: The Liberal-Communitarian Debate', in N Rosenblum (ed), *Liberalism and the Moral Life*, Cambridge, MA: Harvard University Press, 159–82.

Tomkins, A, 2005, *Our Republican Constitution*, Oxford: Hart.

Weiler, J, 1999, *The Constitution of Europe*, Cambridge: Cambridge University Press.

2.3 Law, politics and globalisation

2.3.1 Globalisation and the reconfigured state

In the modern era, the State has been central to debates in law and politics. The main prize for political parties was to gain control of national legislative and executive institutions, with the power to make national laws and policies seen as the means of implementing their policy agenda. This framework remains influential: much political activity is still directed towards national parliaments and governments, and the study of law largely consists of learning rules of the national legal system where the student resides. However, this traditional focus on the State is coming under pressure from claims that we live in a time of globalisation. Globalisation stands for the idea that national borders are becoming less important to the conduct of social life. For example, arguments about the emergence of global patterns of economic organisation, or global forms of culture, have been advanced to show that we are living in a significantly more interconnected world, often in relation to the spread of liberal capitalism and Western-style consumerism.

We can identify three ways in which the idea that the Nation-State is the sole, or principal, location of political authority is coming under pressure in the global era. First is the relocation of power from the national level to supranational entities such as the European Union (EU) and the World Trade Organization (WTO). While the original impetus for this was often framed in relatively narrow terms, such as setting common customs duties, the deliberations of these bodies now affect a wide range of public policy matters, such as agriculture, health, trade and social policy. Other developments that should be included here include the rise of regional and international mechanisms supervising the protection of human rights. The legal instruments issuing from these bodies often have a higher formal status than national laws, and disobedient States can face the threat of sanctions.

Political authority can also be seen to be escaping downwards as well as upwards. Claims for greater devolution of power within existing States are themselves something of a global phenomenon, whether in Canada, the UK, Spain, Germany, Italy or former Soviet States. These present a further challenge to the Nation-State by redistributing political authority to the subnational level, often constitutionally guaranteed against encroachment from the centre. In contrast to this emphasis on new institutions above or below the State, a third challenge highlights the dispersal of power beyond the State. This argues that political authority is now exercised in multiple settings, for example, new forms of decision making within supranational organisations, or networks of international agencies or in the actions of multinational corporations.

As a result, the State is being significantly reconfigured. Some of its former core functions are being performed elsewhere, whether by global regulatory bodies or privatised utilities. Those functions it retains are often subject to new restraints, for example, that they follow market-based ideas such as efficiency and effectiveness. Some argue that it is important to place these developments in geopolitical context, and that the worldwide trend to adopt neoliberal economic policies, that is reduced taxation, fiscal restraint, deregulation, privatisation, free trade and unrestricted currency flows, necessarily leads to a weakened State. The other processes listed above can also be seen to accentuate State weakness: supranational economic and human rights regimes can limit the scope for national policy innovation, while subnational entities have even less power to resist the prevailing global consensus.

Some capture the complexity of contemporary patterns of political authority with the idea of multilayered governance. Where once political activists may have sought to lobby MPs or government ministers, there are now a host of potential actors who may require their attention, whether members of devolved or regional assemblies, MEPs, NGOs, international agencies, social movements or boards of directors. In some cases, it may be unclear as to who are the responsible actors. The result is to remove the State from any preordained position at the centre of the legal and political universe. As Martin Loughlin has put it, '[t]he success of the modern state over the last two hundred years has been based mainly on its ability to promote economic well-being, to maintain physical security and to foster a distinctive cultural identity of its citizens' (Loughlin 2000, p 145). This account is now being called into question by globalisation.

2.3.2 Sovereignty after globalisation

In an earlier section, we characterised sovereignty as a contested concept. If anything, debates over sovereignty have intensified in the context of globalisation. The departure point for these debates is the demise of the Nation-State, understood in terms of a homogeneous people exercising self-governance through a single set of public institutions. In this traditional model, sovereignty was seen as an expression of a State's political autonomy. This political autonomy had an internal and external dimension: internal authority over a particular community, and external independence vis-à-vis other States. We can identify two strands of debate that call this account increasingly into question. One addresses principally the first two developments listed above, that is the rise of new sub- and supranational institutions; while the other considers the consequences of globalisation writ large, that is, the rise of the global economy. Each approach brings a quite different perspective to the questions of what sovereignty is, where it resides and how far it has to be reconceptualised as a result of globalisation.

If we take first the new institutional structures that operate across and within borders, some theorists, such as Neil MacCormick, suggest that in an era of multilayered governance, sovereignty may have outlived its usefulness as a concept. Focusing on the development of the EU, MacCormick argues its Member States do not possess unfettered constitutional power to make laws as this can be overridden by EU law. Furthermore, as a result, these States no longer enjoy unrestrained political power in their external relations. However, this does not mean sovereignty has been transferred to the EU as it does not possess political or legal independence apart from its members. Accordingly, notions of ultimate authority fail to capture the nature of contemporary legal and political relations. Thus as we have seen, MacCormick believes the supposedly sovereign State may well be a transient historical phenomenon, and that we are now in an age of 'post-sovereignty'. This is posited as a preferable framework for the study of law and politics: once we reject the idea of absolute sovereignty, this better tailors discussion about democracy to the reality of a plural legal and political order, for example, by acknowledging that sometimes, citizens' needs are best met at a smaller level of government, other times at a larger.

Other commentators argue that rather than seeing the appropriate response to globalisation as dispensing with the concept of sovereignty, it is better to consider how it is being transformed. They note that despite calls to abandon the language of sovereignty, it persists in political debate, for example, to resist further European integration. Neil Walker, for example, describes the present as a period of 'late sovereignty', to signify that we have not achieved a complete conceptual break with the past. For Walker, the key to overcoming the limits of the Westphalian approach is to shift from describing sovereignty as some objective measurement of power to regarding it as a 'claim concerning the existence and character of a supreme ordering power for a particular polity' (Walker 2003, p 6), whose practical importance depends on its plausibility to key actors in the political system.

The context for Walker's analysis is the growth of non-State entities, such as the EU, as rivals to States in claiming sovereignty. However, what is distinctive about this phase of sovereignty is that these claims are no longer being viewed in absolute terms. This arises because supranational bodies tend not to exercise authority over all matters within a particular territory, but only in respect of certain functions. For example, while the EU claims to be the highest legal authority over matters such as agriculture or fisheries, competences remain with Member States. Accordingly, we can no longer link claims of ultimate authority to territorial exclusivity. Walker argues that this picture of multiple and overlapping – including State and supra-State – claims to authority gives us a better explanation of the emerging global legal configuration. For him, this also has a prescriptive dimension, and provides the guiding ethic that law and politics should be based upon the mutual recognition of different authority claims.

Other theorists regard talk of 'post' or 'late' sovereignty as premature. Loughlin finds the original conceptual underpinnings of sovereignty highly relevant today (see Loughlin 2003). For him, sovereignty expresses a political relationship between rulers and ruled. This relationship combines two facets of sovereignty in the modern State: competence, which refers to its formal legal authority, and capacity, which denotes where political power actually resides. Once this is grasped, he suggests that developments such as the establishment of the EU should not be seen as eroding sovereignty. While Member States may agree to share jurisdictional competence with the EU, this does not amount to a sharing of sovereignty (which in Loughlin's view is conceptually impossible). This is because questions of sovereignty are not determined by new institutional arrangements, but are essentially matters of political capacity. He suggests that the test of continuing sovereignty is whether Member States can withdraw from the EU. Loughlin argues that in the exceptional state of crisis that this scenario envisages, there is little doubt that States retain the right to leave, and for him this shows that they still possess ultimate power and authority.

The debates so far canvassed have focused on public institutional developments, but what of the growth of private political authority beyond the State? An alternative approach is advanced by Saskia Sassen (1996) who sees the relevant challenges to sovereignty as grounded in changes in global political economy. In this connection, she posits a 'new geography of power' whose key sites include supranational organisations, but also global capital markets, transnational legal firms, international commercial arbitration, international human rights codes and electronic economic activity. These combine to reconfigure the interface between territory and sovereignty. For example, for some, New York City is a municipality that runs local services such as rubbish collection, while for others it is a centre for international bond agencies, whose credit ratings can veto national economic policies. In this way, the new geography leads to a partial displacement of economic activity from national territory.

Loughlin acknowledges that these developments may present a stronger challenge to sovereignty as capacity because the power ceded to global markets is not readily recoverable by issuing edicts through formal legal authority (Loughlin 2004). But this raises important questions about the relationship between law and politics: if, as Loughlin suggests, sovereignty ultimately depends on political capacity, is there a point at which the exercise of power by private actors translates into legal competence? Sassen answers this in the affirmative, and highlights new legal regimes that operate outside the public institutional setting, but are instead located in the activities of multinational corporations. These regimes are important in explaining the rules and procedures that apply, for example, to regulating the internet or intellectual property, or aspects of international trade such as insurance and the maritime industry.

Within the supranational debate, there is a strong tendency to attribute sovereignty to expressions of public power, and remove consideration of the private or economic sphere from the discussion. But in the changing land-scape of governance painted by globalisation, distinctions such as that between public and private may now appear outmoded and unhelpful. This casts some of the debates outlined above in a different light. If, as Loughlin tells us, sovereignty is an expression of a political relationship, some of the most important relationships in the global age may be those between indi-viduals and the corporations whose decisions affect the quality of their lives in significant ways, or those that arise from the complex interaction between State, supra-State and non-State forms of normative ordering on which the residual effectiveness of State law may now depend. Or if, as Walker tells us, sovereignty is now better understood as a claim, should sovereignty be restricted to those making self-conscious claims, or should we expand it to cover those private actors who remain silent, perhaps because they do not wish to attract unwanted scrutiny to the political authority they exercise? Accord-ingly, adverting to broader processes of globalisation potentially represents a more radical conceptual rupture with the traditional understandings of sovereignty.

2.3.3 Constitutionalism beyond the State

The diffusion of political authority as a result of globalisation raises import-ant questions about how power is held to account. Traditionally, constitu-tions have provided the institutional and normative framework for discussing questions of law and politics, and in particular the question of the legitimate exercise of power. In modern times, a constitutionally legitimate regime has come to be understood as one that embodies the values of democracy. As with sovereignty, our conceptual apparatus of constitutionalism initially developed with reference to the Nation-State. Thus in its ideal condition, constitutionalism was the means by which a sovereign people within national borders could exercise control over those who governed them, by subjecting politics to the rule of law. But in an age of globalisation, State-centered approaches to constitutionalism may address only part of a broader constel-lation of political authority. For example, while constitutions safeguard free and fair elections to national parliaments, they generally provide for negligible or no popular participation in decisions of supranational bureaucracies or multinational corporations despite the impact that the decisions of these bodies have on people's lives. Accordingly, globalisation can be seen to provoke a legitimation crisis, as national constitutions can no longer guarantee citizens effective democratic control over their rulers.

There has been considerable interest recently in ideas of constitutionalism beyond the State. Neil Walker (2003) argues that constitutionalism – which he sees as the vocabulary for the mutual articulation of law and politics – is intrinsic to the polity understood as the setting for the conduct of politics. In the period of late sovereignty, the polity is not confined to the State, and so we should now associate constitutions with bodies such as the EU or WTO. Walker suggests that we need to understand how some of the traditional functions of national constitutions, such as delineating a formal hierarchy of laws or specifying the rights of citizenship, are now carried out at the supranational level. The extent to which any supranational entity can be characterised in constitutional terms though, is a matter of degree. In this regard, Walker finds that the EU (for example, where the supremacy of EU law is accepted by Member States) is further down the path of constitutionalisation than the WTO (which has no equivalent doctrine).

Supranational constitutionalism does not simply reproduce national constitutional forms on a broader scale. It is in many respects qualitatively different as these new polities, unlike States, are limited in their jurisdictional scope, and do not aspire to provide a comprehensive legal order within hermetically sealed borders. Accordingly, the task of translating State-based constitutional concepts to the supranational level is not straightforward, as the above discussion of the various attempts to adapt sovereignty to the global age demonstrates. However, for Walker the key to accomplishing this is to understand that State constitutional orders have not disappeared, but necessarily exist in relation to non-State sites of constitutionalism, whose purpose is often to influence or direct national legal systems. Accordingly, he suggests we now live in an era of 'constitutional pluralism' (Walker 2002).

For Walker, recovering the language of constitutionalism at the supranational level is important because the often contentious issues which animated traditional constitutionalism, such as the nature of representation and how institutional power should be structured and regulated, remain relevant and important, but have been relocated in the contemporary age. A powerful objection to this project is that it may confer an undeserved legitimacy upon supranational bodies. Given the strong positive connotations of constitutionalism with democracy, to speak, for example, of the WTO as a constitutional entity may suggest a capacity to exert democratic oversight over world trade, which may be absent. Walker's response is that the values and practices of constitutionalism (suitably adapted) are the best available means for engaging in debates over the legitimate exercise of power, and that rather than providing inappropriate closure, they keep dialogue open over how the democratic credentials of the emergent sites of supranational constitutionalism can be improved.

An alternative approach to constitutionalism beyond the State comes under the rubric of 'the new constitutionalism'. According to Stephen Gill, the new constitutionalism is a ' "global economic governance project" designed to "lock-in" the power gains of capital on a world scale' (Gill 2000, pp 11, 6). The context for this project is the rise of neoliberal economic policies (such as privatisation and low taxation) since the 1980s which, Gill argues, seek to discipline national governments so that they do not interfere with the free market. New constitutionalism supports this by placing barriers in the way of more redistributive forms of constitutionalism (which might, for example, promote social democratic goals of lowering material inequality) through legal and political measures that are difficult to reverse. Supranational legal forms are also highlighted here, whether the WTO imposing sanctions on States that deviate from the global economic consensus, or bilateral treaties that may require domestic constitutional reform in order to be eligible for inward investment. Less formal mechanisms are also important, for example, the pressures exerted by corporations on States to lower taxation or reduce domestic regulatory standards if they wish to attract their factories and jobs (resulting in what critics describe as a 'race to the bottom').

The question at the heart of the new constitutionalism is whether economic processes should be regarded as relevant for constitutional analysis. How we answer this has an important implication for how we link constitutionalism and democracy in the global age. In traditional terms, economic actors, like individual persons, were seen as subject to the constitutional jurisdiction of the State. Thus any problems posed to democracy by the growth of private power in the global economy can be addressed by making appropriate adjustments to existing constitutional mechanisms. In this connection, it is argued that developing constitutionalism on a supranational scale may provide the better opportunity for establishing democratic oversight over the forces of the global economy.

But from another point of view, this separation between the economic and the political can no longer be sustained in an era where corporations can be richer and more powerful than many States. For example, comparing annual sales to national GDP, General Motors has a higher annual turnover than Denmark, and Sony is bigger than Pakistan. If corporations should now be seen as important political actors whose actions and decisions have a direct impact on the lives of millions, this implies that political power (or the polity) not be limited to the public institutional setting of States and supranational organisations. It follows that, according to the new constitutionalism, questions about the location of sovereignty and the exercise and accountability of power now have to consider the relation not just between State and supranational, but also non-State sites of constitutionalism. Moreover, the latter may in practice be the most important, so focusing our attention on the first two sites alone may be of limited utility if our objective is to establish some degree of constitutional regulation over the market. This suggests that it may be necessary to craft innovative solutions, which do not adapt, but replace, current constitutional practices. For some, the only means for effective governance over the global economy is to establish a truly global polity – for example, with global (not international) representative institutions – while for others, the answer lies in bottom-up, not top-down, approaches such as the development of new forms of law and politics in global social movements. What seems clear is that in a time of globalisation many long-standing assumptions about law and politics may have to be revisited and rethought.

Reading

For an introduction to the idea of multilayered government, see Ilgen (2003). Loughlin's distinction between right and capacity, or the normative and empirical conceptions of sovereignty is discussed in Loughlin (2000, ch 10). MacCormick's theory of 'post-sovereignty' is concisely set out in MacCormick (1999, ch 8). For Walker's account of 'late sovereignty', see Walker (2003, pp 9–10), and also the responses by Loughlin (2004) and MacCormick (2004). For an application of the ideas of 'constitutional pluralism', and an elaboration of the constitutional attributes of the EU and the WTO, see Walker (2001, pp 28–50). For an application of ideas of the 'new constitutionalism' (Gill 2000) in the context of contemporary investment regimes, see Schneiderman (2000, pp 767–81).

References

Cutler, AC, 2003, *Private Power and Global Authority*, Cambridge: Cambridge University Press, ch 2.

Gill, S, 2000, 'The Constitution of Global Capital', accessed 14 March 2007, www.theglobalsite.ac.uk/press/010gill.pdf

Ilgen, TL, 2003, 'Reconfigured Sovereignty in the Age of Globalization', in TL Ilgen (ed) *Reconfigured Sovereignty: Multi-Layered Governance in the Global Age*, p 6, Aldershot: Ashgate.

Held, D and McGrew, A, 2003, 'The Great Globalization Debate: An Introduction', in Held and McGrew (eds), *The Global Transformations Reader*, 2nd edn, pp 1–50, London: Polity.

Loughlin, M, 2000, *Sword and Scales: An Examination of the Relationship Between Law and Politics*, Oxford: Hart, ch 10.

Loughlin, M, 2003, 'Ten Tenets of Sovereignty' in N Hart Walker (ed), *Sovereignty in Transition*, pp 55–86.

Loughlin, M, 2004, *The Idea of Public Law*, Oxford: Oxford University Press, ch 5.

MacCormick, N, 1999, *Questioning Sovereignty*, Oxford: Oxford University Press, ch 8.

MacCormick, N, 2004, 'Questioning Post-Sovereignty', 29 *Eur L Rev* 852.

Sassen, S, 1996, *Losing Control? Sovereignty in an Age of Globalization*, New York: Columbia University Press, ch 1.

Schneiderman, D, 2000, 'Investment Rules and the New Constitutionalism', 25 *Law & Social Inquiry* 757.

Walker, N, 2001, 'The EU and the WTO: Constitutionalism in a New Key', in G De Burca and J Scott (eds), *The EU and the WTO: Legal and Constitutional Issues*, Oxford: Hart, p 31.

Walker, N, 2002, 'The Idea of Constitutional Pluralism', 65 *Modern Law Review* 317–53.

Walker, N, 2003, 'Late Sovereignty in the European Union', in N Walker (ed), *Sovereignty in Transition*, Oxford: Hart, p 3.

2.4 Problems of the rule of law in political transitions

2.4.1 Dilemmas of the rule of law

Over the last 20 years a theme has come to prominence in legal studies concerning the role of law and legal institutions in political transitions. Under the title of 'transitional jurisprudence', scholars have paid close attention to the various ways in which law has been involved in facilitating countries – from as far apart as central and South America to Africa – in moving from non-democratic forms of political organisation to democratic ones. With the fall of the Berlin Wall and the so-called 'velvet revolutions' of the early 1990s, Europe also saw a burgeoning of jurisprudential reflection on problems of 'how to deal with the past'. What made these recent transitions so interesting – and so important – was due, in part, to the kind of problems thrown up for new governments who wanted to instil a faith in the belief that they would uphold the rule of law. Yet these governments were simultaneously faced with many competing demands to hold to account those who had perpetrated 'historic injustices' under the previous regime. As many people saw it, this produced a kind of rule of law dilemma: on the one hand, as we have already seen, the rule of law means (among other things) securing legal certainty by upholding legal expectations as they have been set out, in advance, by legislatures, courts and constitutions. On the other hand, many of the despotic policies of the previous regimes had been carried out by governments acting under the guise of the laws they had established. Now if the ideal of the rule of law as the upholding of legal expectations was to be respected and aspired to by the new regime, this would mean recognising the laws and legal expectations established by the previous regime, no matter how much suffering they might have caused. For example, in the well-known cases of the East German border guards, soldiers who had shot at escapees were to be prosecuted under the reunified German legal process for the shootings, which were deemed to be criminal offences; yet, the soldiers argued, these actions had been carried out under legally sanctioned orders at the time of their actions and for which they had been rewarded under the East German regime. Would it be legal or fair to find them guilty of criminal acts? Was this not a breach by the new democratic regime of the rule of law (and basic human rights) principle that no one should be punished for an act that was not a crime at the time of its commission? This, in a nutshell, was the dilemma: how to respond to prior injustices of a regime that claimed to be legal at the time? And it presented itself not only in criminal law, but in public and private law too (for example, as claims in restitution in property law). Moreover, bringing in another dimension to this, if reconciliation is important as an ideal for the emerging nation, what are the best approaches to justice and the rule of law in that regard and, significantly, might legal adjudication in these matters not in fact undermine the promise of and conditions for reconciliation, for example, between victims and former oppressors or between victims and current beneficiaries? At the very least we can note that how issues of reconciliation are presented will impact on jurisprudential questions in ways that are not experienced in non-transitional situations.

In this section we will explore in a little more detail some of the jurisprudential issues arising out of such 'transitional' problems. But it should be noted at the outset that although they have become, and remain, highly relevant to contemporary societies throughout the world, these problems are not entirely new. People have always had to deal with the issues of despotic governments and the consequences of their injustices, with problems of coming to terms with the aftermath of wars, civil conflicts and liberation from colonial rule (whether in America in the 1770s, Africa in the second half of the twentieth century, or post-Second World War Europe), and writers and political and legal actors have always had to engage with these problems. The social contract tradition, for example, most vivid in the work of such key thinkers of the modern era as Hobbes, Locke, Kant and Rousseau, was itself centrally concerned with how to establish legitimate government in a transition from what they described (in their different ways) as the state of nature. In that sense, problems of transitional justice are not new. Arguably what is new though, is the legal and international backdrop against which recent transitions have taken place. In a context where the rule of law, democracy and human rights are deemed to establish fundamental values that place limits on the actions of governments, and where – potentially in tension with this – an increasingly powerful and legally established global capitalist economy attempts to set the terms of national and international relations and commerce, the nature of political transitions is itself, we might say, in transition. The point has been reached, it could be argued, where it is law and legal norms in a global setting, rather than simply local politics or violence, which sets the terms of engagement for societies going through radical social and political upheaval. Where this is so, special attention needs to be paid to how the involvement of law and legal mechanisms operate either to limit or create possibilities for genuine social transformation.

In order to make some headway in this broad area of enquiry, we will identify a few key thematic issues in the area of transitional jurisprudence. Mainly, we are concerned here with highlighting the kinds of jurisprudential problems raised, rather than trying to address them in detail.

2.4.2 Difficulties in establishing accountability and responsibility

Where a country has experienced despotic government and injustice resulting in widespread harms, and that regime has now been replaced by a democratic one, one of the key questions faced is how to establish accountability for the harms suffered; that is, who, or which institutions, are to be held to give an account for causing the harms? Establishing accountability in this sense is the first step towards assessing the nature and extent of responsibility for the harms. While at first glance this might appear reasonably straightforward, in countries where this question is asked, a number of problems – some common, others unique to a particular place and time – make it less easy than it may at first seem. When atrocities have occurred on a massive scale, for example, in the commission of genocide or crimes against humanity, establishing accountability and responsibility requires analysing the complex causes, which together facilitated the commission of the harms, and for which conventional criminal law categories may not be adequate. Hannah Arendt, in her famous study of the 'banality of evil', quoted the judgment of the Israeli court in the trial of Adolf Eichmann for his role in the perpetration of the Holocaust:

> in such an enormous and complicated crime as the one we are now considering, wherein many people participated, on various levels and in various modes of activity – the planners, the organizers, and those executing the deeds, according to their various ranks – there is not much point in using the ordinary concepts of counselling and soliciting to commit a crime. For these crimes were committed en masse, not only in regard to the number of victims, but also in regard to the numbers who perpetrated the crime, and the extent to which any one of the many criminals was close to or remote from the actual killer of the victim means nothing, as far as the measure of his responsibility is concerned.
>
> (Arendt 1965, pp 246–7)

It is the extent of the harms, the difficulty of establishing exactly who is to be called to account, and which social institutions (for example, the military or government or the court system) might do this, that make establishing responsibility for them commonly such a daunting task. Despite this, however, there is the desire to see that some kind of justice is done and that impunity – that is, blanket immunity from being held responsible – does not prevail.

2.4.3 Forms of justice

But what kind of justice? Here we encounter different possibilities. One is a form of *retributive justice*, which holds that those who committed or ordered the crimes ought to suffer proportionate punishment for the harm they have caused, that is, they ought to be held criminally liable – assuming they are found guilty by a duly constituted court – and punished accordingly. This was the model adopted post-Second World War in the Nuremberg trials. Again, however, prosecutors and courts face an invidious task. They must establish in the first case the relevant jurisdiction over the offences and the accused, and they must establish that the alleged offences exist as crimes. (In the case of Nuremberg, one of the key crimes to be established was 'crimes against humanity'.) Otherwise, there may be a tendency, rightly or wrongly, to see the prosecutions as merely victors' justice, amounting to the imposition of retroactive laws on the defeated and overlooking offences committed by the victorious side. (This is a common argument, which arises in transitional contexts, most recently, for example, in the prosecution of the former Iraqi leadership.) Moreover, given the further problems of identification and capture of offenders, the potentially vast number of accused, and the difficulties surrounding evidence adequate to the high standard of the criminal trial, the very real possibility exists that only a few people will be brought to justice. Thus in some contexts there may be a sense that some people are being treated as scapegoats, and that a few convictions will work to expiate the crimes or complicity of many others who remain free, while in other contexts it may be perceived that the 'foot soldiers' rather than the senior political agents behind the policies of the regime are singled out unfairly for prosecution. In many such situations then, courts have to engage with the identification of actual perpetrators under conditions in which the 'normal' operation of criminal law seems to be unsettled, since it is often the case that in such scenarios 'the degree of responsibility increases as we draw further away from the man who uses the fatal instrument with his own hands' (Arendt, p 247).

This problem of unequal or uneven treatment is another element of the rule of law dilemma – whether and who to prosecute and for what – and it plays out particularly in the context of criminal law. If the new regime wants to establish its credentials as a rule of law State, then it must be seen to be objective, procedurally proper and not politically biased in its stance towards the prosecution of crime. But in transitional settings, which are often still highly unsettled, it is almost impossible to establish the conventional distance between politics and the criminal law. Would the establishment of the International Criminal Court (ICC) help in dealing with these questions? This is debatable. Even with the establishment of this Court, these doubts and difficulties do not disappear. Moreover, not all states have accepted its jurisdiction – perhaps most problematically, the United States of America – and even those that have may well argue that prosecutions are liable to be politically skewed.

These are perhaps some of the reasons why alternative means of holding to account have arisen in the context of recent political transitions. Under the broad banner of *restorative justice*, there has been an acknowledgement of the limits – though not the complete redundancy – of criminal law as a means of dealing with past injustices, and so attempts have been made to provide a different sense of doing justice to past injustices. Restorative justice is centrally concerned with restoring dignity to victims of injustice, and is also based on a concern that the community itself is in some need of restoration. One of the ways in which this has been promoted is through the use of different forms of tribunal which break the link between a finding of responsibility and punishment. Here, it is argued, it is necessary still to hold to account and find responsible those who committed atrocities, but due to a sensitivity to the conditions of the transition it is deemed desirable, for the sake of social reconciliation, both to establish the truth and give the victims and community a role in ways that criminal trials would not be able to achieve, and to understand the consequences of findings of responsibility in a way that goes beyond punishment and promotes social healing.

Perhaps the most prominent contemporary example of this is the Truth and Reconciliation Commission (TRC), established in South Africa in 1995 after the end of apartheid. The TRC was given the task of finding out the nature and causes of the offences committed under the apartheid regime, and one of its most important mechanisms for doing so was to provide amnesties for those who came forward and gave full disclosure of offences committed that were associated with the conflict between the apartheid government and anti-apartheid resistance. Thus in order to establish the truth about past injustices, and so to begin to promote the possibility of reconciliation in a deeply divided society, it was seen as necessary to sever the link between a finding of responsibility and punishment.

This was controversial, and a number of victims of apartheid policies objected that it failed to take seriously the gravity of the offences, and denied them the right to have justice – of the criminal or tortious variety – established by a court. If wrongs had been committed, they argued, then justice and the law demanded that they be prosecuted. The TRC responded, and the South African Constitutional Court upheld, that unlike blanket amnesties that give no form of accountability for past offences, amnesty of this conditional form was not a denial of justice, but rather provided for an alternative form of justice. This was legitimated by the TRC performing the difficult balancing act between victims' grievances and the need to determine the truth of the past in order to begin to overcome its divisions. This type of conditional amnesty – amnesty on condition of truth-telling – was seen as instrumental to the goal of seeking a shared and peaceable future. Of course, there is a paradox to amnesties in this form: from the same root as 'amnesia' they are about forgetting at least the legal consequences of past acts; but in order to forget, one must first know what to forget, that is, it is necessary to establish the truth about the past. In this tension lies what has been called the 'risk of reconciliation': exposure of too much truth about the past may undermine the restorative process, yet a complete covering over of the past fails to take seriously the injustices of the past and risks ongoing social disharmony and trauma for that reason.

Both these forms of justice in transitional scenarios have however been criticised from a third perspective. Where there is a focus on criminal law sanctions, or on amnesties and reconciliation processes, it has been argued that there tends to be inadequate attention paid to a third form of justice, namely *distributive justice*. Distributive justice is concerned with the distribution of goods, opportunities and liabilities in society. After the fall of the old regime, one of the important sets of decisions to be taken is the extent to which the new democratic regime will upset the distribution of such goods and opportunities as were established prior to the transition. For example, questions will be raised about whether or not to maintain the existing regime of property rights or relations, and the extent to which the effects of systemic discrimination against racial or ethnic groups ought now to weigh heavily in favour of redistribution. We might compare, say, the very different approaches taken to land distribution in Zimbabwe and South Africa after white minority rule came to an end in these countries.

In these instances the new government, or as is often the case, the courts, will face another version of the rule of law dilemma: on the one hand, to uphold legal expectations rooted in the already extant law, and on the other, to deal with the fact that these laws legitimated distributively unjust patterns which, if left in place, would merely continue the legacy of the prior regime. This problem usually reaches its height with regard to property law. Where the right to property is enshrined in the new democratic constitution then those holding property at that time could – again according to a principle of the rule of law – reasonably expect to have their legal rights secured and their property protected. But since this fails to address the problem of material injustice on behalf of the victims of the prior regime, competing claims emerge that challenge the *status quo ante* and demand that redistribution based on redressing past injustice trump the right to property.

One of the important jurisprudential aspects of this involves consideration of what might be called a 'temporal' dimension to justice. This raises the question as to whether the existence of *prior* injustice is relevant to doing justice now. Consider the following two arguments. One is that if there is a group in society who is at the moment disadvantaged, this means they should have a valid claim in distributive justice to address their needs now, and, that this is so, regardless as to how their disadvantage has historically arisen. In that sense, doing justice to their needs is no different from any other group in a society. By way of contrast, the other argument suggests that the disadvantaged group has a *special* claim in distributive justice, based in the nature of their experience in the past, that is, that their claim should be treated differently from others, because the historical causes of current disadvantage need to be taken into account in order that a full understanding and response to contemporary injustice be made meaningful.

Think, for example, of the case of those in the United States who seek reparations for the effects of slavery. Many argue that the historical injustice that was slavery creates special obligations to descendents of that institution that ought to be taken into account in addressing their needs in the present.

Among other things, they argue that were the existence of current disadvantage *not* in fact to take into account the prior injustice that was slavery, then there would be a failure fully to understand and grapple with the nature of the current social and economic inequalities suffered by many descendents of slaves? Of course, we would encounter questions of identity and causation across times that are not easily addressed in legal categories. And for that reason, among others, many suggest that the disadvantages suffered by many contemporary African-Americans should be dealt with merely as a matter of contemporary distributive justice, oriented to current need, irrespective of why or how that need came about. These are urgent debates that often require difficult choices over priorities in the distribution of resources and goods.

Hence the rule of law dilemmas in political and social transitions show up across a range of areas of legal practice, such as criminal, property and human rights law. But they also encounter more fundamental questions, in two senses: first, that these areas of law themselves may conflict as to their demands and benefits and that negotiating such conflicts may overload the legal categories themselves with political or moral pressures, which, in turn, may undermine the claim to any impartial or objective rule of law; second, as such, the value of the rule of law itself may well turn out to be only one factor among many competing social forces and so not only will the benefits of the rule of law be itself unable to negotiate the making of compromises, but that it too may need to be compromised in order to ensure a relatively stable transition.

These deeper problems are ones that are commonly taken to have been settled in stable societies. But it is one of the benefits of thinking about the rule of law in transitional periods that they expose to the light what exactly these 'settled' assumptions are. And this should constantly remind us that, despite them having receded into the background, they never entirely disappear, and this is particularly so in circumstances where past injustices may rear their head again for consideration, or where contemporary conditions may be deemed to be entering a period of insecurity or instability.

Reading

For a good analysis of several of the main themes see Teitel (2000), or Teitel (1997). For more extensive empirical analyses see Kritz (1995) and McAdams (1997).

David Dyzenhaus's review article of several books on this topic gives a good introduction to the literature in this area and some of the central issues it raises: see Dyzenhaus (2003). For his work on the Legal Hearings in the South African TRC, see Dyzenhaus's (1998) *Judging the Judges, Judging Ourselves* (Hart 1998). For a comparative study of truth commissions see Hayner (2002).

For a legal philosophical development of these themes, see the essays in Christodoulidis and Veitch's (2001) (eds) *Lethe's Law: Justice, Law, and Ethics in Reconciliation* (Hart 2001), especially – on South Africa – chapters by D Dyzenhaus and F du Bois. The South African Constitutional Court's validation of the amnesty process in the context of the truth and reconciliation process can be found in *AZAPO v The President of the RSA* (1996) judgment by Mahomed DP (at www.concourt.gov.za/judgment.php?case_id=11939). See also *South African TRC Report* (1998), especially vol 1 ch 5 'Concepts and Principles'.

There is a wealth of literature on restorative justice, but for an introduction, see Johnstone (2003).

On the border guards cases see the essays by Robert Alexy and Julian Rivers in Dyzenhaus (1999). For the cases themselves, see *K-HW v Germany*, and for the military superiors, *Streletz, Kessler and Krenz v Germany*, both decisions of the European Court of Human Rights.

For a thoughtful essay on problems of justice and identity in periods of transition, see Ignatieff (1998), final chapter.

References

Alexy, R, 1999, 'In defence of Radbruch's Formula' and Julian Rivers, 'The Interpretation and Invalidity of Unjust Laws', in D Dyzenhaus (ed), *Recrafting the Rule of Law*, Oxford: Hart.

Arendt, H, 1965, *Eichmann in Jerusalem: A report on the banality of evil*, Harmondsworth: Penguin.

Christodoulidis, E and Veitch, S, 2001 (eds), *Lethe's Law: Justice, Law, and Ethics in Reconciliation*, Oxford: Hart.

Dyzenhaus, D, 1998, *Judging the Judges, Judging Ourselves*, Oxford: Hart.

Dyzenhaus, D, 1999 (ed), *Recrafting the Rule of Law*, Oxford: Hart.

Dyzenhaus, D, 2003, 'Review Essay: Transitional Justice', 1.1 *International Journal of Constitutional Law* 163–75.

Hayner, P, 2002, *Unspeakable Truths: Facing the Challenge of Truth Commissions*, London: Routledge.

Ignatieff, M, 1998, 'The nightmare from which we are trying to awake', in M Ignatieff, *The Warrior's Honor*, London: Chatto & Windus.

Johnstone, G, 2003, *A Restorative Justice Reader: texts, sources and context*, Cullompton: Willan.

Kritz, N, 1995, *Transitional Justice: How Emerging Democracies deal with former regimes*, Washington, US: Institute of Peace Press, 3 vols.

McAdams, A, 1997 (ed) *Transitional Justice and the Rule of Law in New Democracies*, Notre Dame: University of Notre Dame Press.

South African TRC Report, 1998, 5 vols, Cape Town: Juta Press.

Teitel, R, 1997, 'Transitional Jurisprudence: The Role of Law in Political Transformation', 106 *Yale Law Journal* 2009–80.

Teitel, R, 2000, *Transitional Justice*, New York: Oxford University Press.

Cases

K-HW v Germany, Judgment of the European Court of Human Rights, 22 March 2001 (Application no. 37201/97).

Streletz, Kessler and Krenz v Germany, Judgment of the European Court of Human Rights, 22 March 2001 (Application nos. 34044/96, 35532/97 and 44801/98).

2.5 The rule of law and the state of emergency

'Laws fall silent during armed conflicts' – *inter arma silent leges* – must we take this ancient brocard at face value? Surely we can reply that we do now acknowledge laws of war, however rudimentary, and Geneva Conventions on Prisoners of War and Conventions against Torture even in wartime. Yet there is a contemporary trend towards eroding these in the face of a novel type of conflict, the 'war on terror' announced by President Bush, and subsequently endorsed by most other democratic heads of state, after the atrocities in New York, Pennsylvania and Washington on 11 September 2001. The sense of universality of the threat was enhanced by the bombings and mass murders in Madrid in March 2004 and in London in July 2005. The omnipresence of atrocity is, of course, not confined to the 'West'. In an almost routine way innocent lives were being destroyed on a regular basis among Israelis and Palestinians, a Lebanese Prime Minister was blown up by a car bomb, and collateral damage continues to take its toll of civilians in Iraq and Afghanistan, and hostilities in Chechnya rumble on almost incessantly.

Action against terrorists – at any rate against persons suspected of participation in terrorist activity – has been severe, nowhere more so than in the so-called 'Camp Delta' maintained by the United States at Guantanamo Bay. This being in Cuba, it lies outside the United States' courts' jurisdiction. The US Government deems those it holds in detention there to be 'unlawful combatants', not prisoners of war; it accordingly also considers that the normal legal constraints of domestic and international law do not apply. In February 2006, the UN Commission on Human Rights issued a report declaring that the US had committed acts amounting to torture at Guantanamo Bay, and called for it to close its holding pen for suspected terrorists. The response of the US authorities was to dispute the Commission's understanding of the law and to deny the evidentiary basis of the report (see *The Times*, London, 14 February 2006).

The denial that inmates there were suffering torture turned on the claim that ordinary definitions of torture could not be applied during such a conflict as the war on terror. Hence the Commission's findings that the circumstances of solitary confinement and other aspects of the detention at Guantanamo amounted to 'inhuman and degrading treatment' could be dismissed. The classification of detainees as 'unlawful combatants' is represented as entailing that the rules of the Geneva Convention on Prisoners of War do not apply, and rights that would belong to prisoners of war cannot be asserted in favour of these detainees.

In the UK, Mr Blair's Government in one of its early reforms made the European Convention on Human Rights (ECHR) applicable as a part of domestic law, by the Human Rights Act of 1998 and the Scotland Act of the same year. Within three years, however, in the light of the events of '9/11' and emergent threats to the UK, the Government had lodged a declaration derogating from the provisions against detention without trial (Art 5, ECHR). It had, further, obtained Parliament's approval for legislation to facilitate detention without trial of suspected terrorists who were foreign nationals, but who could not be deported on account of the risk of being tortured or put to death were they to return to their country of origin. It had become embroiled in controversy concerning the possible use of evidence obtained by torture in foreign countries without the complicity of the British security forces. Legal constraints thus appeared to be slipping in two of the oldest and most stable democracies, and emergency conditions led to evermore sweeping emergency powers.

Some may find that this calls to mind a famous – or infamous – statement by the legal and political theorist, Carl Schmitt. A leading legal scholar of the Weimar Republic, he entered public life initially as an adviser to the government on constititutional matters, later to become closely affiliated to the National Socialist Party after Hitler's rise to power. Notwithstanding the taint of his association with the Nazi Party, his theoretical contributions (particularly during the Weimar period) have proved difficult to ignore and have become increasingly influential. Among the most famous of his dicta remains the opening sentence of the first of his four Essays in *Political Theology*. 'Sovereign is he who decides on the exception.' As a state of exception Schmitt understands, following 'continental' constitutional parlance, an instance of political turmoil that involves a suspension of rights and other constitutional guarantees under conditions of necessity: *necessitas non habet legem*. Sovereignty is revealed, for Schmitt under conditions where politics necessitates a suspension of law; this subjects law to politics, which is governed by the ever-present possibility of conflict. His point was that in ordinary times it can be unclear who has the ultimate power in a State, especially where some form of separation of powers is in operation. But times can be extraordinary – there can be security crises, such as that triggered by Al Qaïda. For Schmitt, a crisis is 'more interesting than the rule', because 'it confirms not only the rule but also its existence, which derives only from the exception'. Of course the flip-side to the decision to call the state of exception is the sovereign's decision as to whether (political) order and stability have been restored and therefore whether legal normality is to be returned to. Because of course 'for a legal system to make sense, a normal situation must exist, and he is sovereign who definitely decides whether this normal situation actually exists'. In all, to steady the ship of state, measures by way of exceptions to normal constitutional propriety may be called for. Emergency powers have to be exercised. So who decides about this? Whoever decides, and makes that decision stick, said Schmitt, is truly the sovereign. All ordinary law really depends on this sovereign, whose presence may be unknown and unsuspected outside of emergency times. The exception not only proves the rule, it proves the ruler as well, as Schmitt might have said.

This is in some ways a tempting doctrine, seemingly well fitted to the exceptional times that have prevailed since 2001. Yet it is worth noticing where it leads. It points to the conclusion that, despite appearances and theoretical constitutional limits, law is always in the last resort subordinate to politics, and politics is in the last resort a matter of raw power. Such power is doubtless enhanced through successful manipulation of law and legal institutions, but it is never constrained by law except on a strictly voluntary basis, that is, as a matter of appearance, but never of underlying reality. Similar to this is perhaps the view of Jacques Derrida that all States have emerged through the violence of revolutions and there is always a residue of violence behind the civil mask of the most ostensibly consent-based State.

An alternative view is that espoused in the initial sections of the 'general themes', above. Law and politics are genuinely distinct and genuinely interactive. The political activity of governing a State successfully can be carried on under the rule of law, and ideally is. There can be effective, if never complete, institutional arrangements for separation of powers, with resultant checks and balances, which check the tendency of power-holders to seek absolute power, and anyway, normally prevent any one from achieving it. Crises and emergencies are indeed states of exception. Nothing can ever be a cast-iron guarantee against a *coup d'état* that overthrows a previously subsisting constitutional order. Is it not the case, however, that this betokens a momentary *absence* of law, rather than give an insight into law's essence? Here we identify a question that is worthy of debate and discussion.

Readings

For works by Schmitt see in particular Schmitt (1985a), especially the first essay for his account of sovereignty and the exception. For his conceptualisation of the political on the basis of the friend/enemy distinction see Schmitt (1996). For the most complete account of his legal theory in English see Schmitt (2004), and for his critique of liberal parliamentarism Schmitt (1985b), especially pp 22–32.

From the increasing secondary literature on Schmitt, see, in particular, Dyzenhaus's comprehensive and critical account in Dyzenhaus (1997), pp 38–101. From a radical democratic perspective, see Mouffe (1999) (especially the articles by Mouffe, Hirst and Zizek), and for a historical account see Muller (2003). See also MacCormick (2007) ch 10 s 6.

On questions of constitutionalism and emergency see Finn (1991); and for an insightful, but demanding analysis, see Agamben (1998). On questions of constitutionalism and emergency, see Dyzenhaus (2006), in which he defends the rule of law as capable of responding even to those situations that place the legal and political order under great stress.

References

Agamben, G, 1998, *Homo Sacer: Sovereign Power and Bare Life*, Stanford: Stanford University Press.

Dyzenhaus, D, 1997, *Legality and Legitimacy*, Oxford: Clarendon.

Dyzenhaus, D, 2006, *The Constitution of Law: Legality in a Time of Emergency*, Cambridge: Cambridge University Press.

Finn, JE, 1991, *Constitutions in Crisis*, Oxford: Oxford University Press.

MacCormick, N, 2007, *Institutions of Law*, Oxford: Oxford University Press.

Mouffe, C, 1999, *The Challenge of Carl Schmitt*, London: Verso.

Muller, J-W, 2003, *A Dangerous Mind: Carl Schmitt in Post-War European Thought*, New Haven: Yale University Press.

Schmitt, C, 1985a, *Political Theology: Four Chapters on the Concept of Sovereignty* (orig 1922), Cambridge, MA: MIT Press.

Schmitt, C, 1985b, *The Crisis of Parliamentary Democracy*, Cambridge, MA: MIT Press.

Schmitt, C, 1996, *The Concept of the Political*, Chicago: Chicago University Press.

Schmitt, C, 2004, *Legality and Legitimacy*, Durham, NC: Duke University Press.

TUTORIALS

TUTORIAL I

Legality and the rule of law (1): Fuller

Read pp 33–44 and 145–162 of Lon Fuller's *The Morality of Law* (Fuller 1969).

For the purposes of the tutorial you should be ready to explain and evaluate his approach to law. Consider in particular the following questions:

- In what sense is Fuller's theory an 'inner morality' of law? How does this differ from an 'external morality' of law?
- Are any of the eight ways of making law more important or persuasive than others?
- Do the eight principles of legality constrain in any way the substantive content of laws? If so, what examples can you think of?
- Does Fuller's analysis have any impact on how *judges* do or should go about justifying their decisions?
- What values do you believe the doctrine of the Rule of Law upholds? How are these the same or different from Fuller's eight principles of legality?
- Fuller states that 'there is a kind of reciprocity between government and the citizen with respect to the observance of rules.' (Fuller 1969, p 39) In light of his 'principles of legality', how do you understand Fuller's claim? (Select two or three principles by way of example.) Do you find Fuller's analysis persuasive? Why/not?

Corresponding Sections: Part I 1.3–1.4 and 2.1.

TUTORIAL 2

Legality and the rule of law (2)

1. According to Roberto Unger, the idea of constraining power by an impersonal rule of law in liberal societies rests on two assumptions, both of which, he says, turn out to be fictitious: first that the 'most significant sorts of power can be concentrated in government', the second, that 'power can be effectively constrained by rules'. (Unger 1976, pp 178–179.) How do you understand these criticisms of the modern idea of rule of law? To what extent are they correct?

2. '... formal equality before the law is in conflict, and in fact incompatible, with any activity of the government deliberately aiming at material or substantive equality of different people, and any government policy directly aiming at a substantive ideal of distributive justice must lead to the destruction of the Rule of Law.' (Hayek 1944, p 59) Explain what Hayek means by this claim. Is he correct? Why/not?

3. To what extent might certain features of our modern rights culture in the administrative welfare state, (and if so, which ones) operate to undermine the values of the rule of law in practice?

Corresponding Sections: Part I 1.3–1.5.

TUTORIAL 3

Law and politics (1)

Part 1

The province of Cloude, politically a part of the state of Ukania, is an island. Those who believe in independence for Cloude – claiming the right to self-determination – are involved in an armed separatist struggle against Ukania. The separatist movement has major support, gains funds, and espouses its cause mainly from the United States of Amerigo. The Government of Ukania – claiming the right to self-defence – is threatening air strikes against and invasion of those countries suspected of 'harbouring terrorists', including Amerigo.

As a jurisprudentially-informed expert, you have been asked to comment on the following issues for a radio programme:

1. What would be the differences between a legal and a political solution to the problems raised by these events? What are the conditions of success for each, and what are the possible consequences?

2. The Cloudean separatists claim they are freedom fighters; the Ukanian Government claim they are terrorists. Who is correct, and why?

3. Are there any legal limits on what can be done in the name of politics? Should there be?

Part 2

In response to the perceived worsening of events, the Ukanian Parliament declared that the situation amounted to an emergency threatening the peace and security of the State and passed an Act authorising the indefinite detention without charge or trial of those suspected of promoting or carrying out terrorist activities. After the detention of a number of suspects under this Act, its legality was challenged in the Ukanian Supreme Court. The judges were referred to a House of Lords decision that includes the following passages:

A (FC) and others (FC) (Appellants) v Secretary of State for the Home Department (Respondent)

LORD BINGHAM

[29] [The] Home Secretary, his colleagues and Parliament [. . .] were called on to exercise a pre-eminently political judgment. It involved making a factual prediction of what various people around the world might or might not do, and when (if at all) they might do it, and what the consequences might be if they did. Any prediction about the future behaviour of human beings (as opposed to the phases of the moon or high water at London Bridge) is necessarily problematical. Reasonable and informed minds may differ, and a judgment is not shown to be wrong or unreasonable because that which is thought likely to happen does not happen. It would have been irresponsible not to err, if at all, on the side of safety. As will become apparent, I do not accept the full breadth of the Attorney General's argument on what is generally called the deference owed by the courts to the political authorities. It is perhaps preferable to approach this question as one of demarcation of functions or what Liberty in its written case called 'relative institutional competence'. The more purely political (in a broad or narrow sense) a question is, the more appropriate it will be for political resolution and the less likely it is to be an appropriate matter for judicial decision. The smaller, therefore, will be the potential role of the court. It is the function of political and not judicial bodies to resolve political questions. Conversely, the greater the legal content of any issue, the greater the potential role of the court, because under our constitution and subject to the sovereign power of Parliament it is the function of the courts and not of political bodies to resolve legal questions. The present question seems to me to be very much at the political end of the spectrum.

LORD HOFFMAN

[95] But the question is whether such a threat is a threat to the life of the nation. The Attorney General's submissions and the judgment of the Special Immigration Appeals Commission treated a threat of serious physical damage and loss of life as necessarily involving a threat to the life of the nation. But in my opinion this shows a misunderstanding of what is meant by 'threatening the life of the nation'. Of course the government has a duty to protect the lives and property of its citizens. But that is a duty which it owes all the time and which it must discharge without destroying our constitutional freedoms. There may be some nations too fragile or fissiparous to withstand a serious act of violence. But that is not the case in the United Kingdom. When Milton urged the government of his day not to censor the press even in time of civil war, he said:

'Lords and Commons of England, consider what nation it is whereof ye are, and whereof ye are the governours'

96. This is a nation which has been tested in adversity, which has survived physical destruction and catastrophic loss of life. I do not underestimate the ability of fanatical groups of terrorists to kill and destroy, but they do not threaten the life of the nation. Whether we would survive Hitler hung in the

balance, but there is no doubt that we shall survive Al-Qaeda. The Spanish people have not said that what happened in Madrid, hideous crime as it was, threatened the life of their nation. Their legendary pride would not allow it. Terrorist violence, serious as it is, does not threaten our institutions of government or our existence as a civil community.

97. For these reasons I think that the Special Immigration Appeals Commission made an error of law and that the appeal ought to be allowed. Others of your Lordships who are also in favour of allowing the appeal would do so, not because there is no emergency threatening the life of the nation, but on the ground that a power of detention confined to foreigners is irrational and discriminatory. I would prefer not to express a view on this point. I said that the power of detention is at present confined to foreigners and I would not like to give the impression that all that was necessary was to extend the power to United Kingdom citizens as well. In my opinion, such a power in any form is not compatible with our constitution. The real threat to the life of the nation, in the sense of a people living in accordance with its traditional laws and political values, comes not from terrorism but from laws such as these. That is the true measure of what terrorism may achieve. It is for Parliament to decide whether to give the terrorists such a victory.

1. How do the two judges differ in terms of assessing whether or not there is a state of emergency?

2. Which institution – the court or the Parliament – has the ultimate right to determine whether there is a state of emergency?

3. How, in your view, should the judges decide the case before the Ukanian Supreme Court?

Corresponding Sections: Part I 1.1.1–1.1.3 and 2.5.

TUTORIAL 4

Law and politics (2)

Part I

The oppressive government of the state of Ukania was toppled by a democratic revolution in 1997. The new government seeks to act in line with sound constitutional and legal principles such as might be found in European Conventions. One of these principles is that there should be no punishment without a law, while another is that no law is to be retrospective in its effect. The new constitution states that those suspected of gross violations of human rights must be brought to trial. It also states that citizens have the right to have justiciable disputes settled by a court of law.

In its final days the old Parliament passed an Act, it was claimed for reasons of maintaining peace and stability in the transition to the new regime, which gave immunity from criminal and civil liability to all functionaries of the former government.

Three cases are now being brought before the courts.

1. Two victims of torture are bringing a civil suit for damages against their torturer.
2. A prosecutor has decided to bring to trial the former head of the security services and the former Home Secretary for conspiracy to murder 83 political opponents who died as a result of security operations.
3. A former border guard is being prosecuted, despite his claim merely to have been following legitimate orders, for shooting two people who tried to escape the country.

You are the Minister of Justice and have been asked by the Cabinet for your opinion on these cases.

Part 2

The Pinochet 'episode' in British legal history is remarkable: not only did it place the House of Lords at the centre of a national and international political debate about the role of Courts, but also because it generated a debate about the relationship between national and international legal orders and most importantly, for our purposes too, the nature of the relationship between law and politics.

In 1973 General Pinochet assumed power in Chile after a military coup that saw the overthrow of the democratically elected government of Salvador Allende; he became President of the governing Junta and assumed the title of President of the Republic. During his headship of the Chilean State, around 4,000 individuals were killed or disappeared. In 1978 he granted an amnesty to all persons involved in criminal acts since the coup, and thus absolved himself of any violation of human rights committed during the time. In the final of his many official visits to the UK, during which he was always accorded diplomatic courtesies and became a 'close friend' of Margaret Thatcher and other Tories, he was arrested pursuant to a warrant issued under the extradition Act 1989. Judge Garzon in Madrid had issued an international warrant requesting that Pinochet be extradited to Spain to face the charges of genocide, mass murder and hostage-taking, among other crimes. Pinochet made an application to quash the warrant, claiming that he was entitled to immunity as a former Head of State from criminal and civil process in the English Courts; his application succeeded before the Divisional Court. We pick up the story at this point, in the House of Lords decision over, arguably the most significant question as certified by the Divisional Court: 'the **proper interpretation** and scope of the immunity enjoyed by a former head of State from arrest and extradition proceedings in the UK in respect of acts committed while he was Head of State'.

Compare and contrast the following extracts:

LORD LLOYD of Berwick

It would be unjustifiable in theory and unworkable in practice, to impose any restriction on Head of State immunity by reference to the number or gravity of the alleged crimes.

On the issue [of Head of state immunity at common law] I would hold that senator Pinochet is entitled to immunity as former head of State in respect of the crimes alleged against him on well established principles of customary international law, which principles form part of the common law of England.

....

The answer is the same at common law or under statute [the State Immunity Act 1978] And the rationale is the same. The former head of state enjoys continuing immunity in respect of governmental acts which he performed as head of state because in both cases the acts are attributed to the state itself.

LORD SLYNN of Hadley

The Rome Statute of the International Criminal Court provides for jurisdiction in respect of genocide . . . but in each case only with respect to acts committed after the entry into force of this statute.

There is no doubt that States have been moving towards the recognition of some crimes as those which should not be covered by claims of State or Head of State. . . . It has to be said, however, . . . that some of those statements read as aspirations, as embryonic. . . . Nor is there any jus cogens in respect of such breaches of international law which require that a claim of State or Head of State immunity, itself a well established principle of international law, should be overridden.

....

[I]f States wish to exclude the long established immunity of former Heads of State in respect of allegations of specific crimes, or generally, then they must do so in clear terms. They should not leave it to National Courts because of the appalling nature of the crimes alleged.

LORD NICHOLLS

It hardly needs saying that torture of his own subjects, or of aliens, would not be regarded by international law as a function of a head of State. All states disavow the use of torture as abhorrent . . . Similarly [with] the taking of hostages. International law recognises, of course, that the functions of a head of State may include activities which are wrongful, even illegal, by the law of his own state or by the laws of other states. But international law has made plain that certain types of conduct, including torture and hostage-taking are not acceptable conduct on the part of anyone. This applies as much to heads of state, or even more so, as it does to everyone else; the contrary conclusion would make a mockery of international law.

....

[Since] a resolution passed unanimously in 1946 the UN general assembly . . . no head of state could have been in any doubt about his potential personal liability if he participated in acts regarded by international law as crimes against humanity.

LORD STEYN

[For the immunity to obtain] the acts must have been performed by the defendant in the exercise of his functions as Head of State. . . . The Lord Chief Justice observed that a former Head of state is clearly entitled to immunity from process in respect of some crimes. I would accept this proposition. Rhetorically the Chief Justice then posed the question: 'Where does one draw the line?' . . . it is inherent in this stark conclusion [the Chief Lord Justice's and Collins J's] that there is or virtually no line to be drawn. It follows that when Hitler ordered the 'final solution' his act must be regarded as an official act deriving from the exercise of his functions as head of state.

'Why should what was allegedly done in secret in the torture chambers of Santiago on the orders of General Pinochet be regarded as official acts? Why should the murders and disappearances allegedly perpetrated on his orders be regarded as official acts? ... In none of these cases is the essential requirement satisfied, viz. ... that these acts were part of the functions of a head of state. The normative principles of law do not require that such high crimes should be classified as acts performed in the exercise of the functions of the head of State'

1. When Lord Steyn, in the quotation above, talks of the 'normative principles of law' is he relying on an argument about the inner morality of law? Is he relying on a political rather than a legal argument?

2. Is it the business of Courts to argue for what rightly falls under the function of a Head of State and what doesn't?

3. Does an allegation of torture 'trump' a plea of immunity, an issue raised by Lord Lloyd?

4. In your opinion is the fact that Lord Hoffman was at the time a Director of Amnesty International a valid reason to 'vacate' the decision and re-hear the appeal? ⟶ *facts of this case.*

> **Corresponding Sections: Part I 1.1–1.3 and 1.5 and 2.4–2.5.**

p62-68 pg-17

lecture & notes reading

TUTORIAL 5
** Advanced

Law, justice and disobedience

Part I

Whether we think it a law or not we still have to decide what to do. Saying it is immoral and therefore not a law would have the same practical effect as saying it is a law but immoral and therefore we must not obey it. Does the distinction matter?

Reflect on the following two theses:

Thesis 1: 'The strict separation between law and morality cannot be upheld: An unjust law is not valid law. Or at least there is a threshold beyond which a law is too evil to count as law. Those who enforced the apartheid regime in South Africa, the soldiers who shot at Germans trying to flee East Berlin during the Cold War, the officials of the Nazi regime *cannot* claim to have acted according to the law. Some acts – including torture and genocide – should be punished regardless of any prior prohibition.'

Are these merely cases of objectionable law, or are they actually cases of invalid law? If the latter, who is to draw the threshold (every citizen for herself?) and where (does sentencing someone to death row – to the extent that that amounts to torture – invalidate law?)

Thesis 2: The strict separation between law and morality cannot be upheld: there is an important internal link between law and morality but it is to be sought in the *purpose* of law. To explain this: One cannot describe a social institution like law unless one has an idea of what is good for human persons and thus the point of the institution. From there we can see if various laws in the empirical world measure up. To the extent that they do, we can call them laws or, if they do not, approximations of laws. Take an example. We can have two ways of deciding what a university is. We might say that a university is an institution that the State has allowed to be called a university and there may be good universities and bad universities. We might on the other hand, not look at it in this neutral way, but first of all have some idea of the essence and point of a university. We would say then that the purpose of the university has something to do with the pursuit and dissemination of knowledge and only an institution committed to that aspiration is properly called a university. Then we could look at all the institutions the State calls a university and see whether they measure up. We can call some universities, some not universities at all and some approximating to, but not quite, universities. What was said about universities can be said about law. The latter is approximately the way Fuller and Finnis would look at it, the former is more of a legalistic argument.

1. In your opinion, is this argument persuasive in demonstrating that the definition of law necessarily imports value judgements?

2. A member of the British armed forces has objected to going to fight in the Iraq war because he believed it to be illegal on the grounds that it violates the fundamental value of law that it should protect human life. He is now being court martialled for disobeying orders. He has asked you for your advice as to whether there are any jurisprudential grounds for supporting his defence. What do you advise?

Part 2

Read one of the following texts, summarise their arguments, and relate them to the questions outlined in the context set out below.

Dworkin (1986), pp 101–8 and 172–5.

Dyzenhaus (1998)

Christodoulidis (2004)

All South African lawyers who opposed apartheid had to answer the question whether *law could be used to resist law*. Etienne Mureinik was a South African scholar whose work consists of articles that relentlessly criticised the Appellate Court for failing to fulfil its role in considering the *legality* of executive decisions and action taken to sustain apartheid. It may be worth pausing for a moment to consider what questions this injunction throws up for us. In this context, to put it polemically: what would we make of Finnis's argument that law, as an instance of practical reason, by providing the possibility to live under its authority is necessarily a good worth protecting? Of Dworkin's argument that coherence matters, and that we should thus resist taking decisions strategically (to protect the discriminated?) if the coherence of past decisions demand that any current decision must command a *fit* with the legal record of our community?

The case of South Africa under apartheid does of course appear particularly problematic in this respect. It is uncontroversial that laws instituting racial segregation were wicked laws. The question whether the common law gave judges a genuine resource to interpret statute law in ways that modified the oppressive intent of the legislators or whether it became itself infected by this wickedness is one that has troubled legal theorists writing on South Africa. But let us for the sake of argument limit the question to statute, to the laws enacted to implement the principle of separate development, provisions that sought to exclude judicial review for illegality, the security laws that buttressed apartheid and the abundance of subordinate legislation that laid out policy in fantastic detail along lines of race. Altogether these provisions and 'canons' form a weighty, complex and detailed body of statutory law. Integrity does not call us to experiment with latent, subordinate and subversive interpretative options, but calls for fidelity to what becomes entrenched as institutional record, in other words with *what carries the interpretative weight of that record.* And if it is iniquity that entrenches itself legislatively, what is the moral judge to do? What hand does Dworkin deal him? How would Finnis's analysis help solve this problem?

Questions:

Can a legal system of this kind command allegiance for Finnis or Dworkin?

To what extent can one use the law to overcome iniquity? Or does morality, instead, call one to abandon the law since the very categories of its understanding and action are always compromised?

Corresponding Sections: Part I 1.4 and 2.1–2.2.

TUTORIAL 6

Rights culture

Part I

What are the normative justifications for the following rights?

(a) The right to life
(b) The right to property
(c) The right to a fair and public hearing within a reasonable time by an independent and impartial tribunal established by law
(d) The rights to work and to strike
(e) The right not to be discriminated against on grounds of sex, age, race, disability or sexual orientation

Read Waldron 1990 chapter 5.

Part 2

Read Loughlin 2000, chapter 13.

1. What, according to Loughlin, are the principal characteristics of our contemporary rights culture?
2. Are there any reasons to be concerned about rights discourse and its cultural impact?
3. In particular, are there any problems about the role and power of the judiciary, and the doctrine of the Rule of Law?

Part 3

From the *Guardian* newspaper, February 3, 1999:

'A New York Judge yesterday put Americans' constitutional rights to free speech ahead of shielding children from pornography on the Internet. Judge Lowell Reed blocked a law to prevent website operators from making sexually explicit material available to under-17s.'

He said in his ruling: '[p]erhaps we do minors in this country harm if First Amendment protections which they will with age inherit fully are chipped away in the name of their protection.'

Anne Beeson, a civil liberties union lawyer, said: '[t]he Court was able to cut through a lot of very complicated evidence and focus on what this case is really about: first amendment speech.'

Do you agree that this is a victory for civil rights?

Could a liberal consistently argue for rights and defend the protection of children from pornography on the net?

Corresponding Sections: Part I 1.5 and 2.2–2.3.

References

Christodoulidis, E, 2004, 'End of history jurisprudence: Dworkin in South Africa' *Acta Juridica* 64–85.
Dworkin, R, 1986, *Law's Empire*, London: Fontana.
Dyzenhaus, D, 1998, 'Law as Justification' 14, *SAJHR*, 13.
Fuller, LL, 1969, *The Morality of Law,* New Haven: Yale University Press.
Hayek, FA, 1944, *The Road to Serfdom*, London: Routledge & Kegan Paul.
Loughlin, M, 2000, *Sword and Scales*, Oxford: Hart.
Unger, RM, 1976, *Law and Modern Society*, New York: Free Press.
Waldron, J, 1990, *The Law*, London: Routledge.

Cases

A (FC) and others v Secretary of State for the Home Dept [2004] UKHL 56.

Part II

Legal reasoning

General themes

1.1 Introduction to legal reasoning

Consider the following scenario. A woman gives birth to conjoined twins. Unless some attempt is made to separate the twins, both, according to medical opinion, will die a short time after birth. However, while medical intervention to separate them might keep one twin alive, the other would necessarily die. The parents, guided by their religious beliefs, are opposed to any medical intervention, content to let nature take its course. The doctors, on the other hand, are under a professional duty to try to save life and a legal duty to act in the best interests of the children. But what are the best interests of the children? In the face of the parents' unwillingness to have them undergo an operation, the doctors apply to a court to have the legal authority granted to them to go ahead with the operation. How should the court decide? Can they decide on the basis of moral beliefs about life? Are these to play any role at all? Is the cost of treatment a relevant factor at all to be considered? Or must they follow existing legal rules? But what happens in a situation where there are, or seem to be, no pre-existing rules?

The aim of this part of the book is to describe the *kind* of arguments that are employed in legal reasoning, and the normative theories behind them, which focus on what kinds of argument are *appropriate* to legal reasoning.

Of course, we cannot argue about what kinds of arguments are appropriate in legal reasoning unless we have some idea of what law is. If, for example, we think that all that law is, is a system of rules, then we might argue that legal argumentation involves merely the 'mechanical' application of those rules to cases that fall within their ambit. But then we might find it difficult to explain what it is that makes some cases so difficult, and why it is that top lawyers and judges routinely disagree about what the law requires. If, alternatively, we believe that law is to be understood as an argumentative practice that necessarily engages questions of morality and politics, then that belief will incline us to reach very different conclusions about how legal argumentation is to be best understood and carried out. Or again, if we treat law as essentially an open-ended practice, where policies of 'social engineering' or conserving the status quo are the determining factors, then we will have a different view of the nature and purpose of adjudication . . . and so on.

We will look in this part at how theorists and judges approach and answer these questions in different ways, and what they say about the nature of legal reasoning, the nature of law and the connection between the two. If legal argument is about *justifying* the application of the law in terms of principles and values, then the judges may be right in engaging with moral and political justifications, or wrong to artificially exclude them. Conversely, we may be unwilling to grant judges the power to invoke moral and political argument without understanding how their reasoning may be influenced by factors they do not explicitly engage with: their professional or class background, or issues of gender or political bias.

How we answer the more general and abstract questions on the nature of law and legal reasoning bears directly on what we argue is the right solution in each and every case in law. It is in this sense that practices of adjudication and reasoning with law, their underlying features, rationality, or biases, are absolutely central to an understanding of the operation of law, and are therefore in need of closer, critical, examination.

Most law students will learn how judges and lawyers work with the two basic sources of law: *statute* and *precedent*. So they will learn about the different sources of legislation: local, national, European, etc. and how these relate to one another. And they will learn of the various aids to statutory interpretation, covering a set of basic rules: the mischief rule – what mischief or defect did the statute seek to rectify?; the literal rule – that precise words in the statute have to be interpreted literally, according to their natural, ordinary sense, since only then can the legislature's intention be given effect; the golden rule – where the ordinary or literal meaning of words may be deviated from where failure to do so would result in an absurd outcome or one inconsistent with other parts of the legislation; or the purposive approach – that which attempts, in interpreting the words of a statute, to give effect to the true purpose of the legislation.

For a detailed introductory account of these 'rules' of statutory interpretation (better described as 'approaches to' interpretation), McLeod (2005), ch 18. The classic text is Cross (1995), which suggests a 'unified contextual approach' to the 'rules'.

Yet even as a description of what judges purport to do, this is overly simplified and ignores several decades of work in the field. Francis Bennion, the author of the UK's most comprehensive study of statutory interpretation, argues:

There are a great many interpretative criteria, and where these conflict in a particular case there must be a judicial process of weighing and balancing. . . . It is wrong to teach law students, as had almost universally been done, that the interpretative criteria solely consist of the literal rule, the mischief rule and the golden rule, and that courts simply choose between them. . . . Consult even the latest edition of almost any other book on statutory interpretation and you will find the same old parrot cry trotted out: 'the interpretative criteria consist of the literal rule, the mischief rule and the golden rule, and the court chooses between them.' It amounts to a serious breakdown in communication.

(Bennion 2001: 2)

Instead, he insists:

. . . there is no golden rule. Nor is there a mischief rule, or a literal rule, or any other cure-all rule of thumb. Instead there are a thousand and one interpretative *criteria*. Fortunately, not all of these present themselves in any one case; but those that do yield factors that the interpreter must figuratively weigh and balance. That is the nearest we can get to a golden rule, and it is not very near.

(Bennion 2002: 3–4)

With regard to precedent as a source of law, students will learn that attention must be paid to court hierarchies and how they impact upon whether cases referred to are to be considered binding or persuasive. Additionally, they will be referred to the distinction between the *ratio decidendi* of a case (the true reason for the decision), and statements made *obiter dicta* (only by the way and not essential to the reason for judgment). They will be expected to learn how to establish the difference between the two, and also on how to establish what the *ratio* actually amounts to, and how in turn, it may be applied to other cases. They will also be expected to learn the difference between questions of law and questions of fact.

> For a standard introduction to precedent, see McLeod (2005) chs 8–10.
> For a deeper exploration, see Cross and Harris (1991).

In these senses reasoning from sources of law may be portrayed as a more or less technical exercise of rule application. The techniques for doing this will rarely be taught to any level of sophistication – if indeed they are taught at all. Instead, students will be expected to absorb the method by osmosis, as if legal reasoning were simply a skill to be picked up and honed through the practice of example, resulting in a form of mastery of legal materials.

But even at an early stage, students will observe a tension between this image, and the reality of legal practice and adjudication that displays constant signs of genuine and reasonable disagreement about what the law in a particular case requires. This may involve noting contested interpretations of the meaning of a particular word or phrase in the legislation, being asked to assemble a case for or against a specific legal proposition, or how best to understand the meaning or significance of the facts, or it may be gleaned from the reality of reading cases where eminent judges themselves come to opposite conclusions about what the result of a case ought to be. Indeed, the very practice of teaching in law schools is to focus on the supposedly 'pathological' case, the decision so difficult and contested that it must be referred to the highest court of the land. In all this, there will be an awareness that reasoning with law, whether carried out by judges, lawyers, citizens or campaigners, engages deeper questions about the role and meaning of legal pronouncements in creating patterns of behaviour, about the doctrine of the rule of law and the role of the judiciary vis-à-vis the legislature, or about the way in which ordinary obligations and expectations are to be defined or challenged.

In this chapter we will begin to deepen our understanding of these problems by considering a variety of different ways of understanding adjudication and processes of justification. These ways often conflict with each other, and thus demand a critical engagement from the reader. And assessing the persuasiveness of the different positions is crucial, not only for a fuller understanding of institutions of adjudication, but also in order to see how they relate to the other themes addressed in the book.

We do not attempt here to examine the myriad interpretative criteria for understanding statutes, or the debate about the nature of reasoning from precedent, for that is not the role of an introductory text on jurisprudence. But we suggest that those who wish to understand legal reasoning should question, not just whether the law is merely a technical exercise of applying rules, but ask whether the few cursory rules that students are traditionally taught describe even what legal reasoning *purports* to do, let alone whether they describe the reality of legal practice. Whatever their position, radical or conservative, sceptical or committed, students will notice an empty core in law teaching where an explicit and transparent introduction to what purports to be legal method ought to sit. It is then all the more difficult for students to be critical: first, because the early teaching they receive carries the implicit message that law is a technical exercise (an impression which contrasts with the real cases they are then given to study in the rest of their legal studies); and second, because they are not actually taught the complex skills they are told they must acquire. It is hard for students to criticise a practice which is said to be immanent rather than made explicit.

Our aim here is to introduce a debate about whether law is nothing (or little) more than an exercise in rule application. In the remainder of the 'general themes' in this part, first we map the issues and debates over adjudication in terms of the case for formalism in law, the 'revolt' against the formalist position, and the response to that from the prominent English writer HLA Hart; then we will deepen the analysis by considering three contemporary theorists of legal reasoning. The analysis raises questions about whether legal reasoning is – and if so how – open or closed to ethical and political reasoning, and whether it is a special case of practical reasoning with its own particular institutional features.

1.2 Legal formalism, legal realism and the open texture of law

1.2.1 Legal formalism and deduction in law

An image of law that was particularly powerful in the nineteenth century, both in codified legal systems and among common lawyers, might be summarised as follows: the more nearly we could come to constructing a legal system of clear and coherent rules, containing precise and 'scientifically' analysed terms, elaborated out of perfectly analysed and synthesised concepts, the concepts being unvaryingly used in the same sense throughout the whole body of law, the more we may succeed in producing a gapless, highly formalised and thus properly rational system of law, capable of guaranteeing 'the rule of law'.

The more we succeed in this, the more the law will comprise a set of general – and logically consistent – rules capable of being 'deductively' applied to every relevant case of proven facts. The more this is so, the more certain, predictable and uniform will be the law.

Many lawyers and statesmen in nineteenth-century Europe took the project of constructing such systems as a serious ambition. On the continent, the great codes in Germany (the BGB) and in France (the Code Civil) brought together what was to be called the 'jurisprudence of legal concepts' – abstract, conceptual and logical legal scholarship in the exegetical tradition – and a revival of Roman law. (The work of German sociologist Max Weber analysed the historical development of this development (see Part III 1).) In Britain, Bentham argued the case for codification as part of his general attempt to reform the law in an enlightened, liberal fashion. In both cases, codifying the law was seen as a safeguard against arbitrariness in the courts and interference by the executive in the legal process. The idea of the importance of the separation of powers and the ideal of a democratic society resulted in a picture of the law, which saw judges as mere executors of the legislature's will, applying the law mechanically.

Formalism in an extreme form presents a picture in which law is and should be an entirely self-determining system, where judges are never faced with choices or alternative interpretations of such a kind that would lead them to be resolvable only through extra-legal considerations, such as moral or political values. For a formalist, therefore, such considerations never enter into the determination of legal outcomes. Formalism is a realisation of the rule of law ideal in which 'government in all its actions is bound by rules fixed and announced beforehand – rules that make it possible to foresee with fair certainty how the authority will use its coercive powers in given circumstances and to plan one's individual affairs on the basis of that knowledge' (Hayek 1944, p 54). With this statement, it is important to note the *political* stance of the formalist position. That is, legal formalism is not just a theory about how judges do or should decide cases that come before them; it is also an approach that seeks to uphold and promote certain political and moral ends too. This may seem paradoxical. Yet, a belief in the virtues of formalism is bound up with taking a specific stance on the doctrine of the rule of law, the separation of powers, on personal, political and economic autonomy, and to judicial accountability in the political system (see Part I, 1.3).

The promotion of the values of objectivity, impartiality and neutrality are all linked to the formalist concern with determinate rule application. Neil MacCormick has vividly portrayed this:

> A system of positive law, especially the law of a modern state, comprises an attempt to concretize broad principles of conduct in the form of relatively stable, clear, detailed and objectively comprehensible rules, and to provide an interpersonally trustworthy and acceptable process for putting these rules into effect. That process is especially visible in cases where there is some interpersonal dispute or where social order or justice have been held to require the organisation of public agencies to police and enforce observance of rules that might not otherwise be voluntarily obeyed. In these situations, the private complainer or public rule-enforcer must bring forward some assertions about the state of facts in the world, and attempt to show how that state of facts would call for intervention on the ground of some rule that applies to the asserted facts. Accordingly, the logic of rule-application is the central logic of the law within the modern paradigm of legal rationality under the 'rule of law'.
>
> (MacCormick 1994, pp ix–x)

Put at its simplest, the model at work here, says MacCormick (ibid, x), can be written as the following formula:

$$R + F = C \qquad \text{or} \qquad \text{'Rules plus facts yields conclusion'}$$

The legal rule here may have as its source either a statutory provision or a rule based on a binding precedent. In the case of the latter, the *ratio* of the precedent case will need to be established and then stated in the form of a rule. The material or relevant facts as established through the use of rules of evidence are then subsumed under the rule. Legal formalism argues that establishing legal conclusions is therefore a process of rational justification, not one of evaluative or subjective judgement. This is important since it limits the discretion of judges, and also provides for certainty, predictability, and objectivity in the law.

> With regard to a formalist analysis of the application of statutes, see MacCormick and Summers (1991) ch 13, pp 511–25. For an analysis of formalist reasoning from case law, see MacCormick (1994) pp 19–29.

The question we now face, then, is whether formalism as we have sketched it is in any way credible. We should test in particular the assumed connection of legal reasoning with deductive logic.

Here is an example of deductive logic in practice, exemplified in the form of *syllogistic* reasoning used in the presentation of legal determination. In *Daniels* the plaintiffs, having suffered poisoning from drinking a lemonade heavily contaminated with carbolic acid, sued the manufacturer for damages in compensation for their illness, treatment expenses and loss of earnings while ill. Here is the syllogistic translation:

(i) 'In any case if goods sold by one person to another have defects unfitting them for their only proper use but not apparent on ordinary examination, then the goods sold are not of merchantable quality.

(ii) In the instant case, goods sold by one person to another had defects unfitting them for their only proper use but not apparent on ordinary examination

(iii) Therefore in the instant case the goods sold are not of merchantable quality.' (MacCormick 1994: 22)

In technical terminology, sentences (i) and (ii) here are 'premises', while (iii) is the 'conclusion' of this argument. (i) is the 'major premise', the Rule; (ii) is the 'minor premise', the Fact; (iii) the Conclusion. Together this constitutes the argument form called a 'syllogism'. The argument is a deductive argument, where the conclusion is *deduced* from the premises. The important thing about syllogistic deduction is that the *validity* of the argument depends purely on its logical form. So long as the premises are true, the conclusion must also be true; one could not assert the premises and deny the conclusion without self-contradiction. The form of this deductive argument can be expressed formulaically as follows:

All M are P	*eg, famously*:	All men are mortal
S is M		Socrates is a man
S is P		Socrates is mortal

In legal rules, the major premise usually takes the form of a *conditional* statement: an *'if – then'* sentence. For example: 'if a person agrees to do any act which tends to corrupt public morals, [then] that person is guilty of a crime at common law'; or 'if ["where"] the seller sells goods in the course of a business, [then] there is an implied condition that the goods supplied under the contract are of merchantable quality' (Sale of Goods Act, 1979, s 14(2)2). In order for the syllogism to work the material facts of the present case must match the 'operative' facts as stipulated in the major premise. In this way the conclusion – the 'then' component of the sentence – comes into effect as a legally – and logically – justified conclusion.

While judges will seldom literally use logical formulae in their judgments, this itself does not negate the 'essential truth', says MacCormick, of the form R + F = C in legal reasoning.

We have sketched a view of formalism as embodying a vision of legal rationality operating in the sphere of legal adjudication. Law is understood as a system of known general rules – presumed to be clear and, ideally, capable of a purely literal interpretation – that are deductively applied by judges to factual circumstances to yield a conclusion. Correspondingly, the facts of cases must be presentable in readily identifiable typical situations, admitting of simple and uncontroversial application of legal rules. In these circumstances, the legal conclusion necessarily follows and is justified according to the operation of logic. According to MacCormick, so far as legal systems include rules that it is mandatory to apply in every case to which they clearly refer, observance of the requirements of deductive logic is a *necessary element* in legal justification.

It looks as though legal formalism and the belief in deductive logic in law should not just be dismissed out of hand. In part II section 2.1 we will look at how MacCormick develops the initial insights of formalism, but in a way that qualifies the extreme version by extending the analysis of rational factors at play in judicial decision making.

For a short and clear defence of the rule-based account of legal reasoning, read Neil MacCormick's 'Foreword' to MacCormick (1994), and for his reconstruction of *Daniels* in terms of a series of purely deductive syllogisms, see chapter 2 'Deductive Justification' of that book.

1.2.2 Legal realism

The formalist image of law has never gone unchallenged, and the earlier part of the twentieth century saw throughout the Western world various forms of what may even be called a 'revolt' against formalism. This was not simply a revolt against an idealised deductive model of rule application, but was critical of even the more nuanced forms of formal justification. This critique was frequently associated with new approaches in the sociology of law and 'sociological jurisprudence', involving persons such as Roscoe Pound in the US, Francois Geny in France, Rudolf von Ihering, Eugen Ehrlich and various proponents of 'Freirechtsfindung' ('Free law-finding') in Germany. The critique took the form of arguing that formalistic interpretation was not in fact the only available (or commonly used) approach to legal doctrines and codes, and arguing that formalism involved ignoring the social interests on which law was truly based and by reference to which it ought to be interpreted and developed. The revolt against formalism was particularly vigorous in the US in the 1920s and 1930s, at the time of the early conflict between Roosevelt's 'New Deal' and the conservative constitutional activism engaged by the US Supreme Court Judges who would systematically knock down redistributive policies on constitutional grounds. The practice gave rise to some vigorous theoretical debate over formalism and the relation of law to politics, which gave rise to a 'movement' in legal theory that came to be known as 'legal realism' – the doctrines of its main proponents amounting to various forms of more or less extreme scepticism about all aspects of legal formalism.

The American Legal Realists comprised a loose grouping of legal academics and practitioners (such as Llewellyn, Frank, Oliphant, Holmes, Rodell, etc.). They were not concerned to offer a theory of law or even a theory of legal reasoning. They were concerned with changing legal education, legal practice and court processes, so as to bring into the open the policy issues involved in law making by judges. This was important first, for the training of lawyers and judges; second, improvement in the predictability (and therefore the coherence) of judicial decisions; and third, the flexibility that judges should show in updating the law to deal with changing social conditions. The ideas of these thinkers were influenced by pragmatism in philosophy and by a belief in the role that scientific experts could play. They were not rigorous philosophers or social scientists, but they had a profound effect on American legal education and practice and a delayed and patchy influence in Britain.

Two of the forms of realist scepticism that have attracted much attention will be outlined here: *rule scepticism* – the doctrine that rules do not and cannot play the determinative part in legal decision making that formalism credits to them; and *fact-scepticism* – the idea that 'facts' are not so much independent entities that legal processes discover, but rather, propositions about a supposed reality that is generated by legal processes.

1.2.2.1 Rule scepticism

The American Legal Realists argued that the reality of legal decision making should not be concealed by the pretence that law is a system of known rules applied by a judge to produce logical outcomes – the 'myth of legal certainty'. The life of law, Holmes stated, is not logic, but experience: 'the felt necessities of the time, the prevalent moral and political theories, intuitions of public policy, avowed or unconscious, even the prejudices which judges share with their fellow-men, have a good deal more to do than the syllogism in determining the rules by which men should be governed' (Holmes: 1897).

The reality is, they argued, that judges typically cannot decide cases simply by following rules and precedents because these rules are never totally determinate. Again, Holmes stated the position unambiguously: 'no case can be settled by general propositions . . . I will admit any general proposition you like and decide the case either way' (see Rumble 1968, pp 39–40).

According to an early helpful analysis of rule-scepticism provided by Wilfred Rumble (1968),[1] judges face interpretative choices for a number of reasons including, though not limited to, the following:

1. The ambiguity of legal language means cases and statutes are open to different interpretations.
2. The avalanche of precedents: You can find a precedent for either side and for almost any view.
3. Multiplicity of techniques for describing what a precedent established. How is the *ratio decidendi* determined?
4. How broad is the scope of a given precedent? How do you decide between broad and narrow implications? How can you tell in an unprecedented situation whether an old rule was supposed to cover it or not?
5. The potential for distinguishing: No two cases are ever identical. Which are the important differences of law or fact for the purposes of decision?
6. The potential for comparison: Cases that once might have seemed quite separate may come to seem similar in some important respect.

Thus rule sceptics find serious ambiguities both in statutory interpretation and in the use of precedent. Laws do not take the form of clear, general unambiguous rules, but are radically indeterminate. The idea of treating like

---

1 For a magisterial historical account of currents in American legal history see Horwitz (1992).

cases alike poses radical problems about likeness and difference. Consequently, there is always room for some factor *other* than the legal rule that conditions the decision – factors ranging from the influence of prejudice to attention to policy. Such factors may operate randomly or they may offer alternative regularities and predictabilities of law that do not derive from the rules as such.

Realist critiques may thus take different forms. At the level of legal denunciation, realism seeks to unmask hypocrisy and double standards by showing that formalism licenses prejudice and arbitrary decision making cloaked in the form of authority and judicial deference to the rules. At another level, it involves the more everyday observation that predicting judicial outcomes may depend more on knowing about factors that have nothing to do with the rules as such ('Know your court', as lawyers often say).

In any case, the Realists argued, when judges consider a case, they do not work 'forward' from general rules but backwards from the type of outcome that seems appropriate. So any syllogistic logic manifest in the final presentation of a judicial opinion can be contrasted to the logic by which the decision was actually reached.

Finally, the Realists argued that judges were faced with crucial policy questions. Formalism was being used as a cloak for hiding innovations and policy decisions, even, conservatively, to deny the need for change. Recognising that law had become a policy battleground, Realists espoused judges openly taking a stand. Thus they supported the adoption of a form of explicit 'substantive rationality' (see Part III, on Weber) in the search for just and appropriate solutions to particular cases or types of case. It might even be possible to justify conservatism in particular cases or in general, but this had to be argued explicitly and not by the denial of the possibility of change.

However, Realist arguments about policy should not be interpreted too contextually, as a specific response to the idiosyncratic developments of the American legal system. Rather, they reveal one of the underlying tensions between the 'justice' and 'instrumental' aspects of modern law. Since policies are by definition oriented to factors outside the legal system (the social rather than systemic context), how far can a theory of legal interpretation require that judges have to blind themselves to such goals? If the law is deliberately framed with a view to social policy, it seems bizarre to restrict the ways in which such considerations may enter into the application of law. The history of statutory interpretation is dominated by precisely this question and Cross has argued that it is impossible to find a literal meaning for statutes without referring to the context of purposes and intentions.

Realism has had an enormous impact on subsequent arguments about law and legal reasoning. It has inspired the growth of sociolegal studies that attempt to look at the range of non-rule factors influencing the legal process, and to examine the internal perspective of the judicial community. In its more radical Marxist versions – or in Critical legal studies (CLS), as we shall see shortly – the Realist strain is taken to mean not only that the rule of law in its formalist guise is unattainable, but that it is an important myth legitimating an inherently oppressive system, a symbolic/ideational device to make injustice seem morally acceptable to its victims.

The issue raised then, in mainstream jurisprudence at least, has been understood primarily in terms of the questions it raises about judicial decision making. Judicial creativity is seen as a challenge to the doctrine of separation of powers and hence the rule of law ideal. Rule scepticism clearly presents a problem for any theory that claims law can be described purely as a system of rules. Yet in response it might be argued that the Realists conflated, on the one hand, the process of thinking about or reaching a decision (the 'discovery' of the decision) with, on the other hand, the way in which it is justified. Drawing an analogy with the physical sciences, 'discovery' is identified as the moment when a judge has an idea about what the outcome should be, a process that may well be non-syllogistic, involving hunches, personal views and possibly extra-legal considerations, including views about policy (just as great scientific discoveries may be unpredictable and inspirational – in 'Eureka' fashion). But such insights have to be tested to see if they fall within the relevant sphere of legal truth and, only if they do, can they be justified. Syllogistic reasoning only comes in at the second stage of testing and presenting the rationale. Jurisprudence is interested only in the justification process. So long as a decision may be justified by reference to an existing rule of law, then the judiciary has not exceeded their constitutional powers. But arguably this merely postpones the problem. Is this justificatory reasoning *itself* rational and determinate? The Realist criticisms apply here too.

For a classic account of the Realist position read Holmes (1897).

For an influential account, based in an analysis of the British judiciary, of how external factors heavily influence legal outcomes, see Griffith (1977).

1.2.2.2 Fact scepticism

It has been argued that not only formalists, but also rule sceptics ignored the difficulties associated with facts in adjudication. The facts are an essential element in the application of the law, but to what extent is it the case that courts – judges, or lawyers, or juries – actually get at, or even can get at, the 'truth'? Much of a court's, and thus the lawyers' time, is spent on ascertaining or arguing over the facts, yet this has often been neglected when considering processes of justification in legal decision making. Among Realists, it is the 'fact sceptics' that turned their attention to such matters.

They argued that we should look at the challenges that come from the world of the lower courts. From this perspective, the grand debates about legal interpretation appear remote and academic. This 'appeal court jurisprudence' concentrated on prestigious and intellectually stimulating 'hard cases', but thereby ignored many salient if more mundane aspects of the everyday life of the courts. So Jerome Frank, writing in the 1940s–1950s, chastised his fellow legal Realists: rule sceptics concentrated on a very limited aspect of the law in action, whereas most cases were decided on their facts. Like his fellow sceptics, he was extremely dubious about the predictability of legal outcomes. Moreover, the possibility existed that the facts as found by judge and jury did not correspond to actual facts.

At its simplest, Frank's scepticism can be understood in terms of the psychology of fact finding. Witnesses' observations and memory may be extremely hazy, but they will be pressed to produce clear and confident statements in court. Pre-trial interviews with lawyers may even amount to a form of witness coaching in which the witness gets an idea of which version of the facts would best suit prosecution or defence stories. Then, under cross-examination they will be subject to many techniques of double checking and discrediting. By the end of this process, which began in uncertainty in the first place, we may be many degrees from the truth. Ironically, even witnesses who are sure of the truth, and tell it as they saw it, may be 'bad' witnesses. In jury trials these psychological problems are compounded by the jury's complex reactions to witnesses and their capacity to be swayed by the oratory of the lawyers. Yet the jury is supposed to be the 'master of facts'. Even judges in this setting may be less than rational in their reactions and their influence on juries is not inconsiderable. This aspect of Frank's position has been developed subsequently by social psychologists' studies.

To counter such psychological instabilities of truth finding, Frank called upon the expertise of psychology itself. Experts could be brought in to examine witnesses for the accuracy of their perceptual apparatus and their propensity to lie (with reference to standards of reliability and credibility). Juries should be abolished altogether but, failing that, there should be training in jury duties at school, and jury experts to accompany and advise the jury in the court. The confusing and emotional panoply of costumes and ritual should be eliminated. And judges should undergo pyschoanalysis to control their projective tendencies.

Frank focused primarily on the adversarial process, which he likened to a trial by combat with each side's champions trying to do down the others – a 'fight' method of proof. While this may have made sense in the past, when we believed that God was on the side of justice and truth, it is not appropriate to the age of secular rationalism. Instead he proposed an *inquisitorial* system, which would include better training of legal officials, impartial government officials to dig up all the facts, specialisation of judges and state administrators to deal with the complex facts of modern society, and increasing use of expert witnesses.

Today, Frank's belief in the value of scientific expertise, free proof and the managerial legal officials may seem naive, costly and politically worrying. But Frank's basic points have had considerable influence in disturbing the formalist presumption that 'law' divides neatly from 'facts' and that the jury can easily master them. Put polemically, the present system of proof seems self-contradictory. On the one hand, it is based on a presumption that ordinary people can assess and make inferences from the facts as disclosed. On the other hand, legal methods of getting at facts are far from everyday standards of perception or making sense of the world (and, for many, should be). Whether or not legal proof and procedure is as incoherent as Frank would argue, legal virtue and legal vice – confusion and protection, ordeal and ideal – are often embedded in the same legal rules and procedures.

For Frank's account of fact scepticism, see his Frank (1949a), pp 418 23 and Frank (1949b), introduction. See, also, Jackson (1995) for a concise and illuminating account of the following sets of issues: the psychology of fact finding; reliability/credibility of witnesses; advocacy techniques of cross-examination; adversarial process as a way of getting at truth; the construction of narratives.

For further development of these issues, see Part II Advanced Themes 2.3.

We have considered two ways of thinking about legal reasoning – one rooted in a defence of a formalist position, the other drawing inspiration from a critique of that position. In the following two sections we explore some further alternatives to these views, which allow us to shed more light on aspects of legal adjudication.

1.2.3 The open texture of law: easy cases, hard cases and the scope of substantive reasoning

In his article, 'The Legal Nightmare and the Noble Dream', HLA Hart (1983) responded to the Realist picture by presenting a dichotomy between formalism or 'absolutism' (the noble dream) and the picture of total legal anarchy he attributes to rule sceptics. In *The Concept of Law*, while making certain concessions to Realism, Hart suggested that Realists were 'disappointed absolutists', who have grossly exaggerated interpretative leeway because they secretly sought a utopian version of the rule of law ideal.

Read Hart (1961) ch 7 for a concise account of this critique.

Hart argues that while the vast majority of cases where legal rules are applied are straightforward, easy cases, there is inevitably an element of judicial discretion in legal reasoning because of the necessarily 'open texture' of law. Drawing on the work of Wittgenstein, he argues that the *indeterminacy of natural language* makes it impossible for meaning to be somehow 'stilled' and contained in determinate form in rules. Words and phrases may have a 'core' of settled meaning, but there is always a 'penumbra' of doubt and this always leaves room for interpretation and disagreement. Second, there exists a *relative ignorance of fact*. We cannot predict what 'fact situations' the future may generate and in that sense, how our attempts to capture future eventualities through general categories today may be challenged. We cannot predict whether our current legal designations will be *adequate* in the future, although it is precisely *future* behaviour and situations that we are forever at *present* trying to regulate. Third, there exists an *indeterminacy of legal aim* in the legislative process: rules cannot, nor *should* they aim to, cover all eventualities. Such openness is not a weakness, but may be considered desirable, since it allows the law to be developed to meet changing or unforeseen circumstances. Moreover, the law uses *general standards*, which themselves necessarily introduce indeterminacy (or at the very least an underdeterminacy): standards such as 'reasonableness' ('the reasonable man test', 'reasonable foreseeability', etc), 'proximity' (in negligence), 'fairness', 'good faith', 'equitable', and so on, all inevitably allow for leeway in interpretation. These legal standards are not formal rules in the way that we would think of arithmetic rules – they are open to, and demand, interpretation in the instant case.

In addition to this, we know that valid rules or principles in our law come into conflict with *each other*: the right, for example, to free speech claimed by a newspaper publishing details of a celebrity's private life may conflict with that celebrity's right to privacy. Often in these cases there is no simple way of rendering the legal rule as clearly as the formalist position might claim; interpretation – or a balancing of the competing valid rights claims – is required.

Finally, it will also be the case that in legal systems based on precedent, the assessment of the '*ratio decidendi*' of a precedent case is itself a source of indeterminacy. Even in a single judgment, or especially in an appeal court decision where there may be different majority opinions to analyse, there will be room for interpretation in ascertaining what the rule is. This difficulty is magnified where there exists, as often there will do, a series of cases in a particular area of law, many of which may be treated as providing potential precedents, and at least some of which may themselves conflict.

Against both the formalists and, as we have seen, the Realists, Hart argues that legal rules cannot function as simple *predictions* of what judges will do, since they are rules of *adjudication*. Thus in Hart's view, formalism and rule scepticism (the claim, as we have just seen, that rules do not and cannot do the work legal formalists say they do) are both exaggerations. Rules *can* have a clear meaning in legal cases and here formal interpretation works unproblematically. In fact, arguably much of our dealing with the law corresponds to this paradigm.

But where, for any number of the reasons mentioned, the law is not clear, says Hart, there are inevitably going to be *hard cases*. Here the judge must use his or her *discretion* to adapt the pre-existing rules to new cases as they arise. Since the law as established does not supply a clear answer to the case in hand, necessarily the judge must work out a basis for the decision by reference to *substantive* (and therefore not simply formal, deductive) extra-legal moral or political considerations. Yet while in such 'hard' cases judges may have *strong* discretion, it is never total discretion. No matter how the judge reaches his or her decision as a matter of thinking the problem through, they must publicly give *reasons* for their decision in the form of arguments about justice, social policy, morality, etc. and show how these arguments are best weighed up in *justifying* the decision which they give.

On this view then, law is a system of rules supplemented by law-creating exercises of judicial discretion, where adjudication is best thought of as being a middle way between purely formal legal rationality and overstress on substantive rationality after the style of the Realists.

But if it is the case that there are these systematic sources of indeterminacy (of the kind both Hart and the Realists drew attention to), and if it is also true that judges – at least in 'hard' cases – have a great deal of discretion in deciding, would this not be a cause for concern? Wouldn't this tend to undermine the values of judicial objectivity and neutrality, and the predictability offered by the formalist approach? Are there no more *substantive* constraints on how judges reason, or no more to say on how these substantive constraints might operate when we think about how we expect judges to justify their decisions?

We know that lawyers do argue about the meaning or the application of a particular rule of law, and that sometimes even our most senior judges, often by writing dissenting opinions, disagree about what a legal rule requires or how it applies to the facts of the case before them. Given this, we might ask two sorts of questions. First, are there any common types of reasons why reasonable disagreement about the meaning and application of law occurs in a legal system? If so, what are these factors, and how should we understand the role they play? Second, given the fact of disagreement, does this mean that formalism as an approach to legal interpretation is neither in practice, nor even as an ideal, defensible; or, to put it even more strongly – is legal formalism at the end of the day simply a myth? And if it is, what interests would be served by promoting such a myth? Alternatively, is legal formalism – as an approach to how legal decisions are justified – true, but only to an extent, and in practice in need of being supplemented by a range of other justificatory techniques? If so, what are these techniques and how should we understand how they operate? In the next unit we consider three different contemporary approaches to these questions.

The classic statement of Hart's approach can be found in ch 7 of Hart (1961). For a sympathetic interpretation, see, also, Neil MacCormick (1981) ch 10.

1.3 Three theories of legal reasoning

1.3.1 An extended formalism: Neil MacCormick

Drawing on and expanding Hart's theory, Neil MacCormick attempts to develop an account of adjudication, which shows clearly what substantive constraints exist in legal reasoning and how they work. As we have already seen, he seeks to show the – very important – place of established valid legal rules as normally applicable by simple deduction or 'subsumption' in clear cases. Now we can turn to how the underlying logic of legal argumentation in its *non-deductive* phases or elements works. Picking up on the insights of Hart on the open texture of law, MacCormick offers an 'extended formalism' in which the analysis of legal reasoning is true to both common-law reasoning and the justificatory arguments that constrain freewheeling substantive reasoning. This is an account that, he argues, is based on what judges actually do in practice. It is, in other words, a *descriptive* account. But it is a *normative* one too: that is, it is one that argues that the forms of justification he identifies in judicial decision making should be looked on as good practice.

Before looking further it may be helpful to clarify three *types* of problems judges or lawyers will encounter in interpreting legal rules. These are: problems of *relevancy*, problems of *interpretation*, and problems of *classification*.

1. *Relevancy* refers to the question: what is the relevant legal rule? Can it be properly established that the case as averred can be warranted by reference to a valid rule?
2. *Interpretation* refers to the problem: given there is a relevant legal rule, how should it be interpreted?
3. *Classification* refers to whether or not the case as averred can be properly classified as of the type which would fall under – be subsumed under – the relevant legal rule.

In easy cases, where the rule can be established and interpreted clearly and the facts classified without difficulty, the case can be subsumed as an instance of the rule and the legal ruling can be established uncontroversially. Hard cases, by contrast, are those in which problems of any of the three types identified may arise individually or in combination, and so raise the question of how the judge should act to apply his or her discretion where the relevant ruling is not immediately obvious. Problems of relevancy might mean that we identify a 'gap' in the law, or a clash of laws, or a lack of 'fit', or that we allow analogy to do too much work in establishing similarity between cases even where the latter may be somewhat strained. Problems of classification might mean that the case before the judge may not be immediately subsumed under a single legal rule. Problems of interpretation may arise where there is some doubt or contest over whether a condition stipulated in the major premise can be interpreted to include the instance within its ambit. How, then, is the ruling to be given in the case at hand?

In response to these problems, MacCormick identifies a number of constraints in legal reasoning – conditions that any suggested ruling must meet to qualify as a legal ruling. The first is *universalisability*, which, he argues, is and should be a part of all judicial decision making. Indeed, he says, it is of the essence of *justification* as such. That is, to give an adequately justified decision, a judge must make a ruling that deals with the particular case before the court as an instance of a general or universal class. MacCormick suggests that what judges do is to consider whether a proposed decision is capable of *universal* application. For example, in *Donoghue v Stevenson*, the issue of liability was not simply about this specific manufacture's negligence towards Mrs Donoghue. Rather, as Lord Tomlin put it (quoted in MacCormick 1978, p 57):

> I think that if the appellant is to succeed it must be on the proposition that *every* manufacturer or repairer of *any* article is under a duty to *everyone* who may thereafter legitimately use the article . . . It is logically impossible to stop short of this point.

The stress on '*every* manufacturer', '*any* article', '*everyone*' in this passage exemplifies the criterion of universalisability and, MacCormick argues, it is necessary for this to be met if a decision is to be properly justified. Putting the argument that justification is not based on the merits of the particular case, but rather on a universal or general treatment of it, he concludes:

> I cannot for the life of me understand how there can be such a thing as a good reason for deciding any single case which is not a good generic reason for deciding cases of the particular type in view, that is to say, the 'merits' of any individual case are the merits of the type of case to which the individual case belongs.
>
> (MacCormick 1978, p 97)

Universalisability is an extension of the requirement of *formal justice*. This requires us to treat like cases alike and different cases differently. Justification through univeralisation is therefore linked to doing justice to all members of a class in the same way. MacCormick describes this as follows:

> One who has to do *justice* among other persons, and one who seeks this or that as a matter of *justice*, is committed at least to the principle that like cases are to be treated alike and differences of treatment to be grounded in difference of relevant factors in a situation. In so far as we have reason to wish that our public agencies act in relation to citizens in a rationally comprehensible and predictable way, we have reason to wish that they act in accordance with this conception of formal justice.
>
> (MacCormick 1979, p 110)

Formal justice therefore requires that for a decision to be justified, it must treat the instant case in the same way as any other similar case. If there are sufficient relevant differences, then distinguishing this case from another can be justified. (We will see later how this process is in fact less than straight-forward, and indeed is contested at a number of different levels.)

While applying these criteria may be sufficient to dispose of the case at hand, it may be that two competing understandings of the law can be found to be both universalisable and justified by reference to formal justice (treating like cases alike). Thus for example, in *Donoghue v Stevenson*, both the major-ity and minority opinions – the one holding manufacturers liable according to the principle of negligence, the other denying it by reference to the lack of a contract – may be justified in precisely these ways.

In these circumstances then, universalisability can act as a control on *con-sequentialist* calculations, which may be used to test the competing proposi-tions of law. According to MacCormick, 'Among the consequences of a ruling [are included] both (i) the logical implications of the ruling, viewed by reference to the range of hypothetical cases it covers; and (ii) the results of practical outcomes which will or may ensue given the existence of a rule showing those logical implications.' (MacCormick 1979, p 116)

Here, what is properly to be evaluated is not the individual ad hoc decision between parties – it is the consequences of the ruling about the point(s) in issue which matter. What will be the case if this or that among the rival propositions of law proposed by rival parties prevails? How do such con-sequences square with justice, common sense, public policy, etc.? Consequen-tialism may commonly be seen in legal judgments in the form of 'floodgates' arguments, and usually as a form of suggesting why liability say should not be extended. But those are by no means the sole instances, and in fact MacCormick here would include criteria of value ranging from 'justice', to 'common sense', from 'public benefit' to 'convenience'.

Thus in the senses indicated, substantive reasoning in law appears to involve consequentialist argument under the constraint of formal justice, which requires universalisability of grounds of decision. The explicit or implicit ruling by the court on the question(s) before it ought therefore to be tested and justified in terms of the court's evaluation of its consequences.

But if a decision is justifiable on the basis of consequentialist argument, does it follow that judges can act on the basis of any ruling whatever, which they represent as having advantageous or highly acceptable consequences? Are there no other constraints beyond those already identified? MacCormick argues that there are two other important constraints.

The requirement of *consistency* in law: Rulings must not be inconsistent with pre-existing laws, in the sense of not directly contradicting some binding or authoritative rule. If we discover, that is, that the candidate ruling that has met the criteria of 'universalisability' and has the most desirable consequences, contradicts nonetheless a valid rule of the legal system, then it fails as a legal solution and must be ruled out of the competition. If that were not so, the idea of legal systems as being or including systems of valid, binding rules would be necessarily false.

The requirement of *coherence* in law is similar to consistency, yet there is an important difference between them. While consistency is a negative property, consisting in the absence of contradictions, coherence is a positive property. To fulfil its requirements, judges must decide cases only in accordance with rulings that are in keeping with the existing body of law, and supported by it. And this is primarily achieved by reliance on *principles* in legal argument. The ruling in a hard case must be shown to be justifiable by reference to some legal principle, and thus 'coherent' with already settled law. While consistency is an either/or quality, coherence is a matter of degree. For MacCormick 'general principles are to be understood as expressing values which are held to be significant in and for the legal system. They are broad normative generalisations under which more concrete rules and rulings of the system can be subsumed. Hence "coherence" is secured by observance of general principles in legal argumentation, to the extent that sets of rules are made to make sense by being geared together to the pursuance of some supposed value or values' (MacCormick 1981: 118–19).

Another important aspect of 'coherence' is manifested in argument by *analogy*. Arguments from analogy are not *formally* valid in any sense. Rather they work by being more or less *persuasive*. In cases that are partially similar and partially different, an analogy may support without compelling the decision in the case. For example, on the face of it, there is nothing similar between a snail in a ginger beer bottle and a pair of itchy underpants; but on another reading the latter is analogous to – or 'just like' – the former, in that a consumer suffered harm caused by a defective product (*Grant v Australian Knitting Mills*).

Judges use *analogies* reasonably often. And while they do not count as a formal justification, they can often have a direct impact on how the judge treats the case and the light in which s/he expects others to see it. For example, in the case of *In re A (Conjoined Twins)*, the case that provides the fact situation described in the first paragraph of this Part, Ward LJ wrote:

In my judgment, parents who are placed on the horns of such a terrible dilemma simply have to choose the lesser of their inevitable loss. If a family at the gates of a concentration camp were told they might free one of their children but if no choice were made both would die, compassionate parents with equal love for their twins would elect to save the stronger and see the weak one destined for death pass through the gates.

(Ward LJ, *Re A Children* 1009–1010)

For a fascinating account of how analogy works in the common law, with specific reference to the notion of dangerousness in delict as a moving classification system, see Levi (1948) sections I and II, pp 501–19. The 'conjoined twins' case provides the focus for several essays in Bankowski, Z and MacLean, J (2006), which also deal in greater depth with issues of universality and particularity in legal reasoning.

To summarise: MacCormick finds that judges and lawyers use – and can be expected to use – certain *kinds* of argument that on the one hand go beyond deductive reasoning, yet on the other, work to constrain how they may justify their decisions. In this sense where judges do have to make value choices in interpreting the law, particularly in hard cases, these choices are limited by systemic or substantive constraints (see MacCormick 1993, p 18). As such, legal reasoning is best thought of as centrally about rule application and where the formal application is contested, one that remains nonetheless a process of rational justification.

For a concise summary of MacCormick's analysis, see MacCormick (1979). For fuller treatment, see MacCormick (1978, 1994 2nd edn), chs 5–9.

1.3.2 Principles, interpretation and integrity: Dworkin

Since his earliest writings, Ronald Dworkin has consistently maintained that *every* judicial decision requires discretion understood as the exercise of judgement, as interpretation, and yet *none* requires discretion of an unrestricted type. Dworkin's attack on formalism – and its core concept of law as a system of rules – is a powerful one and is oriented to its delimitation of the category of hard cases. Neither do we discover the right legal answer by looking up the right rule, says Dworkin, nor do we 'hit upon' a hard case when we have merely 'run out of rules' in some sense – because, for example, there is a 'gap' in the law, or because of the 'open texture' of the rules (see Hart). Because *how would we know that we have run out of rules?* Dworkin's famous examples (*Riggs v. Palmer, MacPherson v. Buick, Brown v. Board of Education*) are highly convincing attempts to force the rules+discretion model into impasses. Because in none of these cases is it obvious that we have indeed 'run out of rules'. These were cases where the formalist model appeared to give an answer, and yet judges argued passionately about whether it was in fact the right legal answer. Their disagreement, for Dworkin, captures precisely what the 'stuff' of law, as an argumentative practice, is about. They sought the right legal answer by constructing a justification (that subsumes the rule under it) in terms of discussing *principles* embodied in the law. Hard cases in effect are not hard for the reasons formalists would have it: either because of problems of the correct application of the rule or because, in line with how we have described the formalist position, of semantic ambiguities in the language of the specific rules. Hard cases cannot be 'read off' rules in this way. Discerning and arguing a hard case involves a theoretical disagreement about law, involving principles, standards and purposes embodied in the law; in effect, Dworkin sees hard cases not as pathologies that call for a more or less arbitrary decision to be made, but as pivotal, pointing to the law's essential contestability that calls for decisions that are, as he will call them later, always *interpretive*.

For Dworkin's attack on law-as-system-of rules, see Dworkin (1977). For his use of the above cases to 'test' the formalist model, see Dworkin (1986) ch 1. Dworkin's formulation of 'rights as trumps' was developed in Dworkin (1977), but downplayed in his later work.

Let us take things more gradually. The theories of Hart and MacCormick, while accepting some of the Realist claims, maintain that law provides rational constraints to substantive reasoning and that these constraints have to do with the predominantly formalist nature of legal reasoning. It involves a supposition that judges should always seek to make rulings on disputed points of law, should do so consistently with the pre-established law, and should aim at coherence with established law through seeking always to make their judgments conform with legal principles. Such principles, they argue, stand in a rational, justificatory relationship to the valid rules of law. Ronald Dworkin criticises these views because of their acceptance of discretion, judicial law making and retrospectivity. If their view of law-as-a-system-of-rules is correct, according to Dworkin, then rules have an all-or-nothing quality and so, once they run out, there is nothing left in law to appeal to and hence they must give judges a kind of strong discretion that is indeed *unrestricted* by law, given that law comes *only* in the form of rules, and hard cases that require discretion are hard precisely because there is no rule governing the case. The rules have in a crucial sense 'run out'. (Compare Hart's presentation and attack on the Realists.) For Dworkin this inevitable concession is unacceptable. It is unacceptable descriptively, because that is not how judges understand the exercise of legal judgment; if they struggle and agonise over the answer in a hard case, it is not because they think that there is no law to be found covering it and that they therefore need to decide it purely in political or ethical terms. No, it is still the exercise of *legal* judgment that they are involved in. But formalism (and 'extended' formalism) has it wrong prescriptively, too, for Dworkin, because it is an *unacceptable* violation of the values of law and democracy, as they find expression in the rule of law ideal, to concede that judges should in hard cases usurp the role of the legislator.

The discretion that judges have in a legal system, says Dworkin, is only discretion in the 'weak sense', but this is not MacCormick's 'weak sense', which for Dworkin is still a strong discretion, weakened only in that it is 'rationally' constrained. For Dworkin, the discretion that judges have is, and should be, weak in a different sense. Of course as an exercise of judgement, its outcome is never determinable in advance. But this does not mean that there are not right and wrong ways to exercise judgement. He gives the example of an army officer who is given the instruction 'to choose five men' for a mission. The strong discretion he is given in that instruction differs crucially from the weak discretion he would have been given had the instruction been: 'choose the five best men for the mission'. Obviously the latter instruction gives the officer discretion too, but it consists not in the freedom of choice, but in the exercise of informed judgement as to what 'best' means in terms of the requirements of the mission. It is this *kind* of discretion that judges are given. For Dworkin there are always relevant legal standards that will inform the outcome even though, unlike the case of merely deductive reasoning from rules, how to apply them is not always clear and always requires the exercise of judgement. This is difficult to do and often controversial, but there is ultimately a right answer. The judge's task is not to legislate new law. It is to apply existing law. The point is that existing law contains more than the positive rules of law.

In his major work, *Law's Empire*, the insight is integrated in a theory of law as *interpretive practice*. Much has been made of the differences between earlier approaches and that of this book, and although it is fair to say that emphases have been shifted, the later work integrates the earlier insights in a theory of *law-as-interpretation*, fundamentally enriched by the notion that the law is a *practice* and that it occurs in a *community* of interpreters. With this move Dworkin shifts the understanding of the nature of law from text to practice, from settled fact to ongoing revision. In contrast to the concept of law as a matter of past official decisions (positivism), for Dworkin, law is an interpretive concept, the meaning of every law an exercise in interpretation, the very distinction between a hard and an easy case always an interpretive choice. This exercise in interpretation is impossible unless we appreciate that law is a practice and involves us as participants in arguing its meaning. Borrowing from the hermeneutical tradition, Dworkin claims that an understanding of a social practice requires turning to the meaning it has for participants. The meaning of the law, as is the case with every practice and concept can only be retrieved from within a shared context, a shared form of life, a community. As a community of interpreters of the meaning of our legal practice, we share a context of its possible meanings. We can begin to appreciate its demands not because we hold fast to some rigid list of rules, but because we can take the 'internal' point of view of the participant and interpret its point or purpose and how that might inform what it requires of us in each case. So arguing for the *best* among possible understandings involves us participants in an argument over the purpose or point of the practice. To discover what the law requires, each and every time, we must attempt to see the institution in its best light and to understand its requirements in the light of what would most fully realise its implied purpose. This exercise in (what Dworkin calls) 'constructive interpretation' must be performed on objective ground; not, that is, by imposing upon the practice outside moral or personal purposes, but by retrieving purpose from within the practice, as it is intelligible to the people participating in it.

This is as true of all social practices as it is for law. Interpretation is always *justification* for Dworkin: one understands a practice – here legal practice – by justifying what it is about; but this imputation of justificatory principle or purpose needs to be one that is already embodied in the practice, one that we *retrieve* from the best understanding of the practice, not that we impose on it. We may, for example, find that the best justification for awarding damages for delicts is the fair distribution of risks or even the protection of vulnerable members of society. But if that is not what makes sense of the practice of awarding compensation in our legal system, because, for example, the justification for holding people responsible has to do with whether they could have foreseen the injury rather than whether they can pay for it, then however attractive one might find one's own justification, it is not the principle or justification that can be read off the practice; it is imposed not retrieved. And therefore it does not 'see' the practice under scrutiny in *its* best light because it does not *fit* the practice, but instead reconstructs it as something different. The enterprise of 'constructive interpretation' carries great complexity into legal practice and the business of reaching decisions in law. Competing interpretations in law are different rationalisations of the history of the practice competing on the terrain of 'fit'. Justifications command certain 'fits', 'fits' delimit certain justifications. It is a kind of reflexive equilibrium between the two that will allow the best balance of the two – a balancing undertaken against the background of the whole body of the law – to read as the legally *right answer*.

The 'right answer' for Dworkin, is an answer where weight matters. And what weight means, in this respect, is the gravitational pull of principles that need to be deployed to rationalise rules and decisions into coherence. The judge who is guided by integrity will decide on the morally *most attractive* principle, that is a principle that *best fits*, that is, that carries the most weight within that order, having been entrenched in previous decisions. What does this mean in practice? Take an example: someone is before the court having successfully incited a crowd to perform an illegal act. Can we extend criminal liability to her? Perhaps the 'morally most attractive' justification, the principle that the interpreter of law most values, is that *all speech* needs to be immune to prosecution; our political activist should be let off. But testing it against the legal practice of his community, the interpreter may find that it is not the case that this principle 'fits' the practice. The law curtails all kinds of speech acts: from threats to forms of advertising. On the other hand the justification might be overinclusive; perhaps one should limit it to cases of 'political speech', arguing that the best reading of our legal practice demands that political speech acts be protected. In that case, perhaps, the requirement of 'fit' has been met, although, it may also perhaps, now stumble on something different: does the act in question, the incitement of the crowd, fall under the protected category, that is, is it an instance of 'political speech' or has the better 'fit' rendered the justification underinclusive?[2]

Dworkin calls his prescription for the right answer in law *Integrity*. Integrity means *consistency in principle* with past decisions and requires retrieving that principle in precedent as the justification that best fits the institutional record. Dworkin tellingly contrasts integrity to pragmatism, which is the name he gives to his main theoretical adversaries, the CLS movement (see 2.3 below). The pragmatist's recourse to political principles only serves his/her own pursuit of an ideal. There is no commitment to working out common schemes of principle embodied in the law; principles are imputed *strategically* in order for 'judges [and lay participants] to make whatever decisions seem best for the community's future.'(Dworkin 1986, p 95) Unlike pragmatism, '[i]ntegrity demands that the public standards of the community be both made and seen, so far as this is possible, to express a single, coherent scheme of justice and fairness in the right relation'(ibid, p 219). Although every decision about what the law is can be debated as to what the principle to be read into text and precedent ought to be, integrity, unlike pragmatism, does not leave the question open. It insists, as we said, that the operative principle should *fit* the most coherent scheme of justice that can be envisaged for the past history of legal decisions and *morally justifies* that practice. Integrity demands that the rationalising principle of the decision at hand be part of a pattern that coheres as a whole and shows it in its best light.

---

2 For an application of precisely this dilemma to actual political practice in the Scottish context, see Christodoulidis and Finnie (1995).

The concept of 'integrity' is developed in Dworkin (1986) ch 7, where it is usefully contrasted with other prevalent views on legal interpretation. For a concise summary of his theory of legal interpretation, see Dworkin (1990).

To bring the connection between interpretation and coherence forcefully home, Dworkin uses the metaphor of the *chain novel* in which judges assume the roles of the consecutive co-authors. In adding his/her chapter, the author must both assure it reads as a whole as well as the best in its genre; in the same way the judge, if his/her decision is to respect law as integrity, will reconstruct the practice as a meaningful whole, thus sustaining the unity of community by giving coherence to the understanding of its practice of law in which people argue their conceptions of what justice requires. This is for Dworkin, aspirationally, what law is about and he entrusts the momentous task to his imaginary judge *Hercules*. Although every decision about what the law *is* can be debated as to what the principle to be read into text and precedent ought to be, integrity does not leave the question open, but provides Hercules with a guiding ideal that will yield the answer; it insists that the operative principle should fit into the most coherent scheme of justice that can be envisaged for the past history of legal decisions. Integrity demands that the rationalising principle of the decision at hand be part of a pattern that coheres as a whole. And that is the crux of Dworkin's restatement of the right answer thesis. Integrity yields the right answer and thus sustains the rule of law ideal.

1.3.3 Critical legal analysis: Unger

In 1976, a new academic movement was formed when a group of scholars met to form a network called the 'Conference on Critical legal Studies'. Despite considerable opposition in the Academy, the group's influence grew, drawing together a variety of left-wing radical stances towards law into an umbrella movement and giving an institutional unity to those who opposed 'legal orthodoxy'. Picking up the radical moment in American Legal Realism (above), the CLS argue that taking legal doctrine seriously means revealing rather than concealing contrary aspects of law (even teaching law through them). With the Realists they argue against formalism that rules *do not* fix unambiguous meanings; the text of law can be 'deconstructed', they argue, to reveal its inherent ambiguities. Emphasising 'contradictions' means highlighting the choices and possibilities present in law that allow legal scholars, practitioners and judges to tap the resources the law itself makes available in order to argue the case for those who find themselves systematically disempowered by the way legal orthodoxy operates. This ties in with the CLS's second objective – to explore, criticise and eventually reverse the manner in which legal doctrine, legal education and the practices of legal institutions entrench advantage, disempower the vulnerable and sustain the status quo of a pervasive system of oppressive relations in society.

For Unger's critique of 'formalism' and 'objectivism', see Unger (1983), pp 5–14. For a comprehensive introduction to the emergence of the CLS movement in its various strands, see Kelman (1987). For an accessible summary, see Altman (1993) ch 1.

Although it would be wrong to see the CLS as a 'monolithic' movement, it is also not untrue to the variety it harbours, to discern certain common themes. The first has to do with the claim that the law is riddled with *real* (not apparent) contradictions. The second has to do with how power operates in law to conceal these. Both of these moments – the tensions in law and the importance of power and hierarchy – are evident in the way CLS analyses law by stressing the various paired master oppositions that resolve cases in opposite and incompatible ways: mechanically applied rules/situation-sensitive ad hoc standards, values as subjective/values as objective, human action is willed/human action is determined by environment, private/public, individual/group, law/policy, reason/fiat, freedom/coercion. Such pairs are hierarchically structured in that one side of the opposition is dominant, the other subordinate and supplementary. The dominant side sustains the status quo; the subordinate, in exceptional cases, allows us to question it.

Let us look a little more closely at one of the most influential figures in the CLS movement – Brazilian activist and Harvard Professor, Roberto Unger – and approach the complexity of his work, straddling legal, political and social theory, through one of his less demanding examples. Unger contends that because the content of our legal past is inherently indeterminate, it can be made to make sense in different ways depending on the principle we impute each time. He illustrates this with the example of contract law, reading the doctrine alternatively through 'individualistic' and 'communitarian' spectacles, or more accurately, by imputing alternatively the principle of *freedom of contract* and the counter-principle of *fairness of contract*. Both, he will conclude, yield coherent accounts of precedent. He sees in the unleashing of the counter-principle a potential for fresh legal interpretations of the law of contract.

For an application of his work on the concept of 'privacy' in the English law of contract, see Hugh Collins (1987a), pp 92–6; and Collins (1987b).

Unger's argument runs something like this:

1. For every rule, there is an exception.
2. The rule represents the dominant principle; the exception stands for a counter-principle, subordinate but still present in law.
3. Different social visions are in contest in law – individualism vs altruism – and these underlie the rule/dominant principle and the exception/counter-principle.

Applied schematically to the law of contract these yield the following three-fold pairing of oppositions:

Rule	***Exception***
Pacta sunt servanda [contractual obligations must be upheld]	Except when contract is void or voidable
Principle	***Counter-principle***
Freedom of contract: both as to contractual partner(s) and terms	Fairness of contract: agreements are struck down where i) terms are unfair ii) communal aspects of social life are subverted iii) parties acted unconscionably
Value	***Counter-value***
Individualism/Autonomy	Solidarity, protection of the vulnerable, community values

This is of necessity schematic. However, the basic point, as emphasised by Unger, is that the possibility is present in law to argue a case as falling under the rule (*pacta sunt servanda*) or the exception (doctrine of duress, undue influence, unreasonable terms, impossibility, unconscionability, protection of good faith and reliance on less formal representations, etc.); that this opposition at the level of doctrinal interpretation reflects a deeper opposition of competing principles; and that in that opposition of principles a further deeper, and *legally* irresolvable opposition is in turn played out, between two politically irreconcilable value systems – liberal individualism and socialism. The point is not merely that the law provides a wealth of possibilities for lawyers to argue any case either way, but that in fact our legal system acts both as passive enforcer of private transactions and in a paternalistic, active role as protector of vulnerable parties against economic predators. The law does not contain 'right answers' waiting to be discovered. Instead, the law's oppositions in turn correspond to competing normative visions of human association present within law and that the presence of such clashing perspectives should be discussed openly, not least because the suppressed side of law's oppositions are taken to be the more politically progressive. Thus law is to be taken seriously as a means of effecting radical social transformation.

In subsequent work Unger (1987) has gone even further and spoken of the need to institutionalise further categories of rights, including 'solidarity rights'. Although very little is said about the precise content of these rights, one can assume on the basis of Unger's other writings that the content would be retrieved through playing up principles already present – if suppressed – in existing law. The mechanism and logic of this has been elaborated above. In (1996) he renews his call for a 'selective probing of institutions' through the 'dialectical exercise of mapping and criticism'. Unger's suggestion in all of this is for an interpretative method of reasoning that draws on and exploits strategically existing, if latent, institutional possibilities. In the case of solidarity rights, reconstruction would proceed from the protection of solidarity in existing law – of contract and delict basically – such as the protection of reliance and the protection of the disadvantaged party, general clauses of good faith and of abuse of rights, etc., 'by which private law supports communal relations while continuing to represent society as a world of strangers' (Unger 1987b: 537).

Hugh Collins describes a further model for deploying legal analysis in what he describes as a *horizontal* rather than the above *vertical* manner (Collins 1987b). According to the orthodox view of how law functions in society, one can discern broadly three spheres of social life with law applying differently to each. There is the sphere of public life and here our public law provides citizens with robust protection (in the form of civil rights) against the might wielded by the State and organises the democratic system by guaranteeing political rights. Here the law acknowledges a certain asymmetry in the relations of citizen to State and thus affords the vulnerable party protection and guarantees. The second sphere is that of exchange and work. In this sphere liberal law typically treats parties as equal, providing the language and the categories to sanction their dealings with each other, but remaining neutral in the process. Finally there is the third sphere, the sacrosant private sphere of family and intimacy in which the law intervenes minimally in order to maintain it free of State intervention and secure privacy understood as negative freedom.

There are good, political reasons, claim the CLS, why this frozen picture of social life needs to be challenged as maintaining oppression rather than guaranteeing freedom, entrenching advantage rather than opportunity. Family relations, if not put under legal scrutiny, are free to harbour abuse, patriarchal privilege, domestic violence, violation of trust. The sphere of work and exchange is emphatically *not* a sphere where equal parties strike their deals, but instead where corporate giants manipulate individual workers and where economic predators prey on vulnerabilities of contractual partners.

Unger's agenda for radical political change to counter advantage uses law to renegotiate the boundaries between spheres, and manipulate the fragilities and porous nature of those boundaries to stir up social change. More precisely the horizontal application of 'deviationist doctrine' here, of critical legal doctrine, depends again on tracing the paired opposition of principle and counter-principle within each sphere and arguing the case for treating the counter-principle as significant. What gives particular credence to this argumentative strategy here is that what counts as counter-principle in one sphere is indeed dominant in another. For example: while in the sphere of public life our freedom to expose corrupt authority and associate to pursue our claims, the very same rights are denied in the sphere of exchange. The very same activities draw very different legal responses in this sphere: 'whistle-blowing' is not protected and secondary picketing is criminalised. But the logic of this differential legal response is completely flawed and self-contradictory. The sphere of exchange is not a sphere of equality; corporations act increasingly in corrupt ways and their activities need to be exposed to scrutiny, particularly in an era where there are corporate actors who indeed wield much greater power than even Nation-States do; employees are one of the most vulnerable categories in the face of ruthless new management techniques and the threat of unemployment. So why not use the resources the legal system affords us in the form, here, of the protection of rights, and cross the boundaries between spheres, the autonomy of which is becoming increasingly unconvincing, to imaginatively deploy legal argumentation traditionally incongruent to any particular area of social life?

Unger's work is suggestive and radical, both as to its vision for the possibilities of legal analysis and its careful mapping of the ways in which the logic of law can be deployed to stretch those limits. Against an understanding of law as striving for the right answer on the basis of imputation of the one best principle, like Dworkin, CLS propound the possibility of political choice through the imputation of 'counter-principle'. Hence the debate between Dworkin and the CLS is best understood against a background of political theory. CLS are attempting to feed the possibility of transformative political action into law. If law is indeterminate and has to be 'rationalised' each time, then it is a malleable vessel for political vision. What legal answer we see appropriate is relevant to our politics. What reason is 'right' depends on our political choice of what political principle underlying it is right. Dworkin's project is motivated by a typically liberal concern to keep law clean of politics. He professes a theory that will elevate choices from the battleground of politics to the legal forum of principle. On Dworkin's account of it, law provides the politically neutral means of mediating between politically competing positions, so that what one perceives as the right answer in law does not necessarily identify with what one conceives to be politically desirable. The CLS on the other hand not only view it impossible to avoid political choices in legal debate, but view Dworkin's attempt to settle this as itself a political move.

References

Altman, A, 1993, *Critical Legal Studies*, University of California Press.

Bankowski, Z and MacLean, J, 2006 (eds), *The Universal and the Particular in Legal Reasoning*, Aldershot: Ashgate.

Bennion, F, 2001, *Understanding Common Law Legislation*, Oxford: Oxford University Press.

Bennion, F, 2002, *Statutory Interpretation*, 4th edn, London: Butterworths.

Christodoulidis, E, (1996) 'The Inertia of Institutional Imagination: A Reply to Roberto Unger', 59 *Modern Law Review* 377.

Christodoulidis, E and Finnie, W, 1995, 'How the Ace of trumps failed to Win the Trick', *Res Publica*, 131.

Collins, H, 1986, *The Law of Contract*, London: Weidenfield and Nicholson.

Collins, H, 1987a, 'The decline of privacy in private law', 14 *JLS* 91.

Collins, H, 1987b, 'Roberto Unger and the Critical Legal Studies Movement', 14 *JLS* 387.

Cross, R, 1995, *Statutory Interpretation*, 5th edn, London: Butterworths.

Cross, R and Harris, JW, 1991, *Precedent in English Law*, 4th edn, Oxford: Clarendon.

Duxbury, N, 1997, *Patterns of American Jurisprudence*, Oxford: Clarendon.

Dworkin, RM, 1977, 'The Model of Rules', extracted in Dworkin (ed) *The Philosophy of Law*, Oxford: Oxford University Press, and expanded in chapters 2 and 3 of *Taking Rights Seriously*.

Dworkin, R, 1986, *Law's Empire*, London: Fontana.

Dworkin, R, 1990, 'Law, Philosophy and Interpretation [the Kobe lecture for Legal and social Philosophy]', *ARSP*, 1.

Frank, J, 1949a, *Courts on Trial: Myth and Reality in American Justice*. Princeton: Princeton University Press.

Frank, J, 1949b, *Law and the Modern Mind*, London: Stevens.

George, R, 1994 (ed), *Natural Law Theory* Oxford: Clarendon.

Griffith, JAG, 1977, *The Politics of the Judiciary*, London: Fontana.

Hart, HLA, 1961, *The Concept of Law*, Oxford: Clarendon.

Hart, HLA, 1983, 'The Legal Nightmare and the Noble Dream', in ch 4 of *Essays in Jurisprudence and Philosophy*, Oxford: Clarendon.

Hayek, FA, 1944, *The Road to Serfdom*, London: Routledge & Kegan Paul.

Holmes, OW, 1897, 'The Path of Law', 10 *Harvard Law Review* 457.

Horwitz, M, 1992, *The transformation of American law, 1870–1960 : the crisis of legal orthodoxy*, New York: Oxford University Press.

Jackson, B, 1995, *Making Sense in Law*, Merseyside: DC Publications.

Kelman, M, 1987, *A Guide to Critical Legal Studies*, Cambridge, MA: Harvard University Press.

Levi, E, 1948, 'An Introduction to Legal Reasoning', 15 *University of Chicago LR* 501.

MacCormick, N, 1978, *Legal Reasoning and Legal Theory*, Oxford: Clarendon.

MacCormick, N, 1979, 'The Artificial Reason and Judgement of Law', *Rechtstheorie* 105.

MacCormick, N, 1981, *H.L.A. Hart*, London: Arnold.

MacCormick, N, 1989, 'The Ethics of Legalism', *Ratio Juris* 184.

MacCormick, N, 1993, 'Argument and Interpretation in Law', *Ratio Juris* 16.

MacCormick, N, 1994, *Legal Reasoning and Legal Theory*, 2nd edn, Oxford: Clarendon.

MacCormick, N and Summers, R, 1991, *Interpreting Statutes*, Aldershot: Dartmouth.

McLeod, I, 2005, *Legal Method*, 4th edn, Basingstoke: Palgrave Macmillan.

Rumble, WE, 1968, *American Legal Realism*, Ithaca, New York: Cornell University Press.

Twining, W, 1984, 'Some Scepticism about Scepticisms', 1 *Journal of Law and Society*, 137–71.

Unger, RM, 1983, *The Critical Legal Studies Movement*, Cambridge MA: Harvard University Press.

Unger, RM, 1987a, *Social Theory: Its Situation and Its Task*. Vol 1 of *Politics: A Work in Constructive Social Theory*, Cambridge MA: Cambridge University Press.

Unger, RM, 1987b, *False Necessity: Anti-Necessitarian Social Theory in the Service of Radical Democracy*. Vol 2 of *Politics: A Work in Constructive Social Theory*. Cambridge MA: Cambridge University Press.

Unger, RM, 1996, 'Legal Analysis as Institutional Imagination', 59 *Modern Law Review* 1.

Cases

Daniels & Daniels v R White & Sons [1938] 4 All ER 258.

Grant v Australian Knitting Mills [1936] AC 85.

In re A (Conjoined Twins) 4 All ER 961.

Chapter 2

Advanced topics

2.1 Justice, natural law and the limits of rule following

2.1.1 Moral reason and hard cases

In an important House of Lords judgment on the controversial issue of 'wrongful conception', Lord Steyn made the following remark:

> [J]udges ought to strive to give the real reasons for their decision. It is my firm conviction that where courts of law have denied a remedy for the cost of bringing up an unwanted child the real reasons have been grounds of distributive justice. That is, of course, a moral theory. It may be objected that the House must act like a court of law and not like a court of morals. That would only be partly right. The court must apply positive law. But judges' sense of the moral answer to a question, or the justice of the case, has been one of the great shaping forces of the common law. What may count in a situation of difficulty and uncertainty is not the subjective view of the judge but what he reasonably believes that the ordinary citizen would regard as right.[1]

A long debate has existed in jurisprudence over how best to characterise the role of morality in the practice of law. While some authors (legal positivists) claim there is no *necessary* connection between law and morality, many others suggest the interplay between law and morality is more complex and nuanced than this suggests. As this issue is particularly vexed in the case of legal reasoning, it demands our attention here. We need to consider *whether* and *how* legal reasons and justifications can meaningfully be insulated from moral reasons and justifications, and whether it *makes sense* to do so; moreover,

---

1 *McFarlane and Another v. Tayside Health Board* [1999] 4 All ER 961, per Lord Steyn at 977–78.

what is actually *at stake* in our assessment of these questions? In order to explore these issues, we will focus on another landmark medical law case that has been interpreted by John Finnis, a leading jurisprudence scholar, who argues against the legal positivists' position by claiming that the case he discusses exemplifies how legal reasoning is best understood as an *instantiation* of general practical reason.

A much discussed case that throws up the issue of the relation between moral and legal reasons is that of *Airedale National Health Service Trust v Bland*.[2] Anthony Bland had suffered severe injury in the Hillsborough Stadium disaster. He never recovered consciousness and remained in a persistent vegetative state (PVS). Medical experts judged that he had no prospect of recovery or improvement. The Trust applied for a declaration to remove all of the treatment, including feeding, which was keeping him alive. The House of Lords granted the declaration.

In this case, several stark and central issues of morality are at play. Is the outcome morally justified? Is it justified by the state of the law? And more specifically – is it worse directly to intend someone's death than it is to foresee that his or her death will definitely occur? Is it worse to kill than it is to let die? Are either of these distinctions *morally* significant? How are we to assess the boundary between life and death? Is quality of life an issue with which the courts should concern themselves in these cases?

The Lords struggled with these issues and one question that we might want to ask in this context, revealingly, is whether their quandary was a moral or a legal one or even whether the legal answer they gave was one that was morally acceptable (and vice versa). Witness Lord Browne-Wilkinson's agonising over the decision (quoted in Finnis 1993, p 329):

> The conclusion I have reached will appear to some to be almost irrational. How can it be lawful to allow a patient to die slowly, though painlessly, over a period of weeks from lack of food but unlawful to produce his immediate death by a lethal injection, thus saving his family from yet another ordeal . . .? I find it difficult to find a moral answer to that question. But it is undoubtedly the law.

Why was it 'undoubtedly the law' for the Lords? The position in common law is that a failure to act, an omission that causes the death of a 'stranger' (that is, a person to whom one owes no statutory or contractual obligations) is unlawful where, *inter alia*, there is a duty of care, as in the case of a doctor–patient relationship. The duty of care demands that the doctors act in the best interests of their patients. What *Bland* established as the juridical position was that discontinuance of life-sustaining measures is a duty of physicians

2 [1993] 2 WLR 316.

who consider 'invasive', life-sustaining measures to no longer be in the patient's 'best interests'. *But is it rational* to distinguish between two courses of action – a commission of an act (administering a lethal injection) and an omission of an act (withdrawing nutrition and hydration), *both* undertaken by the same actor and both undertaken with the same intention of ending the patient's life? Is it not 'morally and intellectually misshapen' (per Lord Mustil) to establish the distinction between murder and duty of care on that basis? And *is it rational* to argue that it is in someone's 'best interests' to cease to have interests?

2.1.2 John Finnis and the morality of the law

A good way to introduce Finnis's approach is to discuss his opposition to the realist view. Finnis objects to Holmes's aspiration to 'wash with cynical acid' all idealistic fancies about the law, of which, presumably, Finnis's would be one of the more powerful versions. Holmes argued that 'the test of legal principles' is 'the bad man's point of view'. 'What does the notion of legal duty mean to a bad man?' 'Mainly, and in the first place, a prophecy that if he does certain things he will be subjected to disagreeable consequences by way of imprisonment or compulsory payment of money'. 'So much' comments Finnis for 'the widest concept which the law contains – the notion of legal duty' (Finnis 1980, pp 322–4).

To argue against Holmes, Finnis takes the example of contract: according to Holmes, 'the duty to keep a contract at common law means a prediction that you must pay damages if you do not keep it, – and nothing else'. More precisely: 'the only universal consequence of a legally binding promise is, that the law make the promisor pay damages if the promised event does not come to pass. In every case it leaves him free from interference until the time for fulfilment has gone by, and therefore free to break his contract if he chooses' (ibid). For Finnis, this way of viewing it is mis-conceived. For him, 'the virtually universal legal interpretation of contracts and contractual obligation has its significance as an indication that contracts are upheld by the law for the sake of the *common good*, which is positively enhanced (i) by the co-ordination of action, and solution of co-ordination problems, made possible by performance of contracts. . . . and (ii) by the continued existence of a social practice which actively encourages such fully co-ordinate performance and discourages non-performance. Even without collapsing the clear distinction between law and morals, it is possible to see and say that the law's ambitions are higher than this, and its distinctive schemata of thought quite different.' (ibid, p 324) But according to Finnis, Holmes failed to see that contractual obligation, like legal obligation in general, can be explained as the necessity of a type of means uniquely appropriate for attaining a form of good. . . . 'otherwise attainable only imperfectly, if at all'. He failed to see that the social importance of law (as of the practice of promising) derives not only from its ability to mould the 'bad man's' practical reasoning, but also 'from its capacity to give all those citizens who are willing to advance the common good precise directions about what they *must* do *if* they are to follow the way authoritatively chosen as the common way to that good.' (ibid, p 325)

For Finnis, though the law can be seen as a system, it is not from its pedigree that it gets its normativity, but from its function of bringing about the common good. Its normativity comes from the fact that we recognise it as the right thing to do since it instantiates basic values. What are these basic values? Finnis lists seven such values: life, knowledge, play, aesthetic experience, friendship, practical reasonableness and religion (Finnis 1980, pp 85–90). All other values and virtues are subordinate. They are models of realising or participating in basic goods. The basic goods are goods in themselves. For Finnis, law advances the common good by instantiating the basic goods. Much has been written about his analysis of the basic goods, but this is not the place to visit that discussion. What is more important for current purposes is the role of law as providing an instance of practical reasoning and thus an instantiation – a *determinatio* – of the goods. This is a difficult idea and we need to unpack some of its components.

On the one hand, legal reasoning, as a form of practical reason, expresses and substantiates the basic goods. Reasonable and sociable beings must recognise their need for community with others as the necessary context for pursuing the good. The creation of a condition in which all members of a community have full opportunity to participate in the good (to use their practical reasonableness in realising other goods) is the realisation of a good shared by all members of the community. Law facilitates this pursuit. A condition of achieving the common good is a concern for justice, and the example of contract, as we have just seen, illustrates this well.

The second thing that has to be remembered in Finnis's analysis is his emphasis that what any healthy community requires is some common authority. Unless we all in common accede to the authority of some common code of conduct we cannot live together in community at all. And the implementation of any common code of conduct requires the institutionalisation of some agency or agencies, which adjudicate upon breaches of the common code. The more complex a political society becomes, the more rich and varied are the opportunities it presents for diverse manifestations of the good. But the more that is so, the more we face problems of co-ordination, each with another. Hence the more sophisticated are the common public agencies we need for adjudication, administration, enforcement and amendment or enrichment of our common and authoritative code of social conduct.

This, finally, links to another significant point about legal reasoning. Finnis employs the Aristotelian idea of *determinatio* to express how the very abstract requirements of the good acquire specific form and present us with concrete moral imperatives. The flourishing of life, of knowledge, etc., as basic goods, is pitched at too abstract a level to give guidance in practical dilemmas, which require the mediation of practical reason and, paradigmatically in this context, of legal reason. As occupying the middle space between what drives human endeavour (common goods) and concrete situations calling for regulation, legal reasoning, for Finnis, establishes itself, necessarily, as a species of practical reason and this, again necessarily, ties it to morality.

Clear analytical thinking, object positivists, demands that we separate the is and the ought, questions of what the law is from questions of what it ought to be. Picking up a thread from Aristotle, Finnis rehearses a powerful argument that theorists from Aquinas to Leo Russell have used against the positivist injunction. In Finnis, it takes the form of an argument about 'focal meaning'. He argues his methodological commitments at the beginning of his *Natural Law and Natural Rights* (1980). Every attempt, he says, to define an institution, must elevate certain criteria as significant, and this choice necessarily carries an element of evaluation. Why are these – whatever they might be – the criteria that matter? The 'is' and the 'ought' fuse in a zone of indistinction.

But if analytical clarity is our priority, Finnis would insist, how do the positivist judges in *Bland* purport to seriously maintain the distinction between an ethical response and 'what is undoubtedly the law'? Is it really *rational* to distinguish between two courses of action (one 'legal', the other 'illegal') that are undertaken by the same actor (the medical profession) with the same intention and having the same result (the termination of Anthony Bland's life) *because* one is performed through a commission of an act (lethal injection) and the other the omission of an act (starving him to death)? Finnis is of course arguing that a 'basic good', life, should under no rationale – moral or legal – be terminated; we may agree or disagree on the ethics of that. But has he not pointed out in the 'irrationality' of that distinction a certain irrationality of a legal decision – Lord Browne-Wilkinson's 'what is undoubtedly the law' – that is at pains to keep itself pure of ethics, establishing its credentials on what is properly legal?

There are, of course, important counter-arguments to 'natural' law, and these inevitably turn on and into normative questions surrounding legal reasoning. At stake here is the possibility of insulating law from ethics and presenting it as a domain with its proper criteria and methods for reaching outcomes that do not necessarily already engage us in a discussion about ethics. Given the nature of ethical discussions as deeply divisive, indeterminate and subjective, it is no wonder that positivists insist on the need of the 'separation thesis' and advocate its importance for establishing pure, objective and publicly ascertainable *legal* bases for decisions. It is because the stakes are so high that this discussion matters.

To reflect on this consider the following: in his early work *The Unity of Law and Morality* (Detmold 1984) another natural lawyer, Michael Detmold, gives us another argument about the 'necessary connection' of law and morality. It gives us a different angle altogether as we close this discussion for now. Imagine, says Detmold, a judge who is passing sentence on a person guilty of treason. Treason has been established beyond reasonable doubt and carries a mandatory death sentence. Our judge believes that the taking of life is wrong under any circumstance. His dilemma whether to pass sentence is an ethical one; over his duty in law he has no choice. He may decide to fulfil his role as a judge and pass sentence because he might decide that the duty to uphold the law outweighs his personal choice, which his conscience dictates. Or he may decide to step down because he cannot bring himself to send a man to his death. Either way, however, the clash between legal and ethical duty is played out on the ethical plateau. No legal reason can remove that, and this is – what else? – but a subsumption of legal reason to ethical reason.

Reading

For John Finnis's definition of law see (1980) pp 276–90. His methodological stance on the evaluation and description of law, and focal meaning is developed in ch 1 of Finnis (1980). For the full discussion of *Bland*, see Finnis (1993), and for a concise account of the relation of natural law to ethics, see Finnis (1999).

On the positivist/natural law divide that has dominated analytical jurisprudence, see, in particular, HLA Hart in Dworkin (1977) and MacCormick and others in the excellent collection George (1994).

References

Detmold, M, 1984, *The Unity of Law and Morality*, London: Routledge & Kegan Paul.

Dworkin, R, 1977 (ed), *The Philosophy of Law*, Oxford: Oxford University Press.

Finnis, J, 1980, *Natural Law and Natural Rights*, Clarendon: Oxford.

Finnis, J, 1993, '*Bland*: Crossing the Rubicon', 109 *LQR* 329.

Finnis, J, 1999, 'Natural law and the ethics of discourse', 12 *Ratio Juris* 354.

George, R, 1994 (ed), *Natural Law Theory*, Oxford: Clarendon.

MacCormick, DN, 1994, 'On the Separation of Law and Morality', in George (1994).

2.2 Equality, difference and domination: feminist critiques of adjudication

2.2.1 Initial challenges

Some of the most consistently challenging critiques of legal reasoning over the last few decades have come from feminist writers. These critiques are inspired not just by academic analysis, but by an understanding of the very real and detrimental effects of law and its reasoning processes on women's lives. The history of law in westernised societies is the history of laws written by men. It would not be at all surprising then that women's voices and status have been excluded or denigrated, and that processes of legal reasoning have been profoundly implicated in this. While there is a range of divergent positions within feminist analysis, certain strands have emerged that may be considered as critiques – on the one hand of the *substance* of law, and on the other, of the *form* of law itself.

For many feminist writers, notably those writing earlier in the feminist tradition, the aim was to establish formal legal equality between men and women as a matter of the substantive content of the law. Such work inspired – and continues to inspire – much thinking behind anti-discrimination legislation and its application, whose intention is to ensure that men and women have formally equal standing and rights in law. Prominently, for example, in the arena of employment law, women struggled to establish the principle of equal pay for equal work and equal access to employment opportunities, pensions, etc., which could be established in legislation that enshrined the universal principle of non-discrimination on the basis of sex.[3] From this perspective, laws that directly discriminated against women undermined equality under the rule of law. If law's self-image valorised its fairness and impartiality, then those same standards demanded that men and women be treated equally in the eyes of the law. In other words, the principle of formal equality among all citizens should be given full, not partial, effect. Sometimes referred to as 'liberal feminism', this approach argued that women's freedom to participate as equals in society meant holding law to its self-professed standards. Hence already-existing principles of law and legal reasoning could be used to develop full and equal rights for women, in both legislation and adjudication.

This belief in the law's ability to include women, where once they had been excluded, came to be seen as having a number of shortcomings. That is, despite claims to formal equality having been heard, legal interpretation nonetheless still drew on a male perspective in the definition or application of general

---

3 These questions are explored more fully under Part II, 2.4.

categories. On this account, the interpretation of equal rights or standards contained within them biases that meant women continued to be discriminated against. So, for example, with regard to the criminal law defences of provocation or self-defence, the application of the relevant law to cases that did not fit the (masculine) image of an immediate retaliation worked to exclude situations where women responded to male abuse over a long period of time. And, in anti-discrimination law itself, women, in order to find an appropriate comparator against which the question of discrimination could be addressed, had always to compare themselves to a man in the equivalent situation. Hidden here, was that the male standard was always assumed to be the norm, and it was deviation from *that* which was written through the law's assumptions about equality. The general point here is summed up by Naffine (1990, pp 136–7): 'while the law may appear to offer roughly equal rights to men and women, in truth the law organizes around a particular individual who is both male and masculine. The legal person is still very much a man, not a woman, and the law still reserves another place for women: as the other of the man of law.'

Conventional techniques of legal reasoning meant that even where equality was announced in law, the question 'Equal to what?' tended to be answered by treating male standards as the unproblemetised and universal ones. As Naffine (p 144) continues, the underlying question was really this: 'Why can't a woman be more like a man?' In deciding what aspects of the broader social understandings of roles, relationships and expectations were highlighted or downplayed, judges (who are overwhelmingly male) filled in, more or less consciously, the content of abstract legal categories such as legal personality or formal equality by importing male assumptions of these to inform the law's response, while simultaneously legitimating them as expressing equality. In so doing, women's experiences were devalued, or failed to register, in giving content to the law.

2.2.2 Critiquing the form of legal reasoning

These insights raised deeper problems with the liberal feminist approach, which went to the very form of law and legal reasoning itself. The values associated with the formalist position – objectivity, neutrality, universality, formal justice – have all been subjected to criticism by feminist authors. Why would these values be seen as such a cause for concern? The essence of the argument is that while these values purport to treat people equally, they nonetheless operate to do the precisely opposite. There are two kinds of arguments here.

The first is that the very idea of trying to be objective, impartial, neutral, etc., in fact embodies a male perspective on social relations. There are two divergent interpretations of how this impacts on legal reasoning. One argues that men and women have different styles of reasoning. Drawing on analyses of moral reasoning, psychologist Carol Gilligan (1982) found that men tended to emphasise abstract, individualistic and universal or rule-driven approaches to moral problems, while women emphasised connectedness and more particularised or contextualised reasoning. The former she associated with an ethic of justice, the latter with an ethic of care. Moreover, Gilligan noted, the 'justice' style of reasoning was traditionally seen as more 'developed' or 'advanced', and hence the notions of objectivity and impartiality given priority, ahead of those associated with 'care'. Thought of in the legal context, it might be seen that the values of legal formalism replicate such a hierarchy, and in so doing implicitly embody a more male-centred account of what is deemed the most appropriate, 'just' way of approaching legal interpretation. In all this, women's essential experiences could be downplayed, and their 'different voices' excluded from processes of understanding and reasoning.

Such an interpretation has been widely criticised with regard to law and social relations generally. According to Catharine MacKinnon, a feminist legal author, this approach 'essentialises' what is really a matter of contingent power between the sexes, not one of natural differences. Caring, suggests MacKinnon, is just what men want women to do. Rather, she argues, it is not difference but dominance that explains sexual relations in contemporary society. While, as we have seen, treating men and women equally means using the male as comparison, different treatment, she argues is not the result of real differences, but of domination through social practices writ large. Moreover, where exceptions have been made in attempts to recognise 'difference', these are open to the charge of further entrenching male stereotypes and power. Thus even where supposedly well-intentioned judges sought to protect women's differences, 'as a result of their very womanhood', the results could be a form of paternalism that undermined any putative freedom. MacKinnon gives a particularly graphic example of this: where a court decided that it was legitimate to exclude women from a contact job in an all-male prison because they may be raped by inmates, MacKinnon suggests the court took 'the viewpoint of the reasonable rapist on women's employment opportunities' (1989, p 226).

MacKinnon's critique is that the values associated with legal formalism – objectivity, neutrality, impartiality – are themselves suspect since they constitute the basic ways of organising social power to the detriment of women. Central to these are the State – its legislative and adjudication processes – and the doctrine of the rule of law itself when thought of in these terms: 'The state is male in the feminist sense: the law sees and treats women the way men see and treat women. The liberal state coercively and authoritatively constitutes the social order in the interests of men – through its legitimating norms, forms, relation to society, and substantive policies.' (ibid, pp 161–2) The notion of objectivity, for example, so central to the formalist account, does the work in fact of objectifying – that is, turning into objects – women. Hence for MacKinnon, 'Formally the state is male in that its objectivity is its norm . . . The state is male jurisprudentially in that it adopts the standpoint of male power on the relation between law and society.' (ibid, pp 162–3)

As such, understandings of legal interpretation must pay more attention to the *form* of law, and not just its substantive content; or, rather, it must pay attention to the way in which the power of law's form operates to determine its content. And this is true across the whole range of legal regulation: as Finley argues, 'Legal reasoning and its language are patriarchal . . . Privileged white men are the norm for equality law; they are the norm for assessing the reasonable person in tort law; the way men would react is the norm for self-defense law; and the male worker is the prototype for labour law.' (Finley 1989, p 893) It is significant that Finley emphasises the linguistic element in legal reasoning since it shows up both the power of language to normalise social relations of inequality, but also, importantly, its limits; that is, that merely changing to non-sexist language in the law – the reasonable person, rather than the reasonable man in negligence, for example – will not necessarily lead to gender equality where underlying structures of inequality remained unaddressed. It is these observations that point to the intimate links between legal language, formalist values and social domination. As Finley puts it: 'Universal and objective thinking is male language because intellectually, economically, and politically privileged men have had the power to ignore other perspectives and thus to come to think of their situation as the norm, their reality as reality, and their views as objective. Disempowered, marginalized groups are far less likely to mistake their situation, experience, and views as universal.' (ibid, pp 893–4)

Questions remain however, about the extent to which it is persuasive to treat all women's experience as uniform, and whether such accounts tend to downplay other social dynamics such as race, class or culture, across which women's experiences may differ greatly (Fraser 1995, pp 68–93).

2.2.3 Comparing approaches

Let us return to some of the aspects of legal reasoning as identified by MacCormick, earlier, and consider them now in the context of feminist critiques (see above, Part II 1.3.1). It will be recalled that MacCormick considered three central problems associated with legal reasoning: those of relevancy, interpretation and classification. Now, each of these is open to evaluation according to different ways of thinking about how gender bias may be involved.

First, relevancy: what is the relevant legal rule? This is one of the key areas in which contestation has occurred. To give only one example: the question of whether the principle of equal pay for equal work should apply to domestic labour – labour that continues to be carried out predominantly by women. By excluding such work from being recognised within the field of paid employment (and hence attracting the benefits or obligations that may go with it) women's work is devalued in line with what Fraser (1995, p 78) sees more generally as a gendered social hierarchy: gender, she writes, 'structures the fundamental division of labour between paid "productive" labour and unpaid "reproductive" labour, assigning women primary responsibility for the latter.' When considered in addition to discrimination existing across the field of paid employment itself, the result, she concludes, 'is a political-economic structure that generates gender-specific modes of exploitation, marginalisation, and deprivation' (ibid). At this most basic level – the production and reproduction of social goods – the question of relevancy clearly plays a crucial role in being able to recognise and respond to – or, as is more often the case, failing to recognise and respond to – the structured injustices of contemporary gender relations. Establishing the 'relevancy' of a particular law to a particular harm is therefore a crucial way of asserting the applicability of hitherto ignored claims.

Interpretation refers to the problem: given there is a relevant legal rule, how should it be interpreted? Again, here we encounter a whole range of interpretative matters, which can be opened to challenge by feminist encounters with the law. In particular, we might note how certain binary oppositions (or 'dualisms'; see Olsen 1990) operate to construct and naturalise the assumptions within which interpretation takes place. The distinction between public and private is one such opposition, and has a substantial history in legal thought and feminist critiques of it. Here, it has been argued, much of women's experience has been traditionally placed in the 'private' realm into which general legal norms have been only reluctantly applied in order, in theory, that the State respect as fully as possible the autonomy of individuals in their private lives. The effect of this, however, is often to normalise the violence or abuse that may occur in the domestic setting, actions that again impact primarily on women and which would be less likely to be countenanced if they happened 'publicly'. As Lacey points out:

> the practical consequence of non-regulation is the consolidation of the *status quo*: the *de facto* support of pre-existing power relations and distributions of goods within the 'private' sphere ... the ideology of the public/private dichotomy allows government to clean its hands of any *responsibility* for the state of the 'private' world and *depoliticises* the disadvantages which inevitably spill over the alleged divide by affecting the position of the 'privately' disadvantaged in the 'public' world.
>
> (Lacey 1998, p 77)

Although challenging this distinction has been fruitful in raising consciousness – according to the slogan 'the personal is political' – and exposing the failures of legal interpretation to live up to its professed standards, it has also been seen more recently as being descriptively inaccurate and normatively questionable. As legal norms – such as in family or social security law – increasingly regulate or intervene in areas traditionally seen as private, the distinction between the two becomes less clear. Moreover, as Lacey points out, there is an important difference between saying that the 'private' realm should be *repoliticised*, and that it should be legally regulated. Yet despite this, the language and stereotypical associations of the public/private distinction may still operate in an *ideological* way. Lacey's analysis shows how generally, as well as in the context of legal interpretation, 'what happens in this kind of rhetoric is that the labels "public" and "private" are used in question-begging ways which *suppress* the normative arguments which they actually presuppose. This means that the debate sounds common-sensical rather than politically controversial' (Lacey 1998, p 78). It is the importance of that last observation – that what appears as 'common sense' in legal reasoning is itself the result of contingent political victories – that holds the key to understanding the importance of conflicts over interpretation, and especially to the extent that these are involved in continuing sexual discrimination.

Finally, classification refers to whether or not the case can be properly classified under the relevant legal rule. One of the most controversial examples of this concerns the debate over pornography. Should pornography be classified as an actionable harm perpetrated by men against women, or rather as an exercise in free speech or expression and thus be protected by the law? As MacKinnon puts it, 'as a social process and as a form of "speech", pornography amounts to terrorism and promotes not freedom but silence. Rather it promotes freedom for men and enslavement and silence for women.' (MacKinnon 1987, pp 129–30) Then classification of it under the protection of free speech laws merely confirms her observation that the State and its laws are complicit in the reproduction of domination and sexual violence against women. Contrarily, it has been argued that the rights to freedom of speech and expression should be held as paramount, policed only and at the fringes, by obscenity laws. Here, problems of classification clearly refer not to some internal logic of the law or working through of the law's principles, but to how we should understand harm in the context of expressions or violations of sexuality and the extent to which objective, neutral, or impartial accounts of this are possible or indeed desirable, since the very assumptions they make may be part of the problem.

In all these examples, it is clear that attention needs to be paid to the ways in which interpretative leeway and/or the claimed 'naturalness', impartiality or objectivity of legal reasoning may operate to obscure and legitimise gender divisions in the law. This may be referred to as part of the law's ideological role. But it should not be inferred from this that such interpretive leeway is either haphazard, or that its assumptions are set in stone. Rather, the type of arguments presented here suggest that gender discrimination is more or less clearly patterned, that legal categories and interpretive modes of reasoning are implicated in this, but that these forms of exploitation can, and should, be challenged through more creative forms of legal intervention.

Reading

Several of the important statements are set out in the references below. For a general overview, Olsen (1995) provides a helpful starting point. For a recent interesting collection of feminist engagements with the law see Munro and Stychin (2007). Important studies are being carried out across a variety of branches of law, for example, Buss and Manji (2005).

References

Buss, D and Manji, A (eds), 2005, *International law: Modern Feminist Approaches*, Oxford: Hart.

Finley, L, 1989, 'Breaking Women's Silence in Law: the dilemma of the gendered nature of legal reasoning', 64 *Notre Dame LR* 886.

Fraser, N, 1995, 'From Redistribution to Recognition? Dilemmas of Justice in a "Post-Socialist" Age', 212 *New Left Review*, 63.

Gilligan, C, 1982, *In a Different Voice*, Cambridge, MA: Harvard University Press.

Lacey, N, 1998, *Unspeakable Subjects: Feminist essays in legal and social theory*, Oxford: Hart.

MacKinnon, CA, 1987, *Feminism Unmodified: Discourses on Life and Law*, Cambridge, MA: Harvard University Press.

MacKinnon, CA, 1989, *Toward a Feminist Theory of the State*, Cambridge, MA: Harvard University Press.

Munro, V, and Stychin, C (eds), 2007, *Sexuality and the Law: Feminist Engagements*, Oxford: Routledge-Cavendish.

Naffine, N. 1990, *Law and the Sexes*, London and Sydney: Allen & Unwin.

Olsen, F, 1990, 'Feminism and Critical Legal Theory: An American perspective', 18 *International Journal of the Sociology of Law*, 199–215.

Olsen, F, 1995, *Feminist Legal Theory: Foundations and Outlooks*, New York: New York University Press.

2.3 Trials, facts and narratives

2.3.1 The legacy of fact-scepticism

We saw earlier when discussing the American Legal Realists, that one of the main preoccupations of those we called 'fact sceptics', was to argue that the usual critique of law concentrated on a very limited aspect of the law-in-action, whereas most cases were decided on their facts. Jerome Frank, for one, pointed to the likelihood that the facts as found by judge and jury did not correspond to actual facts. While a number of writers had already pointed out that 'the personal bent of the judge' affects his decisions, this was seen as a factor only in the selection of new rules for unprovided cases. This, for Frank, is only a small part of the story. In his own words:

> *In a profound sense the unique circumstances of almost any case make it an 'unprovided case' where no well-established rule authoritatively compels a given result.* The uniqueness of the facts and of the judge's reaction thereto is often concealed because the judge so states the facts that they appear to call for the application of a settled rule. But that concealment does not mean that the judge's personal bent has been inoperative or that his emotive experience is simple and reducible.
>
> (Frank 1970, p 162)

We saw earlier that much of Frank's scepticism revolved around what could be called the psychology of fact-finding. Witnesses' observations and memory may be extremely hazy, but they will be pressed to produce clear and confident statements in court. Pre-trial interviews with lawyers may even amount to a form of witness-coaching in which the witness gets an idea of which version of the facts would best suit prosecution or defence stories. Then, under cross-examination they will be subject to many techniques of discrediting. Jackson examines in some detail the two-tier processes whereby witnesses attempt to make sense of what they say and courts and jurors attempt to make sense of the witness's act of testifying (1995, pp 357–62). Processes of perception are involved in eye-witness testimony, memory and recall, identification evidence, confession and expert statements. In all this, 'to observe a witness testifying in Court is not merely to make sense of what is said. . . . The role of the lawyers is not limited to questioning the witnesses; they also initiate and frame the narrative in their opening and closing statements and provide a running commentary of the acceptability of the performance of the witnesses' (1995, p 15). In fact cross-examination serves as much to reveal as to obscure the 'truth'. One of the prevailing images of our age is that of Milosevic at the Hague, aggressively examining one of the survivors of the atrocious act of ethnic cleansing at Srebernica to the point at which the witness broke down and was unable to recall the details of his aggressors' actions. The pattern has been repeated in numerous political and other trials.[4]

By the end of this process, which began in uncertainty in the first place, we may be many degrees from the truth. In jury trials these psychological problems are compounded by the jury's complex perception and reaction to the facts as narrated. But it is not just witnesses and juries that Frank has in mind:

> Of the many things which have been said of the mystery of the judicial process, the most salient is that *decision is reached after an emotive experience in which principles and logic play only a secondary part.* The function of juristic logic and the principles which it employs seems to be like that of language, to describe the event which has already transpired. These considerations must reveal to us the impotence of general principle to control decision. . . . The reason why the general principle cannot control is because it cannot inform . . . It is obvious that when we have observed a recurrent phenomenon in the decisions of the courts, we may appropriately express the classification in a rule. But the rule will be only a mnemonic device, a useful but hollow diagram of what has been. It will be intelligible only if we relive the experience of the classifier.
>
> (Frank 1970, pp 159–60)

What Frank is stressing here is the subjective and active character of decision making that only *ex post facto* is vested in terms of classification and rule following. This says a great deal about the articulation of rule and fact, though perhaps what Frank is mostly concerned with is the active character of the intervention that is the decision. And to counter such psychological instabilities of truth finding, Frank called upon the expertise of psychology itself. Experts could be brought in to examine witnesses for the accuracy of their perceptual apparatus and their propensity to lie (with reference to reliability and credibility). Juries should be abolished altogether but, failing that, there should be training in jury duties at school, and jury experts to accompany and advise the jury in the court.

More crucially, Frank's argument is not just about psychological reactions and human fallibility. Rather, the unreliability of fact-finding is a direct result of the institutional process of fact-finding itself. For him, the very rules of proof and procedure are antithetical to truth. The whole trial process, as developed over the centuries, is less a unified, scientific and rational method of getting at the truth and far more an archaeological site where successive systems have all left their traces. Archaic legal forms jostle with slightly less archaic forms. Frank focuses primarily on the adversarial process, which he

---

4 For one of the most striking examples see Bilsky (2001) on the Kastner trial.

likened to a trial by combat with each side's champions trying to do down the others – a 'fight' method of proof. While this may have made sense in the past, when we believed that God was on the side of justice and truth, it is not appropriate to the age of secular rationalism. The jury is thus an archaic element whose original task was not to judge facts and individuals they had never come across before, but to deal with a fellow member of the community.

Other writers have made related points. Weber described methods of proof by combat, ordeal and oracle as formally irrational – there was no logical connection between the facts and the outcome (means-end). Substantive irrationality was found in systems of 'khadi' justice typical of traditionalism, individualised decisions pronounced with the wisdom of Solomon or the common-law magistrate (see Part III, 1.2). For Weber, such formal and substantive irrational elements still persisted particularly in the lower courts. Britain had developed what he saw as a 'two-tier' system of justice, legal-rational at the higher level where the powerful (notably capitalists) were seeking to find clear and predictable rules for commercial dealings, yet irrational and summary where the less powerful (notably workers) had their crimes assessed. Other writers (for example LJ Cohen) have described the Roman-canon system, which replaced trial-by-combat-and-ordeal with elaborate rules of evidence (and confession as the centrepiece), maintaining a horror of circumstantial and hearsay evidence and a grading of witnesses by their status credibility. On the continent at least, the use of torture was seen as a small price to pay for the certainty of confession: in replacing absolute divine knowledge with human sources, only the highest standards were acceptable. Modern methods of extracting confessions from suspects, and ranking the credibility of witnesses (the doctor the highest, the unchaste woman the lowest), show that the past is far from superseded. In fact the use of torture has reappeared on the agenda in the context of the West's waging the so-called 'war' on terror. The use of torture in practice (typically the West's practice of 'extraordinary rendition') and the discussion over its 'justifiability' in theory have made a spectacular, and spectacularly alarming, reappearance in the last few years.

As we have become more willing to accept inferences and indirect human knowledge, we have also increased the number of protections against error and injustice by introducing strong corroboration rules (especially in Scotland) and exclusionary rules concerning admissibility of evidence, for example, of bad disposition, etc. Of course for Frank, as for Bentham in the nineteenth century, this series of reforms, undertaken in the very name of fairness and rationality, merely compounds the problem. The whole lot should be swept away in the name of modern scientific rationalism. Such protections could be abolished, he said, if the remnants of the archaic past were totally eliminated and we adopted an inquisitorial system of free proof in which the judge was an investigating magistrate and the jury was no more. Frank's *inquisitorial* system would include better training of legal officials, impartial government

officials to dig up all the facts, specialisation of judges and State administrators to deal with the complex facts of modern society, and increasing use
of expert witnesses.

It may well be that today Frank's belief in the value of scientific expertise,
free proof and the managerial legal official may seem naive, costly and politically worrying. But Frank's basic points have had considerable influence in
disturbing the formalist presumption that 'law' divides neatly from 'facts' and
that the jury can easily master them. The incorporation of facts in narratives,
the possible limitations of legal procedures, the intelligibility of legal language, the aspiration that the courtroom may function as the forum for the
establishment of the truth and of genuine communicative exchange, are all
deeply contested issues in legal theory. It is to these issues, also at the core of
legal reasoning, that we now turn.

2.3.2 Trials and perceptions of fact: language and narrative in the courtroom

The law of evidence provides the structure within which facts may be 'found'
and established as legally relevant. There is of course much that is filtered out
in the process. There are rules about the admissibility of evidence, ruling out
evidence that is unreliable because, for example, it is 'hearsay', and there are
rules about the criteria for the allocation of the burden of truth and the
threshold – 'beyond reasonable doubt' – that establishes what has been
proven as true. Judgments as to whether something counts as relevant or
as to whether the case has been proven occurs 'within this outline structure',
as Jackson (1995, p 390ff) characterises it, and at the point where that judgment must be made, 'common sense' is called to complement 'legal sense',
judges often explicitly instructing juries to use it. At that point of confluence
of the two, of 'legal' and 'common-sense' construction of meaning, the neat
analytical distinctions become blurred in practice. Inferences and intuitive
judgements come to play a crucial role in the reconstruction of the story and
it is different criteria than those stipulated in the rules of evidence that take
centre stage.

In his important work in legal semiotics, Jackson (1988, 1995) surveys
linguistic, semiotic and psychological accounts of sense construction in some
depth. For present purposes it suffices to raise only a few of the basic arguments in these directions, in each case stressing the constructive – rather than
given – elements in the perception of facts and of how that perception is
translated in enunciation in the courtroom. Semiotics alerts us to the dimension of 'signification' – how meanings are constructed within contexts of
interaction. Indicatively:

> Judgements as to the truth of the evidence of witnesses, made by jurors
> who have no direct or personal knowledge of the events, is based in part

on the plausibility and coherence of the stories told by the witnesses: such plausibility is a function of the relative similarity of the rival accounts to *narrative typifications of action* already internalised by the jurors.

(Jackson 1995: 392)

What are these 'typifications' and in what sense do they determine perception and allow selective communicability? Let us take a step back here to look at the kind of stock narratives or stock stories, which as ordering structures, allow us to rationalise or make sense of how things 'hang together', as it were, as meaningful wholes. In *Rethinking Criminal Law* (1978) Fletcher made use of the term 'collective images', which serve as a kind of 'paradigm': the collective image for an offence against property is the 'thief', and 'collective image' of the thief is the nocturnal burglar. These paradigmatic images collect and orient understanding and allow also a certain sharing of understandings (hence 'selective communicability' above). The crucial thing of course is that all collective images are temporally and culturally contingent, and even where those contingencies are shared, often class-specific. This may explain why jurors will be more attuned to picking out certain elements of a situation before them on this basis, why certain forms of offences against property in their eyes are 'privileged' (housebreaks) and other command lesser 'fit' (forms of fraud), why jurors may be keener to see certain offences punished more than others in the sense that they feel more vulnerable to them (to breaking and entering, for example, rather than fraudulent undertakings in financial circles), or, in extreme cases – like the jury in the Rodney King trial in which a community of peers acquitted police officers for a grave assault on a black man in the aftermath of the violent riots in LA – why they are willing to leave offences unpunished. Collective images, obviously, while allowing selective understanding carry tacit evaluations. Jackson's notion of action typifications can be understood on the same continuum: they provide the necessary and sufficient conditions for recognition of fact situations; they allow recognition of what lies within and what outside the situation; they come laden with evaluation; and they are relative to 'semiotic groups', whether these are determined along class, professional, cultural or other social lines (1995, pp 141–63, and for the discussion of examples, pp 163ff). Knowledge is not conveyed in some 'unmediated' way, but through the narration and behaviour of those who present the case in court. We add 'behaviour' here because signification and meaning are not of course limited to what is said, but to a wealth of other factors (body language, signs of sincerity, reliability, nervousness, pace, etc.) to which we attach meaning. Going back to our discussion of truth-telling, these images, typifications, 'frames', 'schemas', or whatever we want to call the narrative frames that 'collect' sense-data as information for us, determine the ways in which we decide who is telling the truth, when and under what circumstances.

In their pioneering early work on narratives in the courtroom, Bennett and

Feldman analyse the form of stories in terms of central action (a 'setting-concern-resolution' sequence) and peripheral action. Battles in court are about who can define the central action successfully and – they claim – success in this matter depends on:

1. Narrative strategies by prosecution and defence (definitional, inferential and validational; defence also uses challenge, redefinition and reconstruction as rhetorical strategies).
2. The cognitive and social functions stories play in everyday life in organising complex information and codifying normative value. Apart from being used to 'narrativising' practices, juries also have stock stories that prosecution or defence may appeal to. Stories thus mediate between law and social life.

Thus unlike MacCormick, they see social bias as a potential element in constructing narrative coherence – but this is no crudely realist account of prejudice distorting law from the outside (for example, gut reactions to individuals on basis of class, race, sex and stereotypes). Rather, bias is structured into stories in terms of 'plausible' action.

Bennett and Feldman also look at another important aspect – *narration* – the way the story is told, particularly the success of witnesses in getting 'their' story across. They draw here on the work of sociolinguistics. From Bernstein (1971), they take the distinction between elaborated codes used in (middle class) formal languages and the restricted codes of (working class) public language. Elaborated codes involve many abstract terms with defined meanings and alternative words to convey and explain; the object of discussion is clearly specified (context-independent). Elaborated codes are thus more mobile in that everything in principle can be explained and defined. They are also more inner-oriented and individualistic. Restricted codes are seen as closed, inflexible and context-bound because they have a fixed vocabulary where knowledge of meanings often depends upon being a member of a particular group (cf. slang) and hence use of this code is also status-oriented. Supposedly, the language used in court by legal professionals is an elaborated middle-class code and working-class witnesses are therefore disadvantaged ('linguistically incompetent') in the courtroom. (But *is* law really an elaborated code? Perhaps a better use of Bernstein would be to see law as a restricted code.) Bennett and Feldman also draw a contrast between 'narrative' and 'fragmented' testimony styles – the extent to which the witness is permitted utterances long enough to constitute an independent narrative string, as against mere responses to questions, and find psychological evidence that the first style is more persuasive and successful.

There lies implicitly and sometimes explicitly in these theories of the trial a more radical, philosophical, objection to correspondence theories of truth that they presuppose some single truth 'out there' waiting to be discovered, perhaps distorted by story forms and linguistic incompetence. For our writers, it is a naive realism that does not recognise that facts are constructed by and within different discourses and thus do not have an independent status. If witnesses suffer cognitive dissonance between their understanding of the facts and the law's understanding, then this is a clash between legal and everyday discourses. Writers from varied perspectives (and not just relativists and postmodernists) challenge the whole notion that there is a distinction between law and fact, arguing that legal norms already determine what can count as legally relevant and indeed how that fact is defined. However, does this necessarily mean that law is a totally closed-off, sealed system? There still seems some plausibility in the idea that stories in the courtroom are *mediating* between legal and social discourses. Or, as Jackson argues (1988: 94–7) that there may be narrative structures that occur in both: he cites a judgment of Lord Denning's involving cricket[5] and analyses, following Greimas, the story involved in terms of paradigms (community) and oppositions (young/old) and narrative sequence in which tradition is disrupted by newcomers. The narrative involves 'value-laden associations [which] are not legally relevant, yet they are inextricable from the narrative understanding of the situation.'

2.3.4 Trials, regulation and justice

Let us finally, in this section, take a step back from the level of the interaction in the courtroom to the function of the trial and look at how the imperatives of State regulation have affected the character of the trial. The question that becomes central from this perspective is this: Is there a growing conflict between the bureaucratic organisational form and due process? For Weber, describing late nineteenth-century-State bureaucracies, there was not a conflict but a fruitful convergence between bureaucratic structure, the spread of formal rationality and the rule of law. These provided a social and administrative guarantee of formal justice and control of the judiciary. The hierarchy of supervision and division of labour was also the most efficient way to handle cases. The uniform and regular application of rules was an effect of the institutional structure. Conversely, however, this guarantee may turn into a threat to the rule of law, for the connection between efficiency and due process is only contingent. If the situation of the administration changes – for example, through increased volume of work – then formal rationality may cease to be the most efficient form of administration. The guarantee has no inherent stability.

Many contemporary analyses of legal administration have thus focused on a general trend towards mechanical regulation and bureaucratic goal

---

5 *Miller v Jackson* [1977] All ER 338

displacement. Internal administrative goals conflict with due process. The increasing volume of work and decreasing resources put the legal system under severe pressure to increase productivity or even to maintain level 'throughput' in processing cases – 'conveyor belt justice'. The response is, on the one hand, to increase the pitch of the bureaucratic logic of standardisation where due process has to be observed in the trial and pre-trial decisions and, on the other hand, to seek ways of avoiding contested trials:

(i)   simplification techniques: no-fault liability; reducing the need to investigate the mental element in crime; standardising sentencing tariffs
(ii) diversion techniques: pre-trial and post-trial diversion; decriminalisation; plea-negotiation; substantial shifts in decision-making powers to the 'paralegal' sphere – police, procurators-fiscal, social workers involved in production of social enquiry reports.

Critics argue that legal decision making thus becomes almost a parody of formalism since legal outcomes will be increasingly uniform and predictable, while leaving the rule of law an empty shell. Legal rationality has no simple protection against this trend since the form of law still remains the 'general application of known [administrative and legal] rules' – the form of the rule of law. Yet simplification techniques mean that crimes and delicts are increasingly put into meaningless categories; for example, the pressure to lose the concept of fault is a major shift away from traditional views of responsibility. Transfer of responsibility to paralegal spheres means decisions are increasingly being made on an extra-legal basis and hence are discretionary in the sense of not being controlled by strictly legal rules. (Their source is no longer internal to law.) Moody and Tombs argue that, in the fiscal service and Crown Office, this does not mean an increase in individual discretionary powers, but rather an increase in bureaucratic rigidity, control and form-filling, which they characterise as 'extra-legal formalism' and a loss of external accountability.

The second trend associated with the growth of the modern state converges with the first in involving an alleged increase in discretionary powers and a shift away from rights-based law to social management. State bureaucracies have increasingly involved themselves in substantive ethical and policy issues associated with a welfare interventionism. This often involves legal formulations that take an overtly discretionary form, thus requiring judges to bring in open-ended considerations. This expansion of judicial discretion is associated with:

(i)   the increasing abstractness or open-endedness of statutory provisions and standards, whereby inherently discretionary concepts such as 'the best interests of the child' replace fault-based legal actions;
(ii) therapeutic and hence offender-specific calculations in respect of

sentencing and the consequent reliance on para-legal judgements of social workers;

(iii) the increase in short-term government-of-the-day policy uses of law – the use of criminal law provisions in industrial disputes, 'football hooliganism', drug abuse, etc;

(iv) the blurring of the boundaries between broad policy – administrative and narrowly legal aspects of legal administration, in the expansion, for example, of welfare law, or the use of equal opportunities legislation. Judges are increasingly expected to adjudicate in fields of expertise – social and economic policy – that lie outside their competence. Increasing use is made of tribunals and regulatory agencies, such as the Equal Opportunities Commission, that rely on informal procedures. Conciliation procedures are increasingly important in family law.

Weber suggested that the features of law that dominated its liberal era – formality and neutrality – were to pervade future development. Neutral rules, thought Weber, were particularly conducive to the workings of bureaucracies and they would persist and expand to new ground without challenge, due to their apparent indispensability to the logic of bureaucratic organisation. While post-liberal law has shifted significantly from legislatures to administration, its form remains what Weber predicted it to remain, formal rational. But that of course is only part of the story. Let us say that between bureaucratisation and welfarism in law there is both a tension and a convergence. Tension because bureaucratic law is rational law, its form that of general abstract rules, while welfarist regulation is substantive, particular and casuistic. Convergence because often welfarist concerns key in with bureaucratic ones, for example, the welfarist shift away from fault (as socially inappropriate) meets with the efficiency demand of bureaucracy, the speedy processing of cases thus far inhibited by the requirement to explore *mens rea*. Other tensions and compatibilities may be traced.

Let us then briefly identify some of these here. First, the 'materialisation' of law marks the tendency towards particularised legislation: the movement towards breaking up the general categories into subcategories towards which law applies differentially. The grand category of the legal person gives way to a specification of categories, and the formal equivalence of the legal subject gives way to a proliferation of different legal statutes: consumer (consumer law), worker/trade union member, employee, welfare recipient, business franchisee. In each case the law addresses the legal subject under that more specific description and there is a move from the formal to the material in this. But further: natural and artificial persons, grouped together under liberal law become differentiated for specific legal purposes, so that, for example, the privacy of the natural person is protected where that of company is not (access to data, freedom of information). Second, the separation of powers, that other lynchpin of liberal law is eroded, for example, once courts are called upon to determine whether a government has acted in the public interest; equally, when the legislature delegates responsibility for fixing the terms of what appear as general directives because the executive state machinery has the resources to do the job better. Finally, formal equality is eroded once 'reverse discrimination' or 'affirmative action', that is, a reverse preference to a disadvantaged group becomes institutionalised in law in order to redress existing inequalities.

Reading

See Cotterrell (1992) for a concise account of the changing forms of regulation (pp 161–6). For an in-depth, comprehensive semiotic approach to narrative construction, see Jackson (1995) and generally for the role of narratives in trials, see Burns in Duff *et al.* (2004). For an analysis of juries, see Redmayne and Schafer & Weigand in Duff *et al.* (2005). On the relationship between truth, standing, participation and due process in the trial, see Duff *et al.* (2007).

References

Bennett, W and Feldman, M, 1981, *Reconstructing Reality in the Courtroom*, New Brunswick: Rutgers University Press.

Bernstein, B, 1971, *Class, Codes and Control*, London: Routledge and Kegan Paul.

Bilsky, L, 2001, 'Justice or Reconciliation? The Politicisation of the Holocaust in the Kastner Trial', in E Christodoulidis and S Veitch (eds), *Lethe's Law*, Oxford: Hart.

Cohen, LJ, 1977, *The Probable and the Provable*, Oxford: Clarendon.

Cotterrell, R, 1992, *Sociology of Law*, 2nd edn, London: Butterworths.

Duff A, Farmer L, Marshall S and Tadros, V, 2005 (eds), *The Trial on Trial*, volumes 1 (2004) and 2 (2005), Oxford: Hart.

Duff, A, Farmer, L, Marshall, S and Tadros, V, 2007, *The Theory of the Trial*, Oxford: Hart.

Fletcher, G, 1978, *Rethinking Criminal Law*, Boston: Little, Brown & Co.

Frank, J, 1970, *Law and the Modern Mind*, Gloucester, MA: Peter Smith.

Jackson, B, 1995, *Making Sense in Law*, Merseyside: DC Publications.

Jackson, B, 1988, *Law, Fact and Narrative Coherence*, Merseyside: DC Publications.

Moody, S and Tombs, J, 1982, *Prosecution in the Public Interest*, Edinburgh: Scottish Academic Press.

2.4 Understanding discrimination

2.4.1 Introduction

In 1993, a researcher sent speculative job applications to the top 100 companies in the UK. These applications were effectively identical – except for the names of the two fictitious job seekers. One, Ramesh Patel, was identifiably Asian. The other, Andrew Evans, had a name that would appear 'white'. Evans received more replies than Patel did, and he was more likely to receive a good response.[6]

Discrimination is rarely so easy to prove. Demonstrating an individual instance of prejudiced treatment often requires witnesses or confessions. It is easier to demonstrate the likely existence of *systemic* discrimination, because social scientists can gather evidence of patterns of differential attainment. When large numbers of people from identifiable groups achieve, overall, less than others with comparable qualifications, experience, skills or other measurable abilities, we can surmise that the explanation lies not with individual failings, but with current discrimination or the effects of historic disadvantage – more often both. Our focus here is with reviewing briefly some aspects of the interpretation of legislation that deal with these concerns, and questioning the extent to which such concerns can be redressed in conventional legal reasoning. But first we will need to consider some background.

One means by which unequal achievement can be demonstrated is through comparisons in employment. If we take the examples of sex and ethnicity and consider recent research, we see abundant evidence of income gaps related to these. Not only do women earn less than men in the UK, but this problem is compounded in old age. The median income of women in retirement is only 57 per cent that of men's, according to findings from the Turner Report in 2006. Women from minority ethnic backgrounds typically fare worse. Again in 2006, researchers for the Equal Opportunities Commission (EOC) analysed statistics from the 2001 Census and found that working Black Caribbean women were 8 per cent more likely to have a degree than white women, yet only 9 per cent of Black Caribbean women were managers or senior managers, compared to 11 per cent of white women. One explanation sometimes offered for this sort of disparity is the supposedly deleterious effect of minority cultures, rather than discrimination; so it is interesting to see the results of an EOC study of 16-year-olds in 2006 which reported that Pakistani, Bangladeshi and Black Caribbean girls are 15–20 per cent *more* likely to want to go to university than white girls. Around 90 per cent planned to work full-

---

6 This famous study is reported by the author in Noon (1993). Many similar studies have been carried out since the 1960s.

time after leaving full-time education, while also raising a family. The great majority stated that their families supported them doing this.

Research can rarely prove conclusively that large groups of people are discriminated against, or even disadvantaged, on the grounds of their sex or ethnicity – but the consistent findings of good quality empirical studies do place the burden of proof on those who deny that discrimination or disadvantage exists. This, however, does not dispose of the questions for law. Even if we can prove that minority ethnic women are suffering discrimination, what is the cause (or causes)? Is it direct discrimination by employers, paying them less for the same job than would be paid to a white man? Is it occupational segregation, driving them disproportionately into traditional women's work, which is undervalued and where they are overqualified and underpaid? Or is it caring responsibilities, where the responsibility for looking after home, children and other relatives holds them back in their careers?

The answer matters, because law may need to identify who is at fault before change can be achieved. Employers, for instance, may justifiably protest that they are not to blame for the detrimental impact of women's family responsibilities (although if they do not offer flexible working, job protection after maternity leave or other appropriate support for their women workers, the effect will be to hinder women's advancement).

Should we manage to answer this, we are faced with a new set of questions. The previous questions were sociolegal: the next are for legal philosophy. What would a non-discriminatory society look like? We should not presume that equal opportunity and equal treatment would denote a fair distribution of social benefits. Are the needs of new mothers equivalent to those of single childless men? To what extent do genuine cultural differences between groups justify different treatment and different rights? If equality comes about only by lowering the pay of privileged groups until it reaches that of disadvantaged groups, is this a desirable outcome? Jurisprudence has much to say on these questions about formal and substantive equality, equality of results and equality of opportunity, disadvantage and discrimination, and other such concepts. Jurisprudes have also had much to say about whether law can bring about radical social change, and the extent to which others can be made to apply such law in the spirit in which its makers intended.

A raft of sex equality legislation has been enacted in the last 30 years, each statute more ingenious than the last, but as we have seen, the problem of the income gap between men and women is far from being solved. Has anything improved? Yes. The UK Civil Service no longer has two formal pay scales for the same jobs (one for men and a lower-paid one for women). Some women now have good careers, flexible working hours, maternity benefits and protection from sexual harassment at work. But unfortunately (although it is not primarily due to fortune) the women least likely to have benefited from legal change are those women in part-time, temporary, insecure jobs requiring few qualifications – and those women are disproportionately likely to be poor, working-class, or Asian or African/Caribbean in origin. Forms of discrimination intersect, and class and race affect life chances just as sex does.

We have seen how complex is the problem of tackling discrimination. Here, we will focus on one analysis of the concept of discrimination and then consider how this can help us cast light on race discrimination and in particular a recent case involving 'race relations' law.

2.4.2 How should we frame the concept of discrimination in law?

Everyone has a picture of what equality and discrimination mean to them, but these concepts become slippery when we attempt to define them. How can we differentiate discrimination that should be unlawful, from discrimination that amounts to reasonable, or equal but different, treatment?

Article 13 of the Treaty of Rome forms the basis for antidiscrimination law in the European Union (EU). Since 2000, a series of directives have produced a core statement of two forms of unlawful discrimination – *direct* discrimination and *indirect* discrimination. Let us consider how these have been defined in the best-known of these directives: the 'General Framework' Directive 2000/78/EC, which deals mainly with discrimination in employment, and the 'Race' Directive 2000/43/EC, which is wider-ranging but deals only with race discrimination.

Between them, the two Directives make it unlawful in certain circumstances (such as employment) to discriminate on any one of six grounds: *(i) racial or ethnic origin; (ii) sex; (iii) religion or belief; (iv) disability; (v) age; (vi) sexual orientation.*

Both Directives define the concepts of 'equal treatment' and 'discrimination' in their respective Articles. Read together, the Articles state:

1. *For the purposes of the Directives the principle of equal treatment shall mean that there shall be no direct or indirect discrimination whatsoever on any of the six grounds*
2. *For the purposes of paragraph 1:*

    *(a) direct discrimination shall be taken to occur **where one person is treated less favourably than another is, has been or would be treated in a comparable situation** on any of the six grounds*
    *(b) indirect discrimination shall be taken to occur **where an apparently neutral provision, criterion or practice would put persons** of a racial or ethnic origin, having a particular religion or belief, a particular disability, a particular age, or a particular sexual orientation **at a particular disadvantage compared with other persons**

unless that provision criterion or practice is objectively justified by a legitimate aim and the means of achieving that aim are appropriate and necessary. (There is also a further exception governing disability, which we need not consider here.)

To show that discrimination has occurred on one of these grounds, then, we must show that there has been a harm caused (someone has been treated 'less favourably' or put by 'an apparently neutral provision, criterion or practice' at a particular disadvantage). But every day harms occur, in every part of people's lives. So which harms count in law?

In an insightful essay on discrimination and the law, John Gardner (1989) argues that there are two ways of identifying such a harm. One is based on the historic disadvantage of groups, while the other is based on what is unfair. These produce very different results in practice. To see this, let us consider an example.

Advocates of the first approach (historic disadvantage) say that we should outlaw discrimination because certain groups in society have suffered serious collective disadvantage and so any discrimination against their members today compounds that historic disadvantage. So, to take the example of race, there is substantial evidence that minority ethnic groups in the UK have in the past been excluded from jobs and housing; paid less when they did the same work as indigenous British people; and criminalised disproportionately when they broke social rules. The relevant harm here is a history of disadvantage, which places people from those backgrounds in a weakened position today when we compare them to their indigenous counterparts. Modern law should therefore attempt to remedy this so that all ethnic groups are treated equally. Hence in this case, discriminating against an indigenous Englishman by excluding him from some opportunity would *not* be a relevant harm, because he is not a person who is likely to suffer repeat exclusions on the grounds of ethnic origin.

An example in law is the case of *Law v Canada*. A Canadian state pension plan enabled widows over the age of 35 to claim survivor's benefits. Mrs Law was aged 30 and so was ineligible. She appealed against this and lost. One of the reasons she lost was because the tribunal held that younger women did not belong to an age group who had suffered pre-existing (historic) disadvantage.

Advocates of the second approach (unfairness) say that we should outlaw discrimination because discriminating between people solely on grounds such as their ethnic origins or their sex is unfair. Sex and ethnicity are not characteristics that say anything about a person's likely moral or intellectual qualities and they should not influence most decisions about whether, say, to give someone a job or to reserve them a room in a hotel. The relevant harm here is the unfairness of taking personal characteristics into account when these should be irrelevant to a decision. Modern law should therefore attempt to prevent people taking such characteristics into account when making important decisions that could harm others' interests. In this case, discriminating against the indigenous Englishman by refusing him an opportunity because of his ethnic background *is* a relevant harm, because it is treating him unfairly and causing him material disadvantage.

The two EU Directives take the second approach. The UK tends to do the same. The key British statute on race discrimination is the Race Relations Act 1976, as amended. Neither the statute itself, nor case law interpreting it, has limited the law to historically disadvantaged groups. It is therefore open to anyone meeting the conditions to bring a case, which places it in our second approach. Let us move on to examine some difficulties posed by the second approach in practice.

2.4.3 Racial discrimination in employment

Our example is the case of *Serco Ltd v Redfearn*. Mr Redfearn was employed by Serco to act as a driver for local authorities, transporting children and adults with physical/mental disabilities in the Bradford area. In May 2004, a local newspaper announced that Mr Redfearn was standing as a councillor for the British National Party (BNP). The BNP's constitution states that membership of the party is limited to 'indigenous Caucasians' (in other words, 'white' people only). It further states that the party is 'wholly opposed to any form of integration between British and non-European peoples' and that it is committed to restoring 'the overwhelmingly white make-up of the British population that existed in Britain prior to 1948'.

When Serco discovered Mr Redfearn's candidature, he was summarily dismissed on the ground that he presented a risk to the health and safety of Serco's customers and employees. (West Yorkshire has suffered a great deal of social unrest with poor relations between the various ethnic communities.) Seventy per cent of Serco's customers were of Asian origin and it was felt that Serco's passengers and carers, who placed much trust in the drivers and escorts, would be made highly anxious by having Mr Redfearn as their driver – while the threat to Serco's reputation could lead it to lose its contract with the council.

Mr Redfearn took his case to an employment tribunal on the grounds that contrary to s 1 of the Race Relations Act 1976 he had suffered race discrimination. The tribunal was then faced with the embarrassing task of deciding whether a person sacked for being a member of a racially discriminatory political party had suffered race discrimination. It held that his dismissal was justified. Mr Redfearn then appealed to the Employment Appeals Tribunal (EAT), which reversed the decision.

Our second approach to identifying harm (the unfairness approach) seems horribly inapposite here. How can it be that a person who is dismissed on the ground (which we will presume for the moment to be accurate) that his racist views threaten others is allowed to turn this around to argue that he himself is the real victim of racial discrimination? It might be fair to argue that he has been discriminated against on political grounds and that he is entitled to freedom of expression. We shall consider the case first as a matter of statutory interpretation.

Section 1(1A) of the 1976 Act, as amended, states:

> *A person discriminates against another in any circumstances relevant for the purposes of any provision of this Act if–*
>
> *(a)* **on racial grounds** *he treats that other less favourably than he treats or would treat other persons . . .*

If persons of any ethnic background can rely upon the legislation, not only those who have been historically disadvantaged, what does 'on racial grounds' mean? If it simply means that there is a racial element, Mr Redfearn could sustain his argument. The case was appealed once more, to the Court of Appeal (which found against him). The Court held that the statutory words had to be understood in the light of the purpose of the 1976 Act, which was to prohibit racial discrimination. He could not credibly make a claim of direct race discrimination against him on the ground that he was white, simply by relying on the decision of his own chosen political party to limit its membership to white people – to discriminate by race. As the court pointed out, dismissal on grounds of party membership is not a racial criterion, and '[t]he BNP cannot make a non-racial criterion (party membership) a racial one by the terms of its constitution limiting membership to white people. Properly analysed Mr Redfearn's complaint is of discrimination on political grounds, which falls outside the anti-discrimination laws.'

The court also held that he could not succeed on the ground of indirect race discrimination. Section 1(1A) of the Act states:

> *(1A) A person also discriminates against another if, in any circumstances relevant for the purposes of any provision referred to in subsection (1B), he applies to that other* **a provision, criterion or practice** *which he applies or would apply equally to persons not of the same race or ethnic or national origins as that other, but–*
>
> *(a) which puts or would put persons of the same race or ethnic or national origins as that other at a particular disadvantage when compared with other persons,*
>
> *(b) which puts that other at that disadvantage, and*
>
> *(c) which he cannot show to be a proportionate means of achieving a legitimate aim.*

No provision, criterion or practice had been identified in the course of the case, but if one was to be identified, the court held, it should be one applying to membership of a political organisation of the type the BNP belonged to, which existed to promote views hostile to members of a different ethnic group from that of its members. This would apply equally to an organisation that was anti-'white', so Mr Redfearn had not been disadvantaged on the ground of his ethnicity.

2.4.4 How satisfactory is the 1976 Act?

Serco demonstrates the difficulty of using law to tackle complex social problems. Had the statute protected only members of ethnic minorities, it would have been open to intense criticism from the ethnic majority. It would require precise definition of who belonged to an ethnic minority, a difficult task given that no such clear biological or geographical boundaries exist, and it would be widely criticised for offering selective protection.

Perhaps the greater concern is the effect of the statute in enshrining discriminatory concepts in law. Sociologist Robert Miles has argued powerfully that to talk about 'race', even when trying to combat it, is to reproduce a misleading and prejudicial discourse. In his view, we should focus on racism, not on supposed 'races', which do not exist. Certainly, the great preponderance of authoritative research in biology indicates that while people can be classified usefully in fairly small groups by their ancestry, there are no large-scale races. There are no consistent groups of features that can be called 'Caucasian' or 'Negroid', or any of the other terms historically used to denote racial divisions. Not only do people vary along continua, rather than being sharply differentiated into different groups: we also do not find that blood types, for instance, belong to one 'race' or another. The groups of people who carry a particular gene, or a blood feature, do not map on to what we would see as racial groups. 'Race' is a social creation rather than a biological reality.

While the preamble to the Race Directive observes that race, as a biological category has no scientific foundation, the Directive includes the concept of 'racial' origin as a term of law. Meanwhile, the words 'race' and 'racial' are used without reservation in the 1976 Act. Is Miles right to warn against this? Consider the BNP's constitution, mentioned above. In support of its claim that only 'white' people can join, it cites not some bogus argument from a disreputable scientific source, but rather the most important case in British 'race relations' law.

'Membership of the BNP is strictly defined within the terms of, and our members also self-define themselves within, the legal ambit of a defined "racial group" this being "indigenous Caucasian" and defined "ethnic groups" emanating from that Race as specified in law in the House of Lords case of *Mandla v Dowell Lee*.'

Miles' advice is easier understood than applied. What statutory language could be devised that would enable law to describe the victims of racist discrimination, while avoiding the trap of classifying them using racist concepts? The discussion in this chapter encounters the same problems: race, white, Asian, even minority ethnic, are all terms which presuppose clearly-identifiable groups of people and implies that – at least for the purposes of the discussion – each is a homogeneous group and that their supposed 'ethnicity' is their most important feature. We are left with the question of whether the benefits of the 1976 Act, and any such antiracist activity, outweigh the detrimental effects.

Finally, it is important to consider the role of legal processes themselves. While it was possible to find an interpretation of s.1 of the 1976 Act, which prevented a person's own racist discrimination from founding a case for a remedy for racial discrimination, some aspects of the legal system are so discriminatory in their effect as to be quite beyond remedial interpretation. Consider, for example, the effects of recent asylum and immigration legislation on the appeals process for asylum-seekers. It is widely accepted that errors are made when the validity of asylum claims is first assessed, and it is of course fundamental to the UK legal system that these sorts of decisions are open to judicial review. Yet the process bears little resemblance to the appeals procedure law students normally study on arriving in law school. Appeal to the higher courts can only take place regarding an error of law, but a great many cases are decided on the credibility of the claimant in the courtroom, which is predominantly regarded as a question of fact, not law. The time limit for an appeal is astonishingly short: the claimant (whose first language may not be English) has only five days to submit an application for reconsideration. Should the applicant be successful in leaping these hurdles, the appeal will not be an oral appeal, but rather a written one, with no opportunity to challenge the other side's arguments after the initial submissions have been made. Yet asylum appeals can literally be life and death cases, since the wrongful return of a genuine refugee to the persecution they have escaped may be fatal. Successive governments have attempted to limit inward migration to the UK, but the provision of asylum is a UK obligation under international law, and it is also inequitable to limit the numbers of people gaining refugee status by removing fundamental legal safeguards that review administrative error.

Tackling discrimination in the legal forum can be achieved both by progressive legislation and by judicial interpretation, but as we have seen in this chapter, we are faced with the triple difficulties of identifying what outcomes we should in fact seek, which formulations of law will bring about these results, and what the individual is able to do when the overarching legal process itself is discriminatory. Elsewhere in this book we consider theories of the legal system which argue that whole societies and their institutions are discriminatory in their structures, processes and discourses, so that it is a risky, or perhaps even worthless strategy to aim to alleviate inequality through law. But even if the reader has faith in what good law can achieve, we have seen that it is very difficult to foresee how this can be done.

Reading

For a good conceptual approach to discrimination law see Feldman (2001). For a brief introduction to the problem of identifying equality, see Stephen Guest's *Ronald Dworkin* (2nd edn, 1997), ch 10. Alternatively, for a more radical perspective on equality and discrimination, see Bartlett (1990). For an introduction to Miles' complex position, see Miles (1993), pp 44–9. For a brief and authoritative introduction to this, see issue 5(8) of *Nature Reviews Genetics* (2004).

References

Bartlett, K, 1990, 'Feminist Legal Methods', 103(4) *Harvard Law Review* 829.
Feldman, S, 2001, *Discrimination Law*, Oxford: Oxford University Press.
Gardner, J, 1989, 'Liberals and Unlawful Discrimination', *OJLS* 1.
Guest, S, 1997, *Ronald Dworkin* (2nd edn), Edinburgh: Edinburgh University Press.
Miles, R, 1993, *Racism after 'Race Relations'*, London: Routledge.
Noon, M, 1993, 'Racial discrimination in speculative application: evidence from the UK's top 100 firms', 3(4) *Human Resource Management Journal* 35–47.

Cases

Mandla v Dowell Lee (1983) All ER 1062, HL.
Law v Canada (Minister of Employment and Immigration) [1999] 1 SCR 497.
Serco Ltd v Redfearn (2006) EWCA Civ 659.

2.5 Judging in an unjust society

Systematic and profound racial discrimination may occur in societies that are committed to principles of formal equality, democracy and the rule of law. It is necessary to try to understand how the operation of basic principles of conventional legal reasoning may be complicit in this situation by operating to entrench injustices, both of the past and present. Australia provides one such contemporary example, and in this section we will look at the High Court decision in *Mabo v The State of Queensland (No.2)* (1992) (hereafter *Mabo*, paragraph references in parentheses). The *Mabo* decision is important and interesting for many reasons, among which, in the current context, are what it tells us about the very assumptions within which legal reasoning takes place, and, about the limits of law in addressing its colonial past and present.

Australia was colonised by the British in 1788. Sovereignty over the territory was claimed under the doctrine of *terra nullius*. According to this doctrine – which means literally 'no man's land' – land that was uninhabited could be acquired for the colonial power – in this instance, technically the British Crown – upon being 'settled'. Of course, the Australian continent was not uninhabited; European 'settlers' encountered the presence of an extensive Aboriginal population and, often, their resistance to invasion. In such instances, however, an 'enlarged' doctrine of *terra nullius* could still be applied by the colonising power, if the following assumption was made: that 'the indigenous inhabitants were not organized in a society that was united permanently for political action.' (33) In essence, this involved an assessment by the imperial power, as the Privy Council put it in *In re Southern Rhodesia* in 1919 (quoted in *Mabo*, 38) that, 'Some tribes are so low on the scale of social organisation that their usages and conceptions of rights and duties are not to be reconciled with the institutions or the legal ideas of civilized society. Such a gulf cannot be bridged.' In other words, the inhabitants of *terra nullius* and their form of society were seen, from an openly racist understanding, as inferior: as Brennan CJ put it: 'The indigenous people of a settled colony were thus taken to be without laws, without a sovereign and primitive in their social organization.' (36).

In *Mabo*, the High Court of Australia was asked to adjudicate a claim on behalf of the Meriam people living on the Murray Islands in the Torres Straight that they had native title to their land, which survived the acquisition of sovereignty by the British Crown. This claim involved the Australian High Court re-evaluating the nature and consequences of this original racist assumption on which Australia was founded, and which had, for over 200 years, denied in law the existence of any such title. As Brennan CJ wrote:

According to the cases, the common law itself took from indigenous inhabitants any right to occupy their traditional land, exposed them to deprivation of the religious, cultural and economic sustenance which the land provides, vested the land effectively in the control of the Imperial authorities without any right to compensation and made the indigenous inhabitants intruders in their own homes and mendicants for a place to live.

(28)

However, continued Brennan CJ:

Judged by any civilized standard, such a law is unjust and its claim to be part of the common law to be applied in contemporary Australia must be questioned.

(28)

Accordingly therefore, he saw that there was:

a choice of legal principle to be made in the present case. This Court can either apply the existing authorities and proceed to inquire whether the Meriam people are higher 'in the scale of social organization' than the Australian Aborigines whose claims were 'utterly disregarded' by the existing authorities or the Court can overrule the existing authorities, discarding the distinction between inhabited colonies that were terra nullius and those which were not.

(39)

According to Brennan CJ, *overruling* the precedent cases was necessary since otherwise their authority:

would destroy the equality of all Australian citizens before the law. The common law of this country would perpetuate injustice if it were to continue to embrace the enlarged notion of terra nullius and to persist in characterizing the indigenous inhabitants of the Australian colonies as people too low in the scale of social organization to be acknowledged as possessing rights and interests in land.

(63)

On the one hand, therefore, Brennan CJ acknowledged that:

Their [Aboriginal] dispossession underwrote the development of the [Australian] nation.

(82)

On the other, however, he argued that:

> the peace and order of Australian society is built on the legal system.
>
> (29)

and that the Court was:

> not free to adopt rules that accord with contemporary notions of justice
> and human rights if their adoption would fracture the skeleton of prin-
> ciple which gives the body of our law its shape and internal consistency.
>
> (28–29)

In other words, the clash of principles to be adjudicated involved confront-
ing the foundational act that dispossessed Aboriginals of their lands, while
simultaneously understanding that that act was the very condition of the ongoing existence of the Australian nation. How then could the racist founding
of Australia be dealt with in accordance with contemporary principles of
justice and equality when that founding was *itself* the one which gave the
Australian State – and hence the law and the High Court – its authority?

The Court's solution to this problem involved making a key distinction
between the acquisition of sovereignty and the consequences of that acquisition. The former, it said, is not subject to review by the court; that is, the
sovereignty established by the initial act of colonisation is *not justiciable* in
the Australian courts – it is that very sovereignty that gives the court *its*
jurisdiction to hear this case. Were the matter to be justiciable – and the
answer given that the act of sovereignty was invalid – then the court would
undermine its own authority to make precisely such a decision.

However, it was open to the Court to review the *consequences* of the
acquisition of sovereignty. And here was where their interpretative leeway
entered. The Court decided that although sovereignty had been acquired
under the doctrine of *terra nullius*, this did not mean the Crown also acquired
'full beneficial ownership' (that is, a complete property right) to the whole
territory. Rather, using a doctrine going back to feudal times, it had only a
'radical' (or ultimate or final) title, according to which it was entitled to *grant*
full property rights under it, even though it did not itself own the land. 'What
the Crown acquired was a radical title to land and a sovereign political power
over land, the sum of which is not tantamount to absolute ownership of
land.' (55) Radical title therefore meant the Crown had sovereign jurisdiction
to create property rights, but where no grant of ownership rights had been
made to another party, then since the Crown did not own the land it was
possible for native title to it to continue to exist 'as a burden' on the radical
title. It was in this space, so to speak, between radical title and full beneficial
ownership that the possibility for a native title claim could exist that survived
the British acquisition of sovereignty.

In this way, where native title had not been extinguished by Crown grants of land, it was open for Aboriginal communities to show that their continued association with the land, from the time of colonisation, qualified them as entitled to native title rights on that land, despite the acquisition of sovereignty by the Crown. For the first time then – and *overruling precedents* to bring Australian law in line with principles of non-discrimination – the common law was able to redress the racist implications of the doctrine *terra nullius* and recognise native title to land.

We might consider two very different types of interpretation of this ruling. The first is congratulatory, and celebrates the much-vaunted virtues of the flexibility of common-law styles of reasoning. According to one commentator, the decision reflects the virtues – the 'genius' and 'spirit' – of the common law, in its ability to uphold basic standards of human rights and to respond in a pragmatic way to 'social, economic and political considerations' (Bartlett 1993, p 181). It also shows something more fundamental, namely how the law can embody – or fail to embody – fundamental human values. On this view, what the *Mabo* decision offered, for the first time in Australia, was the recognition of a full humanity that had hitherto been denied indigenous people by the law and that had in turn played a role in legitimating a broader social and political racism. Moreover, it was only once this full humanity was properly recognised that the further questions of policies directed towards alleviating the suffering that Aboriginals continued to experience could be addressed. Drawing attention to this distinction, Raimond Gaita wrote:

> Fairness is at issue only when the full human status of those who are protesting their unfair treatment is not disputed . . . The justice done by *Mabo* is deeper than anything that can be captured by concepts of equity as they apply to people's access to goods. It brought indigenous Australians into the constituency within which they could intelligibly press claims about unfair treatment.
>
> (Gaita 1999, pp 81–2)

But there is a contrary view. Kerruish and Purdy (1998) make three important observations. First they note that common-law reasoning involves the application of general principles, chief among which in the *Mabo* decision were equality and formal justice (treating like cases alike). But legal equality, they argue, is intimately connected to the concept of the 'legal person'. It is this idea of modern Western law that provides a key legitimating role insofar as it operates according to the idea of treating persons as 'free and equal subjects of the law's address'. According to Kerruish and Purdy, this freedom has two aspects:

> First they are free (in the sense of stripped) of *all* their actual characteristics (from names to locations within basic social relations). Second they

are supposed to have the capacity for choice or free will. Equality at law inheres in this dual freedom; that is, all those who come before the law are *equally* stripped of their actual characteristics and *equally* presumed to be responsible for their own actions.

(150)

There are two criticisms we might draw from this. First, treating people as equal before the law – referring them to or measuring them by the same standard – is in fact to treat them differently by ignoring characteristics about their identity or the context (in this instance violent colonisation) that might be relevant under some other descriptive or normative standards. Moreover, this operation of formal legal reasoning does not in fact attribute no identity to the legal person; rather it imposes its version *as* an identity, in fact as *the* only available identity, against which there is no appeal or recourse. As Aboriginal lawyer Irene Watson noted, the *Mabo* decision 'failed to recognise difference in [the] construction of native title so as to make it fit within a western property paradigm' (Watson 2002, p 257). And this point informs the second criticism: that the idea that those who come before the law are responsible for their own actions is not in fact self-determined, but rather is prescribed and defined *by law* itself. But to the extent that this *misdescribes* the historical reality, it does so in a way that nonetheless provides legitimacy for overlooking this fact.

Second, as we have just seen, the sovereignty established by the initial act of colonisation was not justiciable in the Australian courts, because it is that sovereignty that gives the court its very jurisdiction to hear this case. Such apparently watertight logic marks the limitations of the court's power. But the effect of this is however, that by refusing to engage with the acquisition of sovereignty, the original act of dispossession and its legitimacy based in racist doctrines *remains intact* as the founding act, not removed. This continuity – that Aboriginal dispossession 'underwrote the development of the nation' – is now legally set in stone, but is legitimated in the present by the claim that the common law is acting in a *non*-discriminatory manner. Thus *Mabo* in fact *whitewashes* responsibility for the damages caused by the invasion of Australia since, again in Watson's terms, 'doctrines of state supremacy conjure a magic, which absolves centuries of unlawfulness and violence against indigenous peoples' (ibid, p 265).

Finally, the common-law condition for recognition of native title requiring an ability to demonstrate continuous association with the land since the initial colonisation involved serious drawbacks. Many Aboriginals, because of government policies, had been removed from their traditional lands either to other places or to the cities and towns, which meant that not only would connection with the land be in most cases impossible to show (because of these very colonial practices, but also because, even in these few cases where connection might be shown, the standards of proof required by the common law rely heavily on documentary evidence, which they know to be unavailable because Aboriginal culture was an oral one), but that this very fact of dispossession is now *legitimated* by the common-law's decision in the case. These dispossessed indigenous people are now treated by the law equally as Australian citizens, their dispossession failing to register in law. As Kerruish and Purdy conclude therefore, 'the Australian common law has now managed to strip those Aboriginal people whose connection with the land has been broken of the identity at law of native inhabitants of Australia. It is a *further act of colonisation* that compounds dispossession by non-recognition of Aboriginal identity' (162, emphasis added).

From these observations, we witness the power of common-law reasoning in legitimating – on the very grounds of equality, freedom, and formal justice – ongoing dispossession and discrimination. This is the power of legal reasoning in a colonial context, even where democratic and non-discriminatory principles are espoused. In other words, while the damages and inequalities that exist in Australia for Aboriginal people are ongoing, the integrity of the common law remains intact.

Thus we might finally reflect on both the power and the limits of modern legal thought, by asking whether and to what extent principles of modern law and legal reasoning (of the type we saw in earlier sections) are able to redress the effects of colonial and deeply discriminatory practices, when these very principles have been and continue to be themselves complicit in the legitimation of these discriminatory practices.

Reading

Brennan CJ's judgement in *Mabo v The State of Queensland (No.2)* is the best starting point for the legal and historical matters raised here. An early symposium on the *Mabo* decision can be found in Bartlett (1993) 15:2 *Sydney Law Review*. Ten years on, a critical symposium can be found in 13 *Law & Critique* (2002).

For questions about 'judging in an unjust society' with special reference to Ronald Dworkin's theory of legal reasoning and applied to the context of South Africa, see the special issue of *Acta Juridica* (2004) devoted to that theme. Also in this context see Dyzenhaus (1991), and Mureinik (1988) for a critique of Dworkin.

References

Bartlett, R, 1993, '*Mabo*: Another triumph for the common law', 15:2 *Sydney Law Review* 178–86.

Dyzenhaus, D, 1991, *Hard cases in wicked legal systems: South African law in the perspective of legal philosophy*, Oxford: Clarendon.

Gaita, R, 1999, *A Common Humanity*, Melbourne: Text Publishing.

Kerruish, V and Purdy, J, 1998, 'He "Look" Honest, Big White Thief', 4:1 *Law.Text.Culture* 146–71.

Mureinik, E, 1988, 'Dworkin and apartheid', in H Corder (ed), *Law in Social Practice in South Africa*, Cape Town: Juta.

Watson, I, 2002, 'Buried Alive', 13 *Law & Critique* 253–69.

Cases

Mabo v The State of Queensland (No.2) (1992) 175 CLR 1.

TUTORIALS

TUTORIAL 1

Read the Scottish case *MacLennan v MacLennan* 1958 SLT 12.

The aim of this tutorial is to help students to grasp the essence of *deductive formal reasoning*. *McLellan* was an early Scottish case on artificial insemination by the sperm of a donor without the consent of the husband. The case raised the question whether such an action constitutes adultery and, thus, whether it can provide the basis for an action for divorce. The judge, who appears to follow the model of deductive syllogism quite explicitly reached the opposite conclusion.

Tasks and Questions:

- Summarise the factual basis of the case and the opinion of Lord Wheatley.
- Focus on the precise structuring of the syllogism that sustains his decision and compare it to the 'model' of deductive argumentation provided by MacCormick's theory.
- Focus on the interpretation of the term 'adultery'. Is this a question of open texture, according to Hart's analysis? How does the judge deal with its meaning? Are you satisfied by his approach?
- Critically discuss the explicit contention of the judge that he is not to enter into the moral, philosophical and personal considerations that artificial insemination generates. Are you satisfied by this formalistic approach to the issue?

Corresponding Sections: Part II 1.1–1.2.

TUTORIAL 2

'The case of the Speluncean Explorers'

Aim of this tutorial

The aim of this tutorial is to understand the complexity and contest-ability of legal argument over what is the right answer in hard cases. Look at how judges construct reasonable arguments about the *same* problem departing from radically *different* understandings of the pre-suppositions and meaning of the law and reaching radically different solutions too.

Reading

Lon Fuller: 'The Case of the Speluncean Explorers' (1949)

Tasks

Come prepared to discuss the following questions:

*   How do we identify 'law'? What criteria does each of the judges use to identify law?
*   What kinds of arguments do the judges in this fictitious case offer?
*   Are they convincing?
*   How would you decide the case and why?

Corresponding Sections: Part II 1.1–1.3 and 2.1.

TUTORIAL 3
**Advanced

Part I

In 1989, in Edinburgh, JD Stallard was charged with raping his wife in the matrimonial home while they were living together there. He challenged the relevancy of the charge, relying on Hume's statement (see below) that a husband cannot rape his wife because she has 'surrendered her person' to him. The plea was repelled at a preliminary diet, and Stallard appealed to the High Court.

Here are the facts

Johnston David Stallard was charged on indictment that, inter alia:

'(2) [Y]ou being married to Evelyn Stewart or Stallard, care of Police Office, Bridge of Allan, and while residing with her at said house at . . . Stirling, did on 25th August 1988 at said house

(a) assault said Evelyn Stewart or Stallard and did strike her on the face and punch her on the leg, to her injury;

(b) order said Evelyn Stewart or Stallard to a bedroom within said house, there order her to remove her clothing and threaten to rip said clothing from her body if she refused, and she having removed her clothing you did assault her, place and lock a set of handcuffs on her wrists, order her to lie on a bed, lie on top of her, threaten her with violence if she screamed for help, have sexual intercourse with her against her will and thereafter kneel by her and emit semen on her face and did rape her; and

(c) further assault said Evelyn Stewart or Stallard, tie her body and legs to said bed with ropes, force a sock or similar object into her mouth and place Sellotape over her mouth and face, and all this you did to her severe injury.'

Read the following extract from HMA v Stallard *from the decision on appeal (emphases added):*

LORD JUSTICE GENERAL (Emslie)

There is no doubt that if it was the law of Scotland that a husband is not amenable to a charge of raping his wife, the rule rests solely upon the sentence in Hume which was simply adopted and repeated in different language by the later commentators and writers on the criminal law. The statement in Hume that 'a man cannot himself commit a rape on his wife' appears in a passage in relation to a discourse on art and part of rape against a background of abduction. All who assist are involved in the same guilt as the actor.

' "This is true without exception even of the husband of the woman; who, though he cannot himself commit a rape on his own wife, who has surrendered her person to him in that sort, may however be accessory to that crime ... committed on her by another.' ... The view expressed by Hume and echoed by, inter alios, Burnett, was taken from Hale's Historia Plactiroum Coronae published in England in 1736 in which he said this [vol 1, p 629]:

'But the husband cannot be guilty of a rape committed by himself upon his lawful wife, for by their mutual matrimonial consent and contract the wife hath given up herself in this kind unto her husband, which she cannot retract.'

The first question accordingly comes to be whether, even in the eighteenth and early nineteenth centuries, the reason given for the husband's supposed immunity for the commission upon his wife of acts which would constitute the crime of rape was a sound one. That reason was, according to Hume, that the wife had 'surrendered her person' to her husband 'in that sort'. This is the first opportunity which the court in Scotland has had to consider whether Hume's statement of the law was sound when it was written and whether it is sound today. It was not necessary in HM Advocate v Duffy or in HM Advocate v Paxton for the court to consider whether Hume's view was and is a sound one in any circumstances during the subsistence of a marriage, but we must do so now. In our opinion, the soundness of Hume's view, and its application in the late twentieth century, depends entirely upon the reason which is said to justify it. Our first observation is that if what Hume meant was that by marriage a wife expressly or impliedly consented to sexual intercourse with her husband as a normal incident of marriage, the reason given affords no justification for his statement of the law because rape has always been essentially a crime of violence and indeed no more than an aggravated assault. Even in Hume's time there was no immunity for a husband who assaulted his wife even if the assault contained elements of the grossest indecency. If, on the other hand, Hume meant that by marriage a wife consented to intercourse against her will and obtained by force, **we take leave to doubt whether this was ever contemplated by the common law** which was derived from the canon law, regulating the relationship of husband and wife. We say no more on this matter which was not the subject of debate before us, because we are satisfied that the Solicitor-General was well founded in his contention that whether or not the reason for the husband's immunity given by Hume was a good one in the eighteenth and early nineteenth centuries, it has since disappeared altogether. **What Hume meant to encompass in the concept of a wife's 'surrender of her person' to her husband 'in that sort', the concept is to be understood against the background of the status of women and the position of a married woman at the time when he wrote.** Then, no doubt, a married woman could be said to have subjected herself to her husband's dominion in all things. She was required to obey him in all things. Leaving out of account the absence of rights of property, a wife's freedoms were virtually non-existent, and she had in particular no right whatever to interfere in her husband's control over the lives and upbringing of any children of the marriage. By the second half of the twentieth century, however, the status of women, and the status of a married woman, in our law have changed quite dramatically. A husband and wife are now for all practical purposes equal partners in marriage and both husband and wife are tutors and curators of their children. A wife is not obliged to obey her husband in all things nor to suffer excessive sexual demands on the part of her husband. She may rely on such demands as evidence of unreasonable behaviour for the purposes of divorce. **A live system of law will always have regard to changing circumstances to test the justification for any exception to the application of a general rule**. Nowadays, it cannot seriously be maintained that by marriage a wife submits herself irrevocably to sexual intercourse in all circumstances. It cannot be affirmed nowadays, whatever the position may have been in earlier centuries, that it is an incident of modern marriage that a wife consents to intercourse in all circumstances, including sexual intercourse obtained only by force. There is no doubt that a wife does not consent to assault upon her person and there is no plausible justification for saying today that she nevertheless is to be taken to consent to intercourse by assault.

This development of the law since Hume's time immediately prompts the question: is revocation of a wife's implied consent to intercourse, which is revocable, only capable of being established by the act of separation? In our opinion the answer to that question must be no. Revocation of a consent which is revocable must depend on the circumstances. Where there is no separation this may be harder to prove but the critical question in any case must simply be whether or not consent has been withheld. **The fiction of implied consent has no useful purpose to serve today in the law of rape in Scotland**. The reason given by Hume for the husband's immunity from prosecution upon a charge of rape of his wife, if it ever was a good reason, no longer applies today. There is now, accordingly, no justification for the supposed immunity of a husband. Logically the only question is whether or not as matter of fact the wife consented to the acts complained of, and we affirm the decision of the trial judge that charge (2)(b) is a relevant charge against the appellant to go to trial.

Questions:

*1. What **kind** of argument is the Lord Justice General relying on in the above quote? Is it an argument from principle? Is it an interpretation of existing law or does it involve a change of the law? How might the theories of Hart and/or Dworkin help us to make sense of the legal reasoning in this case? Is the Rule of Law – or any aspect of it – sacrificed in the process?*

Part 2

Read the Lord Advocate's Reference No 1 of 2001. It is reported at 2002 SLT 466 and 2002 SCCR 435.

The case was a Reference following the acquittal of an Aberdeen law student on a rape charge.

1. Summarise the arguments of EITHER the Lord Justice General OR Lady Cosgrove AND the dissenting opinion of Lord McLuskey

2. Explain the point of disagreement and the legal arguments used to support the opposite opinions.

3. How do the judges view their role here? Do they view it as applying or as creating the law? What do you think is their proper role?

4. Compare with the reasoning in *Stallard*. What, if any, similar issues arise?

Part 3

Critically read L Farmer's 'The Genius of Our Law' (Farmer 1992). What does it say about the judges' 'practical legal approach' and does it help us understand the development of Scots Law as a 'living body of law'? In your opinion is it correct to sacrifice 'abstract legal rules' in the name of this more pragmatic approach?

> **Corresponding Sections: Part II 1.1–1.3.**

TUTORIAL 4

Rules and principles

Donoghue v Stevenson is one of the most famous common law cases. Read the following extracts of the opinions:

LORD BUCKMASTER

My Lords, the facts of this case are simple. On August 26, 1928, the appellant drank a bottle of ginger-beer, manufactured by the respondent, which a friend had bought from a retailer and given to her. The bottle contained the decomposed remains of a snail which were not, and could not be, detected until the greater part of the contents of the bottle had been consumed. As a result she alleged, and at this stage her allegations must be accepted as true, that she suffered from shock and severe gastro-enteritis. She accordingly instituted the proceedings against the manufacturer which have given rise to this appeal.

The law applicable is the common law, and, though its principles are capable of application to meet new conditions not contemplated when the law was laid down, these principles cannot be changed nor can additions be made to them because any particular meritorious case seems outside their ambit.

LORD ATKIN

. . . The liability for negligence, whether you style it such or treat it as in other systems as a species of 'culpa,' is no doubt based upon a general public sentiment of moral wrongdoing for which the offender must pay. But acts or omissions which any moral code would censure cannot in a practical world be treated so as to give a right to every person injured by them to demand relief. In this way rules of law arise which limit the range of complainants and the extent of their remedy. The rule that you are to love your neighbour becomes in law, you must not injure your neighbour; and the lawyer's question, Who is my neighbour? receives a restricted reply. You must take reasonable care to avoid acts or omissions which you can reasonably foresee would be likely to injure your neighbour. Who, then, in law is my neighbour? The answer seems to be – persons who are so closely and directly affected by my act that I ought reasonably to have them in contemplation as being so affected when I am directing my mind to the acts or omissions which are called in question.

It will be found, I think, on examination that there is no case in which the circumstances have been such as I have just suggested where the liability has been negatived. There are numerous cases, where the relations were much more remote, where the duty has been held not to exist. There are also dicta in such cases which go further than was necessary for the determination of the particular issues, which have caused the difficulty experienced by the Courts below. I venture to say that in the branch of the law which deals with civil wrongs, dependent in England at any rate entirely upon the application by judges of general principles also formulated by judges, it is of particular importance to guard against the danger of stating propositions of law in wider terms than is necessary, lest essential factors be omitted in the wider survey and the inherent adaptability of English law be unduly restricted. For this reason it is very necessary in considering reported cases in the law of torts that the actual decision alone should carry authority, proper weight, of course, being given to the dicta of the judges.

. . .

I have already pointed out that this distinction is unfounded in fact, for in Elliott v. Hall (4), as in Hawkins v. Smith (5) (the defective sack), the defendant exercised no control over the article and the accident did not occur on his premises. With all respect, I think that the judgments in the case err by seeking to confine the law to rigid and exclusive categories, and by not giving sufficient attention to the general principle which governs the whole law of negligence in the duty owed to those who will be immediately injured by lack of care.

LORD TOMLIN

My Lords, I have had an opportunity of considering the opinion (which I have already read) prepared by my noble and learned friend, Lord Buckmaster. As the reasoning of that opinion and the conclusions reached therein accord in every respect with my own views, I propose to say only a few words.

First, I think that if the appellant is to succeed it must be upon the proposition that every manufacturer or repairer of any article is under a duty to every one who may thereafter legitimately use the article to exercise due care in the manufacture or repair. It is logically impossible to stop short of this point. There can be no distinction between food and any other article. Moreover, the fact that an article of food is sent out in a sealed container can have no relevancy on the question of duty; it is only a factor which may render it easier to bring negligence home to the manufacturer.

The alarming consequences of accepting the validity of this proposition were pointed out by the defendant's counsel, who said: 'For example, every one of the sufferers by such an accident as that which recently happened on the Versailles Railway might have his action against the manufacturer of the defective axle.'

LORD MacMILLAN

What, then, are the circumstances which give rise to this duty to take care? In the daily contacts of social and business life human beings are thrown into, or place themselves in, an infinite variety of relations with their fellows; and the law can refer only to the standards of the reasonable man in order to determine whether any particular relation gives rise to a duty to take care as between those who stand in that relation to each other. The grounds of action may be as various and manifold as human errancy; and the conception of legal responsibility may develop in adaptation to altering social conditions and standards. The criterion of judgment must adjust and adapt itself to the changing circumstances of life. The categories of negligence are never closed. The cardinal principle of liability is that the party complained of should owe to the party complaining a duty to take care, and that the party complaining should be able to prove that he has suffered damage in consequence of a breach of that duty. Where there is room for diversity of view, it is in determining what circumstances will establish such a relationship between the parties as to give rise, on the one side, to a duty to take care, and on the other side to a right to have care taken.

I am happy to think that in their relation to the practical problem of everyday life which this appeal presents the legal systems of the two countries are in no way at variance, and that the principles of both alike are sufficiently consonant with justice and common sense to admit of the claim which appellant seeks to establish.

Discuss the following questions:

[General:]

* Is the 'neighbour principle' a legal or a moral principle?

* If, as Lord Atkin asserts, it is indeed 'found on examination that there is no case in which the circumstances have been such as I have just suggested where the liability has been negatived', then in what sense is *Donoghue* a hard case?

[In relation to MacCormick:]

* Is it any of the business of the courts to decide cases on the basis of consequences they may have?

* Discuss the role of coherence in law on the basis of the arguments made by the judges in this case.

[In relation to Dworkin:]

* How would integrity's balance of 'fit' and 'justification' require Hercules to decide the case?

[In relation to the CLS:]

* Discuss the contention that Donoghue exhibits nothing else but an early expression of a *politics* of legal reasoning in the judges' conviction that values of social solidarity should inform all social interaction

Corresponding Section: Part II 1.3.

TUTORIAL 5
**Advanced

Discrimination and legal reasoning

1. *Read the paper* by Ronald Dworkin : 'Bakke's Case: Are Quotas Unfair?' (Dworkin 1985)

Answer the following questions:

Summarise and explain the structure of Dworkin's argument.

In your opinion does Dworkin resolve the clash between the protection of individual rights and the pursuit of the common good in a satisfactory way?

2. *Consider the following scenario:*

The medical school of Aberlour University in Scotland is concerned about the makeup of its student population. Measured against the overall population, too many of its students are female (75%), and they do not attract enough ethnic minority students or students from state schools. Recent research shows that state school students perform better at university than public school pupils with the same grades. As a result, the medical school introduces a quota in favour of state school pupils to address the imbalance. Since statistically, most ethnic minority students are also state school educated, the medical school hopes that as an indirect result, this policy will also increase the number of ethnic minority students.

John is a black African student, who studied at Fettes, an expensive private school in Edinburgh. His application to the university is rejected in favour of a lesser qualified female student who studied at a Scottish state school.

Questions:

(i)   Do you think that the introduction of the quota achieves a proper balance between the right to education and other social and political demands?

(ii) Do you think that John has been treated fairly?

(iii) In your view how might Dworkin answer this problem? How might Unger? Which approach do you find most persuasive?

Corresponding Sections: Pt II 1.1–1.3. See also Pt II 2.4.

TUTORIAL 6
**Advanced

Part 1

Essay Questions:

(1) All legal systems, argues Hart, 'compromise between two social needs: the need for *certain* rules, which can . . . safely be applied without weighing up social issues, and the need to *leave open for later settlement* issues which can only be properly appreciated and settled when they arise in a concrete case.' (Hart 1961, p 127)

(i)   Do you agree?

(ii) In your opinion can these two 'social needs' be reconciled?

(iii) Is this a result of the 'open texture' of the law?

(iv) Discuss this statement with reference to Dworkin

(2) 'Clearly there is something wrong in regarding adversarial jurisprudence as an efficient tool for arriving at the truth. After all we know that others searching after facts – in history, geography, medicine, whatever – do not emulate our adversary system.'

Discuss

(3) If law is a matter of rules, why does it matter that the vast majority of judges are male, white, upper class and educated in private schools?

(4) 'Law's attitude is constructive: it aims, in the interpretive spirit, to lay principle over practice to show the best route to a better future, keeping the right faith with the past.' (Dworkin 1986)

(i)   Do the terms 'best', 'better' and 'right' in the above quote introduce an irreducibly 'subjective' element in legal reasoning?

(ii) Discuss the contention that Dworkin's theory is a robust defence of the Rule of Law.

Corresponding Sections: (1) Part II 1.2; (2) Part II 1.2 and 2.3; (3) Part II 1.2–1.3 and 2.2; (4) Part II 1.2–1.3.

Part 2

(1) 'To regard the jury simply as a judicial institution would be taking too narrow a view of the matter for great though its influence on the

outcome of lawsuits is, influence on the fate of society is much greater still. The jury above all is a political institution and it is from this point of view that it must always be judged.'

De Tocqueville, *Democracy in America*

In your opinion is a compromise possible between the role of the jury in deciding on the truth of the matter and its role as a 'political institution'?

(2) '[J]udges ought to strive to give the real reasons for their decision. It is my firm conviction that where courts of law have denied a remedy for the cost of bringing up an unwanted child the real reasons have been grounds of distributive justice. That is, of course, a moral theory. It may be objected that the House must act like a court of law and not like a court of morals. That would only be partly right. The court must apply positive law. But judges' sense of the moral answer to a question, or the justice of the case, has been one of the great shaping forces of the common law. What may count in a situation of difficulty and uncertainty is not the subjective view of the judge but what he reasonably believes that the ordinary citizen would regard as right.'

McFarlane and Another v. Tayside Health Board [1999]
4 All ER 961, per Lord Steyn at 977–78.

Discuss

(3) 'A law of society prescribes what we may or may not do. It *can* be broken – indeed if we could not break it there would be no need to have it.'

Discuss

(4) *Discuss either of the following contentions:*

(i) 'Legal reasoning is an inherently repressive form of interpretive thought which limits our comprehension of the social world and its possibilities.' (P Gabel)

(ii) 'The intellectual core of the [formalist] ideology is the distinction between law and policy. Teachers convince students that legal reasoning exists, by bullying them into accepting as valid in particular cases arguments about legal correctness that are circular, question-begging, incoherent, or so vague as to be meaningless.' (Kelman)

Corresponding Sections: Part II, all sections.

References

Dworkin, R, 1985, *A Matter of Principle*, Oxford: Oxford University Press.
Dworkin, R, 1986, *Law's Empire*, London: Fontana.
Fuller, L, 1949, 'The case of the speluncean explorers', 62 *Harvard LR* 616.
Hart, HLA, 1961, *The Concept of Law*, Oxford: Clarendon.

Part III

Law and modernity

General themes

1.1 Law in modern society and legal modernity

In this part of the book we change the focus of analysis to ask how some of the issues that have been addressed in the first two parts of the book might be understood as being specific to modern law. This requires that we ask whether there are legal issues or features of law that have developed only in the modern period, and what this can tell us about law as an institution. Further, if as many theorists have suggested, we are moving into a period of late- or postmodernity, this raises questions about how the functions of law might be changing and how we might need to revise our understanding of law. However, before we can begin to answer such questions, we must first consider what we mean when we talk about modernity, and more specifically, what we mean by the term legal modernity.

While the term 'modern' is often used in ordinary speech to describe something that is up to date or contemporary, the term modernity has a more specific meaning when used in social or political thought. In this context it is used to refer both to a specific period of time – roughly the period following the European Enlightenment in the eighteenth century to the late twentieth century – and a specific set of beliefs or ideas that were manifested in different areas such as the arts and literature, architecture, politics, philosophy and, of course, law. While there is a danger of oversimplification in the reduction of any complex set of ideas to one or two claims, we can begin by describing the characteristic beliefs of modernity as the belief in progress and in the capacity of rational thought to understand and organise the world. In the field of science, for example, this has led to the belief that the natural world operates according to natural laws (such as gravity, evolution and so on) as opposed to magical or mysterious forces, and that science can be applied to the understanding and eradication of particular social problems (such as disease or famine). An understanding of the project of modernity has been thrown into particular relief by the development of ideas about postmodernity, or the recognition of the postmodern condition, in which it is argued that the project of modernity has reached its limits.

> For a classic statement of the 'Enlightenment project' see Kant (1991). For an analysis of the limits of this approach see Foucault (1984).

In this section we shall suggest that there is an intrinsic relationship between a set of beliefs about rationality and modern Western law, such that we can refer to the specific phenomenon of legal modernity. We shall argue that an understanding of this phenomenon opens up a distinct perspective on some of the problems faced by modern law, and we shall also examine some of the social and economic developments that have led some writers to question whether or not we have reached the limits of the modern law. Before doing so, however, we want to look at the social and cultural transformations that have taken place in the modern period, and how these have had an impact on our understanding of the role of law.

Most social theorists would agree on the nature of the massive economic and social transformations of the last 200 years. These transformations are often described in contrast to an earlier pre-modern, pre-capitalist or traditional society. Where pre-modern societies relied on agricultural forms of subsistence and were largely rural, modern society is industrialised, organised around a capitalist economy, and is largely urbanised. If traditional societies were based on face-to-face interaction with family and acquaintances in small, self-contained, communities, modern society is based on various forms of mediated communication and exchange with strangers. And if traditional societies were structured by beliefs in magic and religious or mystical symbols played an active role in the organisation of social life, modern society is characterised by the declining importance of religion, and the belief that the social and natural world can be demystified through the application of science. These transformations have had a huge impact, not only on how we live, but also on how we think about ourselves and our relation to the world that we live in. Indeed, it is not surprising that sociology – the science of society – has its origins in the thought of the eighteenth and nineteenth centuries as writers struggled to understand the nature of the social changes that they were living through.

A key problem for such writers was the question of social order – what it was that held society together in spite of the growing social divisions and tensions in a period in which traditional forms of social ordering were being destroyed. This led in turn to an interest in the social functions of law as an instrument for the production of social order.

Two perspectives are particularly influential here. The first, exemplified by the work of French sociologist Emile Durkheim (1858–1917), stresses the themes of social cohesion and collective belief, arguing that the changing forms of law can be seen as indices of different types of social solidarity. The second, exemplified by the work of Karl Marx (1818–1883), focuses, by contrast, on the theme of social conflict and dissensus, and the role played by institutions such as the law in the suppression of class conflict and in supporting the dominance of particular class interests.

Durkheim analysed the transformation of the modern world in terms of the development of the division of labour – the extent to which work on particular tasks is subdivided between members of a community, and the subdivision of the labour involved in the production of particular objects – and its impact on the organisation of social life. He identified two forms of social solidarity, each of which was associated with a characteristic form of law. The first – *mechanical* solidarity – existed in small, undeveloped societies, where each clan or social group was a separate economic unit. In these societies labour was shared, and was geared primarily towards the subsistence and reproduction of that unit. Such groups were characterised by shared beliefs and values. Law in such societies was *repressive* – that is to say that it was primarily aimed at the reinforcement of social solidarity and the punishment or expulsion of those who threatened collective beliefs. The most prominent type of law was criminal law. The second – *organic* solidarity – was typified by modern industrial societies. In these societies there are high levels of economic interdependence, as individuals typically work at the production of objects that must be sold to other economic producers, and are not producing their own means of subsistence. However, there are fewer shared beliefs, and Durkheim was concerned with the pressures that were created towards *anomie* (normlessness) or social disorder in such societies. The form of law corresponding to organic solidarity was *restitutive* law, which was aimed at the regulation and co-ordination of relations arising from the division of labour. The most prominent, but not exclusive, type of law was contract law, governing relations between producers and consumers in the marketplace. For Durkheim, then, the form and functions of modern law were to be studied as a means of understanding the nature of social solidarity.

Marx also regarded the contract as the distinctive form of modern law, but on the basis of a fundamentally different analysis of social relations. The primary category of analysis for Marx was social class, and classes were defined and understood in terms of their position in relation to the means of production. Industrial capitalism was understood as a system in which one class – the bourgeoisie – owned the means of production (factories, etc.) and exploited the proletariat or labouring classes who were forced to sell their labour in order to live. The bourgeoisie extracted profits from labour by forcing down the price of labour and maintaining the price of the objects produced through control of supply and demand in the market. The economic *means* of production was thus accompanied by distinctive social *relations* of production, which aimed at the reproduction of the social position and power of the dominant class.

One way in which Marx explained this relation between the means and relations of production was the 'base-superstructure' metaphor. According to this metaphor, the base of social relations in any society is the economic mode of production, and the form of social relations such as law, religion, politics and so on is understood as superstructure. The form of social relations in the superstructure is determined by transformations in the material or economic base. Law is primarily to be analysed as superstructural: its form is determined by the economic base of society, and its function is to sustain and regulate capitalist economic and social relations. The contract is the characteristic form of modern law, because the form of the contract governs economic relations – particularly the sale of labour. However, the form of law, which sees the contract as a fair exchange between two equal individuals, masks social inequalities, and the fact that contract law systematically reproduces the economic interests of the bourgeoisie. For Marx, then, the form of law was a means of systematically reproducing the interests of a particular social class and masking or repressing the underlying economic inequalities.

See Durkheim (1933) chs 2 and 3 for a discussion of social solidarity and the division of labour. The base-superstructure metaphor is set out in Marx (1977), and this also provides a useful (and brief) introduction to some of the themes of Marx's thought. Both are discussed in Giddens (1971).

Durkheim and Marx raised important questions about the relationship between law and modern society, but they saw this relation as largely external and contingent – that is to say, social changes were reflected in law, and that changes in the form or practice of law were best studied as a guide to understanding these broader shifts. However, we want now to turn to a third writer who, while also being centrally concerned with the relations between law and modern Western capitalism, studied law as a distinctive form of modern rationality. This is the German sociologist Max Weber (1864–1920). The following two sections will be devoted to the exposition and discussion of his understanding of legal modernity. The final section of this part explores the extent to which the paradigm of modernity remains a useful framework for understanding the function of law.

1.2 Formal legal rationality and legal modernity

Weber's major work was carried out between the years of 1904 and 1905 – when he first published the essays that subsequently made up the book *The Protestant Ethic and the Spirit of Capitalism* (Weber 1930) – and his death in 1920. The bulk of his great synthetic work – *Economy and Society* (Weber 1968) – was published posthumously in 1921. Weber's central project was a historical sociology of the distinctive forms of modern Western rationality. Central achievements of occidental rationality were seen as the capitalist economy, organised religion, the Nation-State and modern forms of bureaucracy or political administration, and the rule of law. His sociology of law was an attempt to analyse the distinctive features of modern Western law by focusing on the conditions that he saw as central to its unique development, and to trace the relationship between the law and the other forms of rational organisation of social life.

Weber saw modern Western law as having certain distinct features. It was a system of general norms of universal application, organised and backed by the power of the State, applied and interpreted by a specially qualified staff of lawyers. In addition, modern law was relatively independent from politics, although the modern bureaucratic State was itself dependent on a particular legal form. These were not viewed as necessary features of all law, but were understood as the outcome of a particular process of historical development. The study of the form of modern law (as with the study of all other forms of rationality) thus required the development of a particular methodology, focusing on the forms of legal rationality and political authority and the relationships between them. We shall look at this, before going on to see how Weber used them in his historical sociology of the development of modern law.

> Weber provides an excellent short introduction to the questions that animate his sociology in the introduction to *The Protestant Ethic and the Spirit of Capitalism*: Weber (1930, pp 13–31). Weber's theory generally is discussed in Turner (1996) and Murphy (1997).

1.2.1 Forms of legal rationality

Legal rationality was analysed in terms of four forms, combining formal and substantive (informal) rationality and irrationality. These were 'ideal-typical' forms, not intended to refer to any actually existing legal system, but to allow the analysis of the principal characteristics of specific legal systems on the basis of variations in legal technique and forms of political organisation. There are two major dimensions of comparison: the degree of *rationality* and the degree of *formality*. The former measures the generality of the rules employed by the system and the systematic character of the legal order, the latter the extent to which criteria of decision intrinsic to the legal system are used. Thus the degree of rationality is aimed at the analysis of the internal consistency of a legal system, while the criteria of formality are concerned additionally both with the extent to which legal norms are formally articulated and with the autonomy of the legal system from political institutions and pressures. It must, therefore, be noted that these forms refer not only to the internal characteristics of legal systems, but also to the relation between legal systems and other forms of social and political organisation.

If we look at each of the different types of rationality, we can distinguish the following principal types of legal systems:

informal irrational	**formal irrational**
informal rational	**formal rational**

1.2.1.1 Informal irrational

In these types of systems there may be no formally established body of laws, and no established criteria on which decisions are to be made in individual cases. There may or may not be recognised judges, and each case will be judged on its own merits. Decisions will commonly have no binding force beyond the particular case to be adjudicated. Weber sometimes referred to this as 'khadi-justice' after the practice in certain Muslim courts (Weber 1968, pp 845, 976–8).

1.2.1.2 Formal irrational

This refers to those types of systems where there is some form of established law, but the law derives its authority from the lawgiver, as in the case of sacred law, or from a formalised set of customary practices. This was regarded as irrational in the sense that the authority of the law was not related to an internal quality of the rules themselves or their efficacy in organising social life, but was derived wholly from the oracular quality of their source (for example forms of sacred or religious law). Thus in the sphere of law-finding, there might be recognised judges who follow certain established procedures for the settling of disputes, but the criteria of decision making are unknowable. A good example of this type of practice would be the trial by ordeal or battle, which was a highly formalised system, but which appealed to divine intervention for the determination of guilt.

1.2.1.3 Informal rational

This refers to those systems where there is a rational process for the making and enactment of law, but this is directed towards set extrinsic or external aims, such as ethical imperatives, utilitarian ends or political purposes. Law is used instrumentally, and its authority depends on the extent to which it is able to fulfil these ends. The application of law must meet similar criteria. It would therefore be conceivable that in cases where the facts were similar, different decisions might be reached depending on, for example, the status or social class of the litigants as a matter of the policy or values to which the law was oriented.

1.2.1.4 Formal rational

This refers to systems with a formal process for the enactment of laws, but where the laws would be regarded as relatively autonomous from particular social policies or ethical ideals. There would be specialised institutions for the application of the law, and the discretion of judges would be limited. There would be a strong expectation that cases that were alike in their relevant legal characteristics would be treated alike. This requires the development of techniques for determining the relevant legal characteristics of a case and for the identification and application of general rules. Alternatively, it may simply demand the adherence to certain external characteristics of the facts, such as a signature on a deed or the utterance of certain words. This is to distinguish two different variants of formal rationality, which can be referred to as logical formality and the formal recognition of extrinsic characteristics. The former is in many respects the key to Weber's analysis of modern law, and we shall be examining it at some length below. It is first necessary, however, to look at his analysis of the forms of political authority.

> The classic analysis of Weber's sociology of law in these terms can be found in M Rheinstein (1954, pp xlvii lxiii). A similar account can be found in Kronman (1983, ch 4). See, also, Parts I 2.4 and II 1.1 for a discussion of legal formalism.

1.2.2 Forms of political authority

Weber defined a State as 'a human community that (successfully) claims the *monopoly of the legitimate use of physical force* within a given territory'

(1948a, p 78), arguing that political organisation could not typically rely on coercion alone, but would have also to establish some legitimate grounds for political authority. The forms of political authority or domination were, therefore, analysed in terms of the types of legitimacy that were typically claimed by, or which actors ascribed to, political orders. Political authority or domination was also seen as taking certain characteristic or ideal-typical forms. Weber identified three pure types of legitimate domination:

1. Traditional domination, which rested on the 'established belief in the sanctity of immemorial traditions and the legitimacy of those exercising authority under them.' (Weber 1968, p 215)
2. Charismatic domination, which rested upon the extraordinary heroism or exemplary character of an individual leader and the order created or revealed by him or her.
3. Legal domination, which rested on the belief in the legality of a consciously created order and the right to give commands vested in certain persons designated by that order. This is seen as the specifically modern type of administration.

The last is an impersonal form of order where obedience is demanded and given out of respect for the order itself, while the other two depend on the status of an office or the characteristics of certain individuals. In legal domination legitimation is thus intrinsic to the order, rather than being dependent on external factors. However, Weber goes on to argue that, to the extent that legal domination is a rational form of domination, it will tend to have certain further characteristics relating to its administrative staff: official business is bound by rules; it is carried out within certain demarcated spheres or jurisdictions; it takes place within an official hierarchy of rule and supervision; and it requires some degree of professional training of officials. In addition, in a rational system there is a strict separation between the ownership and the means of administration, with no office being owned by its incumbent: that is to say that there is a separation between the office and the individual, which guarantees the impartiality and technical efficiency of the bureaucracy. Thus 'the purest type of exercise of legal authority is that which employs a bureaucratic administrative staff' (Weber 1968, p 220), for this leads to an increase in the technical knowledge and competency of the administration, which is essential to economic organisation and organisation of social life under the conditions of the division of labour. In this sense, then, rational bureaucratic organisation is essential to modernity, since it alone is capable of dealing with the problems of distribution of goods and management of the economy, as well as ensuring the continuous regulation of social life.

> The types of legitimate domination are set out in Weber 1968, ch III.
> You should read pp 217–26 for an analysis of legal authority. See, also,
> the discussion in Cotterrell (1995).

Through these ideal types Weber establishes an affinity between formal
rational law and legal domination – legal domination as the rule of law, but
also seeing bureaucracies as rule-bound institutions of government – a relationship that would be confirmed by his historical sociology of Western law.
However, it is important to note that there are ambiguities here that reflect
tensions between law and politics in the modern State.

The key point here is the distinction between forms of legal and political
organisation and the way that the different forms of law could interact with
the types of legitimate political domination. Thus while certain forms of law
require some sort of extrinsic guarantee for the legal order, as informal
rational law relies on religious (charismatic) or political ends and authority,
formal rational law claims an intrinsic authority or validity based on the
legal form itself. In this way it makes a claim to autonomy from political or
economic or ethical ends or rationality (although as we have suggested in
Part II.1.1 the commitment to formalism is in itself a commitment to a
particular set of political values). The question of legitimacy, however, is
primarily a political question, and legal domination is a form of *political*
legitimacy. This is a claim to a form of intrinsic authority (while the other two
types rely on extrinsic factors) that depends on, for example, the legal codification of political relationships in the form of a constitution and the legal
definition of the scope of political offices or powers. It thus overlaps conceptually and historically with formal rational law. The ambiguity lies in the
fact that while legal domination appears to rest on an internal claim to validity (government by laws not men, the rule of law), it in fact depends on the
organisation of the legal system and the sustainability of the distinction
between law and politics. There is a necessary tension in the juxtaposition of
formal rational law and legal legitimacy, for though the latter would seem to
require the former, the reverse of this is not the case. This captures an important feature of the relationship between law and politics in the modern State.
This relationship is slanted towards the question of how law can guarantee
political order, rather than vice versa. This means that the question of the
legitimacy of the legal system itself can appear as a problem under certain
conditions, such as, for example, when legal questions become politicised or
where law is required to adjudicate in political disputes, because while the
political system might draw on the formal rational law for legitimacy, this can
come at a cost for law. Historically, Weber suggests, the difficulty is bridged
through the conjunction between formal legal rationality and the development of bureaucracy as the highest forms of rational and autonomous

administration in the modern State. However, as we shall see, the distinction between law and politics has become increasingly unstable.

1.2.3 The development of legal modernity

The relationship between forms of law and political organisation becomes clearer if we consider it in the context of Weber's basic outline of a historical sociology of Western law, the central feature of which was the increasing rationalisation of legal thought and the triumph of formal rational law. In this we can illustrate how Weber uses the ideal types as a means of analysing a specific pattern of development, as well as seeing how the development of legal modernity relates to the forms of political organisation.

The broad outline of development of legal modernity is laid out in the following passage:

> From a theoretical point of view, the general development of law and procedure may be viewed as passing through the following stages: first, charismatic legal revelation through 'law prophets'; second, empirical creation and finding of law by legal *honoriatores*, i.e. law creation through cautelary [reasoning on a case-by-case basis] jurisprudence and adherence to precedent; third, imposition of law by secular or theocratic powers; fourth and finally, the systematic elaboration of law and professionalised administration of justice by persons who have received their legal training in a learned and formally logical manner. From this perspective, the formal qualities of the law emerge as follows: arising in primitive legal procedure from a combination of magically conditioned formalism and irrationality conditioned by revelation, they proceed to increasingly specialised juridical and logical rationality and systematisation, sometimes passing through the detour of theocratically or patrimonially conditioned substantive and informal expediency. Finally, they assume, at least from an external viewpoint, an increasingly logical sublimation and deductive rigour and develop an increasingly rational technique in procedure.
>
> (Weber 1968, p 882)

This describes a double movement combining the increasing rationalisation of law, in the sense of generalisation in its elaboration and enactment, and the increasing formalisation of the law and its autonomy from systems of religious and political power. At the same time, however, this describes the subjection of political power to the forms of legal rationality, one of the more significant achievements of formal rational law and a characteristic of legal modernity.

These achievements can be broken down into four broad categories. First, the development of rational law frees the individual from traditional forms of power based in superstition, religion or arbitrary sovereign action, through the development of universalisable norms and the rational administration of justice. The development of modernity thus establishes a particular kind of relationship between formal legal rationality and political power, which is constituted in legal form. This form of legitimacy enables those holding political power to do certain things, in particular when associated with the development of the capacities of rational bureaucratic administration, but (in its formal rational expression) the law now sets limits on arbitrary power. It is thus (paradoxically) both a means of achieving individual and political freedom and the means through which the rational administration of the modern State is constructed.

The second achievement is the creation of a law of general validity and universal application. As the State has a monopoly over the means of violence within certain territorial boundaries – the classic definition of the modern Nation-State – this leads to the creation of law that is universal within the territory, superseding all local laws and privileges based on status and special jurisdictions. Formal rational law achieves its ideal expression in the form of a code. Laws must be published in advance in a form that can be understood by all subjects, and are merely applied by judges and other legal officials who are formally independent of the sovereign. The actions of the State and its officers are subjected to legal controls, and so become more predictable. Equally, in the area of private law, the protection of private property and the enforcement of contracts become more secure and predictable, allowing the more certain regulation and future planning of economic affairs. By this means the rule of law creates and sustains security in economic, governmental and social life.

Third, there is the development of a sophisticated and specialised type of reasoning that requires that those interpreting and applying the law receive professional training. The idea that the law is both gapless and internally consistent with itself is derived from the reception of Roman law, which took rules that were developed by an inductive process and were context-dependent and generalised them to the level of abstract principles that could be applied deductively since they were believed to be the highest achievements of reason. Legal problems are thus seen as individuated cases that can be solved in a systematic manner by identifying the legally relevant facts and subsuming them within abstract legal norms. Cases are to be solved only by looking at the combination of law and facts, and by excluding consideration of factors such as moral values or social status.

Finally, as part of a wider process of secularisation, the law is separated from the sphere of ethics. Although this was initially understood in terms of the separation of law and religion, both at the level of the disestablishment of State religion and in terms of the content of individual laws, this has a number of important consequences for our understanding of modernity. Weber traced the reception of Roman law through its transformation into modern or revolutionary natural law, in which the legitimacy of the norms was derived from the immanent or teleological qualities of the law – the working out of the principles of 'reason and justice' – which allowed it to transcend its origins in princely or priestly power. This, he argued, was the 'only consistent type of legitimacy of a legal order which can remain once religious revelation and the authoritarian sacredness of a tradition and its bearers have lost their force' (Weber 1968, p 867). However, he also pointed out that this form of legitimacy was undermined by the development of a formal rational law whose authority was grounded only in the formal question of the internal validity of the norm. The development of legal modernity thus broke the connection between law and reason or justice. Formal positive law need have no particular content, and is limited by no other ethical or moral principles. It is non-interventionist – not pursuing particular social or policy ends – and it is clearly differentiated from other sources of normative ordering. It is therefore implicit in both the idea and the historical development of formal rational law that there be some form of specialisation and autonomy from other spheres of values and social life.

From this brief account we can see how Weber's conception of formal rational law describes important features of legal modernity. It is tempting to see these achievements as the inevitable result of the unfolding of an immanent process of rationalisation – a march of progress towards better, more rational, law – a temptation that is exacerbated by the language of ideal types and Weber's description of formal rational law as the highest form of rationality. However, it is necessary to ask why this form of law should have developed uniquely in the West, for this was not an inevitable process, even when considered in conjunction with the development of the capitalist economy. In other words, what were the general social and political factors that contributed to the development of the distinctive forms of modern Western law?

To begin with, it is important to note that Weber did not see this question as one simply of the relation between law and economy, or between forms of legal and economic thought, although he clearly regarded this relation as being of central importance. Indeed, he was at pains to deny the existence of a strict correlation or causal relation between the two: changes in external conditions, such as changes in the form of the economy might have some impact on individual or collective conduct, but could not in any sense be regarded as determinants of such conduct. Equally, the law might protect certain economic interests, but it was clear both that these interests might be protected in others ways, and that the law also served other interests that could not be reduced to purely economic factors. It is thus important to note that while Weber wished to place the forms of economic organisation at the centre of his sociology, he was also distancing himself in two important respects from Marx's analysis of the development of law and the capitalist economy. First, he was concerned to establish the full range of relations between the economy and other relevant social spheres, without seeing these relationships as being uni-causally determined in any way. Second, in contrast to Marx's class analysis, Weber was concerned with individual activity and orientations towards forms of conduct or ideas as a means of understanding social and economic activities: 'the ability and disposition of men to adopt certain types of practical rational conduct' (Weber 1930, p 26; Ewing 1987). However, unlike many forms of methodological individualism that begin from the assumption of certain natural or intrinsic characteristics, such as self-interest or the ability to reason, for Weber there is no intrinsic quality attaching to human actions or persons, and thus there can be no organising principles beyond the orientation towards certain rationally structured activities. This problematises the idea of rationality, for it is implicit in this view that the world is fundamentally non-rational. This gives his analysis of the rise of formal rational law further distinctive characteristics, notably an emphasis on the contingency of social relations and a scepticism about the capacity of rationality to organise human affairs. The explanation for the rise of formal rational law was sought, then, in the coincidence of, or affinity between, certain interests, combined with an analysis of the intrinsic or internal demands of a developing legal profession.

This can be seen in his treatment of the rise of the national economic system and its impact on traditional forms of economic and political organisation. Weber argued that an economic system of the modern type could not exist without a legal order backed by the State that could guarantee the predictability and stability of economic relations:

[M]odern economic life by its very nature has destroyed those other associations which used to be the bearers of law and thus of legal guaranties. This has been the result of the development of the market. The universal predominance of the market consociation requires on the one hand a legal system the functioning of which is *calculable* in accordance with rational rules. On the other hand, the constant expansion of the market consociation has favoured the monopolisation and regulation of all 'legitimate' coercive power by *one* universal coercive institution through the disintegration of all particular status-determined and other coercive structures which have been resting mainly on economic monopolies.

(Weber 1968, p 337)

In this passage Weber points to the central importance of legal order in counteracting the social effects of economic development, as well as the way in which economic development created the conditions in which a rational legal system could supersede other forms of social and political organisation. Law functioned to promote the security of the interests of commerce and business and the protection of property. It did so by structuring economic relations in ways that made them more efficient, predictable and enforceable, specifically through the contractual form, but also through the development of devices such as agency and negotiable instruments, which facilitated economic transactions. However, Weber was also at pains to point out that this was not a function of legal rationality as such, for 'the consequences of the purely logical construction often bear very irrational or even unforeseen relations to the expectations of the commercial interests' (Weber 1968, p 855). The formal abstract character of law was also of decisive merit to those with economic power in securing freedom from arbitrary government interference, as it was to those 'who on ideological grounds attempt to break down authoritarian control or to restrain irrational mass emotions for the purpose of opening up individual opportunities and liberating capacities' (Weber 1968, p 813). Once again, however, this was accompanied with a caveat, pointing out that there was no necessary connection between economic freedom of contract and political freedom.

Weber identified two other principal factors in the rise of formal rational law: the influence of political authority and autonomous developments in the study and professional organisation of the law. With respect to the former, he argued that the more rational the administrative machinery of princes or religious leaders became (in the sense of the use of paid, qualified, officials and the development of a permanent bureaucracy), then the more rational would become the law. This, however, was not a matter of articulated policy, but was generally driven by the immanent needs of their own organisation, whether fiscal or administrative. In general, Weber identified princely or patrimonial forms of law with either arbitrary command or the creation of privileges in the 'estates', but he argued that this limited the effectiveness of princely rule, since the administration was limited by the fragmentation of the realm and the discontinuity of laws across special jurisdictions. The elimination of these privileges served the interests of officials in the expansion of the extent of the law and the creation of order and unity, also coinciding with the interests of the bourgeoisie in a more objective and rational law. In fiscal terms, as the size of the administration grew beyond the household of the prince, the costs of maintenance increased, and these needs were met by increasingly rational (regular and general) rather than arbitrary forms of taxation as the princes sought to tie themselves to certain economic interest groups. Perhaps most importantly of all, however, Weber stressed the importance of technical factors associated with learning and professionalisation that drove the autonomous development of the law. The crucial factor here was the reception of Roman law, initially in the canon law and later as a more abstract system of legal learning, which offered the basis for a universalisation of law that transcended traditional forms and particularistic norms. This had important consequences for the education of lawyers in the early universities. The study of law based on the formal qualities of Roman law became a specialised form of knowledge and encouraged the formation of the legal profession (though these did not necessarily serve economic interests). It also had important consequences for the administration of justice as trained lawyers, whether acting as officials or judges, demanded the rationalisation of law and procedure. This underlines, once again, the close connections that Weber drew between formal rational law – the development of rational administration in the form of bureaucracy – and legal domination.

In summary, then, legal modernity was characterised by the development of formal rational law, a development that coincided with, and contributed to the development of the capitalist economy. The notable achievements of this form of law were to provide a legal form that enabled both the stable and continuous regulation of the economy and social life and the constitutionalisation of political power, through the creation of an autonomous, specialised form of legal reasoning. However, as we shall see in the following section, both internal and external pressures on the law have threatened these achievements.

1.3 Dilemmas of modern law

Although Weber's account of the development of legal modernity would appear to culminate in the triumph of formal rational law, it is nonetheless clear that he viewed this as an inherently unstable form. The final pages of the sociology of law in *Economy and Society* are devoted to a discussion of how formal rational law was being undermined, both by virtue of its own internal qualities and as a result of external pressures, which asks questions of his preceding analysis. This discussion, moreover, is consistent with the more pessimistic tone of his analysis of modernity, and certainly gives his analysis of legal modernity a more ambiguous quality than might at first appear. In this section, then, we will discuss these pressures before linking this to the broader analysis of modernity and Weber's methodology more generally.

Read Weber (1968, p 880 9) where he identifies the 'anti-formalistic' tendencies in modern law. For a similar analysis (with clear Weberian roots), see Unger (1976, pp 192 223).

Lying at the heart of Weber's analysis of legal modernity was his belief in the inevitability of the continuing technical rationalisation of the law. The modern system of the administration of justice linked formal rational law to the political legitimacy of the modern State. However, as we have noted, this meant the validity of the law was founded in either the political authority of the legislator or the internal characteristics of the norm. There was no external *normative* basis for the authority of law (such as that provided by modern natural law), and this meant that the law was put at the service of the political system becoming an instrument for the pursuit of particular policy ends. This undermined the authority of the legal system. He argued that:

> Consequently, legal positivism has, at least for the time being, advanced irresistibly. The disappearance of the old natural law conceptions has destroyed all possibility of providing the law with a metaphysical dignity by virtue of its immanent qualities. In the great majority of its most important provisions, it has been unmasked all too visibly, indeed, as the product or the technical means of a compromise between conflicting interests.
>
> (Weber 1968, pp 874–5)

These circumstances, he suggested, led to an increased scepticism about the dignity of the law, while simultaneously requiring an increased obedience to the law from those holding legitimate political power.

Weber thus argued that modern law was an autonomous and technical discipline, which, at least in the sphere of bureaucratic administration, had to fulfil the ends of legitimising the political system. While bureaucracy is rational, it is oriented to law instrumentally rather than formally – that is to say that it is a tool for the implementation and pursuit of certain political ends, and cannot provide any normative basis for legal authority. There is thus an inherent tension between political power and law as forms of bureaucratic organisation become more predominant, since the political demand for the implementation of particular policies undermines the formal rationality of the legal system. The law, having no deeper normative foundation, is unable to resist the demands of power. 'Juridical formalism', in Weber's formulation, 'enables the legal system to operate like a technically rational machine' (1968, p 811) – implementing policy through legislation – but with the consequence of undermining its capacity to stand opposed to political power. Legal modernity had created a formal rationality without ideals, where the legal profession act as technicians serving established power, and where law is used to promote instrumental ends. Thus:

> [i]nevitably the notion must expand that the law is a rational technical apparatus which is continually transformable in the light of expediential considerations and devoid of all sacredness of content. This fate may be obscured by the tendency of acquiescence in the existing law, which is growing in many ways for several reasons, but it cannot really be stayed.
>
> (Weber 1968, p 895)

He identified three developments, which were bringing specific pressure to bear on the formal rationality of modern law. In the first place, he noted the revival and growth of 'particularism' in the law specifically, though not exclusively, in the areas of commercial and labour law. While, as we have seen, the development of modernity had been characterised by the removal of status privileges and jurisdictions and their replacement by universal law, writing in the early part of the twentieth century, Weber noted a trend towards the weakening of legal formalism by considerations of substantive expediency. Thus he noted that in the area of commercial transactions the application of the law was coming to be determined by the substantive qualities of a transaction, that is to say the economic purpose of the transaction, rather than the formal properties of the transaction. This was accompanied by the development of special tribunals, such as commercial courts, which explicitly sought to develop principles of adjudication that were adapted to the activity that they sought to regulate. This was a result of an occupational differentiation that combined with an effective political organisation, through trade bodies, for example, to demand solutions that were better adapted to the circumstances of particular conflicts or disputes. The continuation of this trend has been noted by later theorists who have observed, for example, that the outcomes of commercial contractual disputes are more likely to be determined by the relationship between the contracting parties than the letter of the contract, and that the law is used only as final resort. We can also note the continued development of specialised informal dispute settlement institutions, such as tribunals or courts of arbitration, which have their own specialised jurisdiction and rules.

Second, Weber noted the operation of the status demands of lawyers. Legal formalism seeks to minimise the contribution of the lawyer by bowing to the political demand that the law be accessible and intelligible and attempting to reduce judicial discretion in the interpretation and application of the law. Weber, however, argues that this conflicts with the professional ideology of lawyers, which claims that the law is a complex science, the understanding of which requires specialised training and knowledge. Lawyers have an interest in maintaining the complexity of the law, and react to political movements for legal codification by seeking to defend their interests and preserve their social status. There is thus a fundamental conflict between professional demands for complexity and political demands for intelligibility, the outcome of which in practice has been the development of increasingly technical and internally differentiated bodies of law.

Third, he noted the impact of social conflict and inequality in the law, as the law was increasingly used as a tool for the management of class conflict with the development of the welfare state. This, he argued, affected the ability of the law to be an abstract and impartial system of adjudication in one of two ways. On the one hand, the existence of social conflict called into question the abstract claims of the law to treat all individuals as equals, which led to political demands for a more social law that would be responsive to certain inequalities. There was thus a politicising of law – that is to say the use of law as a means of achieving certain policy ends – in order to preserve the legitimacy of political authority. On the other hand, in the process of legal interpretation and application there was an assertion of the need for judicial creativity to supplement the abstract formulation of the law with evidence relating to the meaning and context of certain disputes. Thus lawyers would claim to discover the 'real' intentions of the parties to a contract, rather than looking at its purely formal qualities, and demand the recognition of categories such as 'good faith' or 'fair usage', which would require the judge to be more evaluative. This reflects an inherent incompatibility between the 'utilitarian' meaning of a proposition and its formal legal meaning as this was governed by the demands of logical consistency. These could only be brought together at the cost of the renunciation of the formal qualities of law, and in particular the idea that the law was complete and 'gapless', in favour of more amorphous and ethical standards of substantive justice.

The classic account of the uses of contract law in commercial disputes is Macaulay (1963). For a more recent discussion, see the symposium on contract law and legal theory (*Social & Legal Studies* 2000, pp 397–447).

Larson (1977) analyses the development of professions in terms of the ability of the occupational group to control supply of its services in the market to its own benefit. This perspective is applied to the development of the legal profession in England and Wales in Abel (1986).

Although his analysis concentrates mainly on the external pressures that were being placed on the law, it is worth noting that it reflects a general and underlying internal tension in the legal form. This can be seen in the two different aspects of the positivisation of the law – a development that (as we have already noted) Weber regarded as a central achievement of legal modernity. On the one hand, positivisation reflects a fundamental conflict between legal and social fact, which can be traced to the relation between formal and substantive legitimacy in modern natural law. Modern natural law sought to establish the normative legitimacy of the law by codifying the natural qualities of social relations. It thus claimed a direct relation between legal and social fact. However, this form of law is vulnerable to disruption by the evidence of actual social facts or substantive demands made in the name of an ethical claim about legal justice. There is thus a necessary gap between legal and social fact that follows from the failures of social life to correspond to the model of law. Thus while the model of formal law is apparently founded on the premise that legal and social justice are commensurate, the experience of modernity suggests that this is not the case, and the law in practice swings between retreating into formalism and its dissolution in the pursuit of particular substantive ends. That is to say that there is a privileging of either the normative quality of the legal or that of the social, as a result of the unbridgeable gap that has been created between law and society. On the other hand, the positivisation of the law results in the specialisation of the legal sphere and the autonomy of the legal system. This establishes a fundamental tension between the universalism of the ideology of the legal form and the more limited capacity of the law to resolve social conflicts.

Weber's account of the development of legal modernity as a process of increasing and irreversible rationalisation and specialisation can readily be located within his account of modernity. In general, modernity was depicted as a state of liberation from superstition and tradition in all spheres of social life, a state which had been achieved not only through the use of reason in the guiding of human conduct and the understanding of the world (disenchantment), but also through the institutionalisation of reason in certain spheres of human activity (rationalisation). Reason is the means to the disenchantment of the world and the universalisation of standards and values. It thus became its own form of sovereignty, and rationality was a medium of power through which the sovereign command could be conveyed, allowing the domination of nature (through the institutionalisation of science) and society (through the institutionalisation of law and politics). Yet, at the same time, Weber's account of modernity is marked by a deep scepticism, a personal disenchantment that reflected the disenchantment of the world, about both the achievements and potential of rationality. This was most famously expressed in the metaphor of the 'iron cage' of modernity with which he concluded his essay on the protestant ethic and the rise of capitalism:

> The tremendous cosmos of the modern economic order . . . now bound to the technical and economic conditions of machine production which today determine the lives of all the individuals who are born into this mechanism . . . [F]ate decreed that the cloak [of rationality] should become an iron cage . . . Specialists without spirit, sensualists without heart; this nullity imagines that it has attained a level of civilisation never before achieved.
>
> (Weber 1930, pp 181–2)

This passage is striking not only for its apparent pessimism about the achievements of Western modernity, but also because the language of 'fate' seems to conflict both with the subject matter of modernity and Weber's methodological 'anti-determinism'. Notwithstanding this, the idea of fate neatly combines the relation between the objective conditions of social life and the meaning of individual conduct that lies at the heart of his sociology, to suggest that the conditions under which individual personality can be developed are being eroded in modernity. As rationality increasingly becomes a medium, obedience and docility are required as the means for the efficient functioning of the institutional machinery. The individual is reduced to an instrument, trained to function as a cog in the machinery of bureaucracy, carrying out commands without question. The idea of individuality was diminished or levelled, as the idea of personality was increasingly replaced by that of function.

This is a process in which rationality undermines itself. Reason had been the means of expression of freedom from tradition and superstition (enlightenment), but rationality was becoming the principal form of closure against which critique had to be directed. Reason had been the means of producing universal norms, but the scope of these norms was increasingly limited by the process of the specialisation of different spheres of social life. Reason broke the bonds of traditional values and beliefs, but was then unable to replace these with any new values. Science could contribute to the technology for the controlling of human life by calculation and observation, but can provide no objective answer to the meaning of life: ' "scientific" pleading is meaningless in principle because the various value spheres of the world stand in irreconcilable conflict with each other' (Weber 1948b, p 147).

The state of disenchantment thus corresponded to Weber's own understanding of the function of social science. In his writings on method he insisted on the importance of a 'value-free' sociology, in the sense that it should consider the analysis of data as an end in itself, detached from any ultimate values. It was, he argued, an inescapable condition of our historical situation that objective facts could not reveal any larger or underlying truths about the world. In making this claim, he did not suggest that the social scientist brought no presuppositions to the study of society. Indeed it is clear, for example, that in placing the concept of formal rationality at the core of his sociology of law, he was making a series of assumptions about the nature of rationality (and irrationality), as well as of the importance of law and government to the construction and maintenance of the modern social order. However, it was not possible either to assume that any of the institutions or practices that were studied had any intrinsic value in themselves or that the social scientist could discover any patterns of rationality that were intrinsic or natural to human behaviour. A consequence of both specialisation and disenchantment was that in modernity science can neither create nor discover values, and could not ground the presupposition of its own value. Moreover, by being value-free it opened up the possibility of the questioning of values. Thus in the definition of the ideal types of law, Weber is not arguing that the characteristics of universality and formality are necessary or intrinsic to the definition of law, nor that the law is essential to social order. His concern is rather with the ways that people accord law a certain social function and attribute validity to legal norms – and indeed with the way that the question of validity or legality takes on a particular form and importance under conditions of modernity. The study of law, therefore, was not merely a matter of the justification of legal norms, but of understanding the means by which legal norms could be regarded as justifiable. The problem that this left open, of course, was the question of how to choose between competing conceptions of law. Scientific reason opened up the field of study, but was unable to guide between competing value conceptions. The transformation of science in the direction of technical knowledge and of politics into technical decision making on the grounds of material interests thus results in a loss of direction:

> The fate of our times is characterised by rationalisation and intel-lectualisation and, above all, by the 'disenchantment of the world.' Precisely the ultimate and most sublime values have retreated from public life either into the transcendental realm of mystic life or into the brotherliness of direct and personal human relations.
>
> (Weber 1948b, p 155)

The collapse of any criteria of public morality thus led to either the flight from the meaningless of the world into mysticism or to the instrumentalisa-tion of the self. Although we cannot address this question of the loss of value at any length at this point, it is worth noting something of Weber's response. The outlines of this can be found in the two famous lectures, 'Politics as a Vocation' and 'Science as a Vocation', delivered at Munich University in 1918 (Weber 1948a, b). In these lectures he addressed the questions of how the professional politician should act in the world of the party machine, and how the scientist should respond to the absence of values. In other words, the question was that of how the professional was to act with a sense of responsibility in a calling independent of the technical pursuit of particular goals. While noting that this question would require to be answered differently in each specialised life sphere according to its own particular characteristics – politics, for example, was characterised as power backed by violence – he argued that there were two fundamental maxims for the conduct of life. These were described as an ethic of ultimate ends and an ethic of responsibil-ity. The former was the attempt to act in the 'right' manner according to some fundamental beliefs and to disregard the results, and the latter was where one had to 'give an account of the foreseeable results of one's action' (1948a, p 120) or to 'give an account of the ultimate meaning of his own conduct' (1948b, p 152). The former is unconditional and must either disregard the means in pursuit of the ends, or reject all means that are morally dangerous. Con-sequently, he argued, an ethic of ultimate ends was unable to stand up to the 'ethical irrationality of the world' (1948a, p 122) and must ultimately repre-sent a withdrawal from it. The latter not only must recognise the means, but also must give an account of the relationship between means and ends. It was in the combination of these two ethics that the 'genuine' man could be consti-tuted, with the ability to maintain a sense of distance towards the self, which was essential to the formation of personality in the pursuit of a vocation: 'what is decisive is the trained relentlessness in viewing the realities of life, and the ability to face such realities and to measure up to them inwardly' (1948a, pp 126–7). This was a requirement of integrity, in the scientist as an 'irrational' commitment to the possibility of truth and in the politician in the subjective commitment to the objective use of power, as well as commitment to certain ultimate values and meanings. And we should note that this attempt to address the meaning of a vocation, independently of its particular aims, replicates Weber's personal commitment to the objective study of society and the impact of these conditions on the soul or personality of the modern man.

> Anyone interested in pursuing these questions should read 'Politics as a Vocation' and 'Science as a Vocation' (Weber 1948a, b).

1.4 After modernity? Law and globalisation

Weber's analysis of legal modernity, and in particular of the dilemmas of modern law, has been extremely influential, and we find echoes of it in the writings of many contemporary theorists of law and society. However, a recent strand in legal theory addresses the question of the extent to which Weber's paradigm of modernity is still able to offer insight into the nature of modern law, or the relation between law and society. These theorists argue that fundamental shifts in the social function of law in the post-welfare state, and in the relationship between law and the Nation-State mean that the paradigm of legal modernity developed by theorists such as Weber has been superseded, and that it is necessary to develop a new theoretical understanding of law. Central to such challenges has been the phenomenon of globalisation, for this challenges many of the core assumptions that underpin this account of legal modernity. Thus for example, where Weber sees legal modernity in the consolidation and singularity of state law, globalisation sees the fragmentation of sovereignty; and where our understanding of legal modernity is based on the generality and universality of state law, globalisation sees the pluralisation and diversity of legal orders. To what extent then does this require us to revise or replace our understanding of legal modernity?

The literature on globalisation is vast, covering a wide range of subjects often unfamiliar to the legal curriculum. The question of where to start elaborating the relevance of globalisation studies for legal theory can appear quite daunting. It is therefore important to be clear what our purpose is in referring to debates about globalisation. Here, we focus on the key issue of whether the pressures on the Nation-State discussed under the rubric of globalisation represent the demise of the paradigm of modernity. This has important implications for legal theory, given the close relationship outlined above between modernity and contemporary understandings of law: if modernity is in crisis, this may require us to revisit some core assumptions of current legal thought. We set the context for this discussion by outlining the main contours of the debates on globalisation, before considering in more detail why this has led to claims of epochal change. We then contrast the response that these challenges can be accommodated by adapting existing legal concepts with the argument that we need to transform the basis of existing legal knowledge. We conclude by considering what law, after modernity, might look like.

Debates about globalisation often divide between globalists, who argue that the Nation-State is no longer the main organising principle of society, and sceptics, for whom globalisation means very little. One key issue is whether the link between national territory and politics is being undermined, with the state being supplanted at the supra-, sub-, and non-State levels as the primary locus of political authority. Claims that technological innovations that compress business time and space have led to the organisation of economic activity on a global scale are met with the response that the global economy is a myth designed to suggest there is no alternative to prevailing neoliberal policies. Some argue that a global culture is being created, evocatively referred to as 'McWorld', while others highlight the still powerful connection between national identity and cultural institutions. These two perspectives on political, economic and cultural globalisation provide helpful tools for engaging with the debates, but they are only a starting point. Moreover, they are far from distinct positions, being connected with varying degrees of complexity. For example, does the development of institutions for regulating the global economy limit the scope for national policy innovation? Are cultural changes driving other forms of globalisation or are they secondary phenomena?

> For an introduction to debates about globalisation, see Held and McGrew (2003).

The question that runs through these debates is whether globalisation represents a period of paradigmatic transition. In other words, do the changes discussed above signal the intensification (but continuation) of existing processes, or do they represent a more fundamental rupture with the past? Are forms of knowledge that take the Nation-State as the privileged unit of analysis still adequate for understanding ongoing changes? This also engages with claims of modernity's political failure: some see the crises attending globalisation as evidence of the Nation-State's inability to deliver its promise of greater emancipation, while others emphasise the resilience of existing institutions. These debates are necessarily linked, and give us a flavour of the politics of globalisation. A paradigmatic reading, which advocates a new framework of inquiry, is generally linked to a transformative political strategy that imagines forms of social organisation beyond neo-liberalism. A sub-paradigmatic reading tends to assume capitalism's continuation, but seeks to adapt the resources of modernity to manage its excesses.

> For an account of paradigmatic and sub-paradigmatic readings of globalisation, see Santos (2002, pp 172 7).

It is fair to say that debates about globalisation were considerably advanced in other disciplines before they caught the attention of lawyers. However, it is now clear that claims that modernity is in paradigmatic crisis require us to consider how this affects our dominant paradigm of law. As with globalisation debates generally, the conceptual and political dimensions are emphasised to varying degrees in the literature. The first concerns the effect of these claims on a knowledge of law rooted in the close connection between territory and formal political authority in the modern State. The second considers the implications of modernity's political failure for the instru-mentalist conception of formal rational law as the principal means of engineering social change, and thus securing progress. As we will see, these dimensions are not unconnected, but we will introduce the discussion by focusing on the conceptual challenges.

We can identify three important ways in which globalisation undermines some deep-rooted assumptions of modern legal thought. First, it makes it increasingly difficult for legal study to be contained within the territorial boundaries of national legal systems. To understand the operation of formal State law, we have to take into account the proliferation of supranational sources of law, such as those emanating from the European Union (EU) or the World Trade Organization (WTO). The obverse of this is that at the international level, sovereignty is being undermined by greater acceptance of interference in the internal affairs of States, for example, through the doctrine of humanitarian intervention. Second, while traditional jurisprudence focused exclusively on municipal and public international law, globalisation requires notice of other forms of legal ordering, such as the *sui generis* legal order of the EU. But not all have a formal pedigree. One prominent example is transnational *lex mercatoria*, which regulates interactions between global commercial firms outside official law through practices such as international arbitration. Other types not readily slotted into standard categorisations include Islamic law, which operates across national boundaries, sometimes in opposition to State law. A third challenge addresses how globalisation may be undermining the cultural specificity of law, and asks whether in response, we can construct a theory of law that reaches across legal cultures. In other words, can we develop a conceptual language that can make sense of the relations between, for example, national and supranational, formal and informal, sub-State and non-State contexts?

Two recent attempts to address the challenges arising from globalisation are found in the work of William Twining and Boaventura de Sousa Santos. In *Globalisation and Legal Theory* (2000), Twining argues that legal theory should respond to these fundamental challenges by reviving general jurisprudence. He distinguishes between particular jurisprudence, which focuses on general aspects of one legal system, and general jurisprudence, which focuses on legal phenomena across jurisdictions. As local legal phenomena need to be viewed in relation to ever-broader contexts, developing general jurisprudence on a global scale is necessary to gain a complete picture of the contemporary global world. This project is linked to rethinking comparative law. For Twining, globalisation highlights the limits of approaches, which are unconcerned with non-State law. However, he believes that a reformulated comparative project can provide students with a helpful account of 'law-in-the-world'. Such a rethinking involves a more serious theoretical engagement with issues of comparison, and could provide maps for navigating between different types of law, such as Scots law, Islamic law and EU law. He suggests that an important task here is to expand the list of concepts included in general jurisprudence to provide more apposite terminology for enhancing understanding across legal cultures. Another is to broaden the range and type of comparators beyond positive State law.[1]

This rethinking of comparative law addresses some of the recurring questions of legal theory, in particular how we separate the legal from the non-legal. Twining sees part of the answer in the unbuckling of law from the State, which attests to the growing importance of legal pluralism. The distinction here is between the view of law as consisting exclusively of State law, and the idea that there are multiple forms of law, whether customary and State law coexisting in postcolonial societies, or non-State forms of law, such as *lex mercatoria*. For Twining, a global perspective reveals 'the coexistence and interaction of legal orders at different levels' (2000, p 228), making legal pluralism central to his general jurisprudence project. However, he does not offer a definitive means of delineating the legal. Instead, he suggests we should see the attributes of law as resting on a continuum, so as not to erect unnecessary barriers between similar phenomena, such as formal and informal ways of resolving disputes.

Twining helps concretise the relation between globalisation and legal study. This changes who the important actors are now, to include, for example,

---

1 To include concepts such as 'group, dispute, institution, process, function, decision, regulation, efficiency and effectiveness'. (2000, p 190).

transnational nongovernmental organisations (NGOs) and multinational companies. It also leads us to expand the places and settings where we would expect to find law. In short, it requires a critical re-examination of core conceptual tools in legal theory. He demonstrates the often-complex relation between paradigmatic and sub-paradigmatic approaches. In conceptual terms, his pluralist account of law is a shift from the dominant statist paradigm. However, in political terms, he is not motivated by a transformative agenda; rather his project is to rework our heritage of ideas so they 'can fit the modern facts'. This is not a purely abstract endeavour, but one that he suggests can yield practical benefits: for example, understanding the limits of current notions of public international law is vital for dealing with problems such as environmental despoliation. However, to the extent he is adapting an existing institutional framework to better address globalisation's challenges, this can be seen to be a sub-paradigmatic approach.

For further discussion of these points, see Twining (2000, especially chs 1, 3 and 7).

By contrast, Boaventura de Sousa Santos contends that the problems engendered by modernity cannot be solved within the latter's intellectual and political resources. His primary motivation is to develop an emancipatory conception of law in response to the political crisis of modernity, ushered in by globalisation. While overtly socio-political, Santos's response to globalisation also addresses our categories of legal knowledge. For him, the two are deeply connected, as it is only by 'unthinking' the current basis of legal knowledge that law's emancipatory potential can be realised.

Santos's theory of law and globalisation is situated within his broader account of the demise of modernity. Modernity established a dynamic tension between regulation (or order) and emancipation (or good order). Its success was predicated on the promise that a sufficient weight of expectations (of emancipation) could be translated into experiences (emancipatory struggles translated into new forms of regulation), so that incompatible values, such as equality and freedom, could be held in balance. This was to be delivered through the Nation-State, applying scientific knowledge through legal instruments. However, he argues that what marks our time is the wholesale collapse of emancipation into regulation, as, for example, the welfare state comes under pressure from the global economy in neoliberal mode.

Santos defines globalisation as 'the process by which a given local condition or entity succeeds in extending its reach over the globe and, by doing so, develops the capacity to designate a rival social condition or entity as local' (2003, p 178). He distinguishes first between two hegemonic forms of globalisation: '*globalized localism*', which is 'the process by which a given local phenomenon is successfully globalized' – for example, the spread of US popular culture – and '*localized globalism*', which connotes 'the specific impact of transnational practices and imperatives on local conditions that are thereby destructured and restructured in order to respond to transnational imperatives' (2003, p 179) – such as the emergence of free trade areas. The core industrialised countries specialise in exporting the former, whereas developing peripheral countries are the prime importers of localised globalisms. Each operates in subparadigmatic mode as they assume the continued existence of global capitalism. Alongside these, he outlines two forms of counterhegemonic globalisation: *subaltern cosmopolitanism*, referring to transnational resistance to hegemonic globalisation, for example, the new forms of political activism under the umbrella of the World Social Forum; and the *common heritage of humankind*, which motivates political struggle around issues such as the depletion of the ozone layer and the proliferation of nuclear weapons. These represent paradigmatic approaches to globalisation as they are addressed to audiences that seek to imagine different forms of social organisation beyond capitalism. Santos is critical of those approaches to law and globalisation that concentrate solely on hegemonic processes, as this neglects the significance of new forms of law, which are emerging from daily struggles in diverse settings.

Santos sees the 'globalisation of the legal field' as a constitutive element in these processes. An important example is the spread of liberal democratic constitutional reforms to newly established democracies in Central and Eastern Europe, and Latin America. While often sponsored by international agencies as the epitome of good governance, Santos sees these reforms as globalised localisms, elevating Western-style democracy as the single global model. However, these processes are not just hegemonic in substance, reinforcing North–South power asymmetries, but also in form through their partial understanding of legal phenomena. Accompanying these reforms is a series of measures designed to shore up the rule of law, for example, by providing for the protection of property rights. Not only is law understood here solely in terms of formal State law, but also this conception is seen as vital to providing the infrastructure for global capitalist activity.

This brings us to the key point of Santos's critique, namely that the reduction of law to State law is a deeply contingent political product of modernity, and which helps explain the latter's emancipatory limits. For Santos, this reduction rests on an artificial distinction between the State and civil society, which obscures the existence of political authority beyond official processes, for example, in the workplace. Moreover, the identification of law solely with the State played a key role in sustaining capitalism. First, autonomous and scientific State law was held up as the instrument for securing societal progress by managing capitalism's worst excesses. But this was also a strategy of depoliticisation, which legitimated the confinement of democratic politics to the State, while excluding them from other sites of social power. So although modernity has, for example, promoted formal democracy in the State, by legislating for equal voting rights among citizens, it has left in place unequal power relations in the workplace.

Santos argues that globalisation makes this limited conception of law implausible when it attempts to describe law as it is and unacceptable as a vision of what law should be. For him, one feature of the paradigmatic transition is the increasing visibility of forms of law beyond the State. This requires us to widen our knowledge to include *inter alia*, the laws generated by transnational corporations, resurgent forms of indigenous law such as the assertion of historic rights by aboriginal peoples, and the broad international human rights regime, which covers the activities of both international agencies and NGOs. The objective is not simply to catalogue different types of law, but also to account for the uneven ways in which they interact with and influence each other – what Santos calls *interlegality*. In this picture, State law is one of a number of legal orders and not necessarily the most influential – often, for example, operating in the shadow of the (legal) norms of the neoliberal global economy.

While Santos appears to share Twining's view that globalisation expands the sites of law production, it is important to see how he links this reconceptualisation of law to the political dimension of globalisation. For Santos, the recoupling of law with social power lies at the heart of the counter-hegemonic agenda. This is not just aspirational rhetoric, as his later work discusses the various struggles, whether campaigns against water privatisation in Latin America or the fight for affordable antiretroviral drugs in Africa, which he sees as providing the basis for new international legal regimes. Thus Santos emphasises the need to consider both hegemonic globalisation from above, but also counter-hegemonic globalisation from below. This necessarily changes how we think about State law, as now only one route among many open to legal activists; but to the extent it can be successfully deployed in a broader campaign of resistance it may retain an emancipatory character. For example, he discusses the transnational coalition for the elimination of sweatshops as an attempt to politicise the law of the workplace in a counter-hegemonic way.

Santos's work provides an ambitious framework for making sense of law and globalisation as part of a broader account of paradigmatic change. His strategic rejection of modernity goes further than Twining in questioning the basic assumptions of Western legal thought. While he shares some of Twining's diagnosis, he parts from him in terms of prescription, casting the project of general jurisprudence as a globalised localism, that wrongly sees conceptual clarification as the urgent task of legal theory in the context of globalisation. The project instead lies in returning law to its emancipatory potential. This requires us to shift our focus away from traditional State legal forms to the practices of oppressed groups. These new forms of law, found in the interstices of the State and in non-Western settings, may appear alien subjects for *legal* study to students educated in the Western tradition. But that is precisely his point: that the paradigmatic transition highlights the ways in which old certainties are being undermined, and which require us to 'unthink' many core assumptions of the modernist conception of law.

See, further, Santos (2003, pp 1–11, 89–98, 177–93 and 465–70). For a discussion of Santos's theory by Twining, see (2000, ch 8).

References

Abel, R, 1986, 'The Decline of Professionalism', 49 *Mod LR* 1.

Cotterrell, R, 1995, 'Legality and Legitimacy: The Sociology of Max Weber', in Cotterrell, *Law's Community*, Oxford: Clarendon.

Durkheim, E, 1933, *The Division of Labour in Society*, New York: The Free Press.

Ewing, S, 1987, 'Formal Justice and the Spirit of Capitalism: Max Weber's Sociology of Law', 21 *Law and Soc Rev* 487–512.

Foucault, M, 1984, 'What is Enlightenment?' in P Rabinow (ed), *The Foucault Reader*, Harmondsworth: Penguin.

Giddens, A, 1971, *Capitalism and Modern Social Theory*, Cambridge: Cambridge University Press.

Held, D and McGrew, A, 2003, 'The Great Globalization Debate: An Introduction', in D Held and A McGrew (eds), *The Global Transformations Reader*, 2nd edn, Cambridge: Polity Press, pp 1–50.

Kant, I, 1991, 'What is Enlightenment?' in H Reiss (ed), *Political Writings*, Cambridge: Cambridge University Press.

Kronman, A, 1983, *Max Weber*, London: Edward Arnold.

Larson, SM, 1977, *The Rise of Professionalism: A Sociological Analysis*, Berkeley: California University Press.

Macaulay, S, 1963, 'Non-contractual Relations in Business: A Preliminary Study', 28 *Am Soc Rev* 55–67.

Marx, K, 1977, 'Preface to *A Critique of Political Economy*', in D McLellan (ed) *Karl Marx. Selected Writings*, Oxford: Oxford University Press.

Murphy, WT, 1997, *The Oldest Social Science? Configurations of Law and Modernity*, Oxford: Oxford University Press.

Rheinstein, M 1954, 'Introduction', in M Rheinstein (ed), *Max Weber on Law in Economy and Society*, Cambridge MA: Harvard University Press.

Santos, B de Sousa, 2002, *Toward a New Legal Common Sense*, 2nd edn, London: Butterworths.

Social & Legal Studies, 2000, Symposium on Contract Law and Legal Theory 397–447.

Turner, B, 1996, *For Weber. Essays on the Sociology of Fate*, London: Sage.

Twining, W, 2000, *Globalisation & Legal Theory*, London: Butterworths.

Unger, RM, 1976, *Law in Modern Society*, New York: The Free Press.

Weber, M, 1930, *The Protestant Ethic and the Spirit of Capitalism*, London: Allen & Unwin.

Weber, M, 1948a, 'Politics as a Vocation', in HH Gerth and CW Mills (eds), *For Max Weber*, London: Routledge & Kegan Paul.

Weber, M, 1948b, 'Science as a Vocation', in HH Gerth and CW Mills, *For Max Weber*, London: Routledge & Kegan Paul.

Weber, M, 1968, *Economy and Society, An Outline of Interpretive Sociology* (2 vols), Berkeley: University of California Press.

Chapter 2

Advanced topics

2.1.1 Introduction

The question at the heart of legal pluralism is what separates law from non-law? For many students, teachers and practitioners of law, the instinctive answer to this is that law is the formal product of the State, consisting primarily of statutes made by legislatures, or the decisions of courts. According to this view, special training is required to become 'learned in the law', and so be able to administer and use it. Legal pluralism contends that this view of law – sometimes referred to as 'lawyers' law' – gives us only a partial account of the nature and scope of law. Instead it is argued that there are many other non-official, often unwritten, normative orders operating in society – whether setting standards for conduct in workplaces, within clubs and associations or among neighbours – which should also be regarded as sources and forms of law.

Legal pluralism presents an alternative paradigm of law to that of legal modernity. As discussed above, the dominant legal understanding that emerged from the eighteenth century onwards saw law as one of the principal achievements of Enlightenment rationality. This view emphasised law's singularity, its universality and its effectiveness. Law was regarded as a coherent body of norms, emanating from a single source – the State; rational law was the culmination of human progress, and the aspiration and mark of all 'civilised' societies; and law was one of the primary instruments of social engineering available to the State, shaping society through various inducements and sanctions. Legal pluralism challenges not only the State-centredness of legal modernity, but also its main attributes. In place of singularity and unity, legal pluralism sees multiplicity and relative disorder; in place of universality, legal pluralism sees legal modernity as but one, deeply contingent, way of imagining law, tied to a particular (European) time and place; in place of effectiveness, legal pluralism highlights the ways in which State law is often stymied by non-State law, and so fails to live up to its own standards of instrumental rationality.

Renewed interest in ideas of legal pluralism is generally attributed to anthropological research, conducted in colonial societies in the mid-twentieth century. The nature of this work – often focused on the customary habits of tribal communities – led to legal pluralism being depicted as 'exotic,' and so kept on the margins of legal study. However, in the 1970s, interest in non-State forms of law extended to the mainstream law and society movement, and more recently ideas of legal pluralism have become a central feature of debates about globalisation. While much of this scholarship was conducted over the past 50 or so years, it is important to note that exponents of legal pluralism claim that they are recovering an older tradition, which was temporarily displaced by legal modernity. We now consider some of the key claims from each of these periods to illustrate the more specific arguments advanced by legal pluralists.

2.1.2 Classical and contemporary legal pluralism

The issue of the basis of legal authority in colonial societies crystallises some of the principal themes of legal pluralism. The paradigm of legal modernity played an important role in justifying European colonialism. According to the Europeans, if land was unoccupied – *terra nullius* – it was open to settlement and governed according to the law of the coloniser. But the territories that the settlers encountered were still occupied by their original inhabitants, and in many cases had been for thousands of years. This problem was overcome by contrasting the stage of development of European societies, with their formal, rational laws, with indigenous forms of social organisation that were deemed 'so low in the scale of social organisation' that they could not be 'reconciled with the institutions or legal ideas of civilized society'.[1] Without law, there could be no rights of ownership on the part of aboriginal peoples and so, as John Locke put it, there could be no injury to them by the assertion of European sovereignty.

Various legal anthropological studies over the past century have disputed the idea that law arrived in modern-day North America, sub-Saharan Africa or Australasia with the European settlers. These studies – often referred to as 'classical legal pluralism' – emphasised two points. First, that indigenous peoples formed relatively complex societies with their own normative structures and forms of political organisation. Legal anthropologists identified many developed systems for regulating social life, whether for exchanging goods, raising children, exploiting the land or settling disputes. These rules were often expressed through (to Western eyes) unfamiliar forms, such as woven belts, and operated within different cultural assumptions – private

---

1 *Re Southern Rhodesia* (1919) AC (PC) 210 at 233.

ownership of land is simply incomprehensible to many indigenous peoples. The settlers did not recognise this as law because it failed to meet their own cultural predispositions (as would be the case with Western law for the aboriginals). The second argument running through classical legal pluralism is that indigenous forms of law did not disappear in the colonial state. Indeed, the coexistence of both formal and indigenous law is said to be the more accurate account of the colonial era (Asch 1997). For example, the early settlers often entered into treaties with aboriginal groups, adopting the latter's rites of solemnification, such as exchange of wampum belts (although, when inconvenient, these treaties were dispensed with by asserting the ultimate authority of the colonial state). Moreover, colonial officials often found it more pragmatic to license the use of customary norms, which in many cases continued to be followed by the local population, to govern areas of social life such as the family (Chanock 1985). Thus legal pluralists argue that claims that official State law provides the sole criterion for legal order simply do not accord with reality.

The key development that marked a move from classical to 'new' or 'postcolonial' legal pluralism was the growth in empirical sociolegal studies. This research adopted a different approach to traditional legal scholarship, concerned less with doctrinal analysis – 'law in the books' – and more with how it operated in practice – 'law in action'. This led many to conclude that an exclusive focus upon State law only gave a limited picture of legal relations in developed countries. An important impetus here was research on forms of alternative dispute resolution (ADR). This demonstrated that citizens who lacked the wherewithal to have access to the formal machinery of justice often cultivated their own informal means of settling disputes (Abel 1982). The idea that informal law was not only to be found in colonial societies was taken forward by other studies, for example, in the field of industrial relations. Legal pluralists here contrasted State labour law with the 'indigenous law of the workplace', such as codes of conduct, informal agreements and customary patterns of behaviour, and argued that the latter were often more important in shaping workers' day-to-day activities (Arthurs 1985b).

The advent of globalisation has further refocused attention on plural forms of legal ordering. This is unsurprising, given that the principal argument across the globalisation literature is that the Nation-State should no longer be the privileged object of study. Some commentators highlight the profusion of sites of formal political authority in the global era, and suggest that citizenship is now necessarily multiple, and that we negotiate our rights and obligations within overlapping legal orders at the subnational, national and supranational levels (see Part III, 1.4 on globalisation). Others argue that the new legal forms, which have helped lubricate the operation of the global economy, can only be explained by a pluralist perspective. For example, an important feature of contemporary economic activity is global *lex mercatoria*, which includes various business practices, codes of conduct, standard form contracts and arbitration awards, all of which can be described without reference to State law. Economic globalisation may also recast what we regard as sources of law, and see multinational corporations as exercising significant normative authority, for example, in setting standards in the fields of agricultural production or medical research (Hertz 2001).

2.1.3 Strong and weak legal pluralism, and the position of the State

It should already be clear that legal pluralism itself takes many forms. One way in which we might characterise different approaches adopted in the various phases is the distinction between 'strong' and 'weak' legal pluralism. According to John Griffiths, 'weak' legal pluralism entails the 'formal acquiescence by the state' in accepting 'different bodies of law for different groups in the population' (1986, pp 7, 5). The archetypal, but not only, example of this is the coexistence within the colonial state of Western and indigenous legal rules, with the State's courts authorising reliance on customary law to resolve disputes before it. Griffiths argues that this situation should not count as proper legal pluralism, as it accepts the State as the ultimate sovereign authority: in our example, customary norms apply because the State legal system 'recognises' them. He contrasts this with 'strong' legal pluralism, which he defines as 'that state of affairs, for any social field, in which behaviour pursuant to more than one legal order occurs' (1986, p 2). Accordingly, State law is but one legal order, whose authorisation is unnecessary for the empirical operation of other forms of law.

A leading account of 'strong' legal pluralism is found in the work of Boaventura de Sousa Santos, in particular his complex 'structure-agency map' of modern capitalist society. Santos posits six structural places – the householdplace, the workplace, the marketplace, the communityplace, the citizenplace and the worldplace. Each generates its own distinct form of law: for example, the domestic law of the householdplace refers to the unwritten codes that govern social relations within the family, while the exchange law of the marketplace denotes the trade customs and normative standards operating among producers, merchants and consumers. For Santos, the actual legal rules that apply at any one time are not dependent on one type of law, but will necessarily be a combination of the different forms. For example, the legal regulation of the family includes a mixture of formal State law and informal domestic law.

The distinction between strong and weak legal pluralism is a controversial one, and not everyone accepts Griffiths's dismissive stance towards the latter. It highlights though that attitudes towards the State remain an important fault line within legal pluralist scholarship. This raises important methodological and normative issues. Regarding the former, legal pluralists have sought to provide a definition of law that captures the full range of legal phenomena.[2] However, Brian Tamanaha (1993) claims that many of these attempts underscore the difficulty of conceiving of law without reference to the State. He argues that legal pluralists tend to posit their criteria for law by focusing on what appears essential to State law – whether the enforcement of norms or the resolution of disputes – but then subtracting the indicia of the State from this equation. For him, this shows that the State remains the starting point even for some leading pluralist accounts of law.

A related question is whether, even if legal pluralism could escape the analytical framework of State law, it is desirable that it should. This addresses the connection between description and prescription in legal pluralism. While Griffiths argues that legal pluralism is simply a fact, it is part of his mission to debunk the 'ideology' of centralising approaches that hold that law *ought* to be the law of the State. It would seem to follow that legal pluralists think that law ought to be regarded other than in State-centred terms, and some writers appear to valorise non-State forms of law for their own sake. Others though are concerned by the normative implications of this position. First, they suggest there is no special reason to believe that plural forms of law will be necessarily progressive: for example, some sociolegal scholars saw the rise of ADR as problematic as it potentially restored the advantages of the financially and socially powerful, which the formal law had sought to equalise. Moreover, to confer the term 'law', with its connotations that what is lawful is right or moral, on some aspects of social life, is to confer upon them a legitimacy that they do not deserve (for example, the often oppressive regimes generated within prisons) (Tamanaha 2000).

These are important questions, but to some extent, they are unanswerable within their own terms: how, for example, do we 'prove' what law is? Rather, they direct us to an inquiry into the usefulness of plural understandings of law, and the objectives that they serve, to which we now turn.

2.1.4 Empirical, conceptual and political approaches to legal pluralism

The points just discussed highlight the importance of the qualifying adjective. In traditional terms, State law is simply 'law,' while plural forms of law, such as indigenous or informal law, require qualification or demotion, so that they are customs, or habits, or social norms, but not law. There are various strategies that legal pluralists employ to cast off the burden of the qualifying adjective, and so affirm that they are indeed talking about law. We might

---

2 Santos (2002, p 86) defines law as 'a body of regularized procedures and normative standards, considered justiciable – i.e. susceptible of being enforced by a judicial authority – in any given group, which contributes to the creation and prevention of disputes, and to their settlement through an argumentative discourse, coupled with the threat of force'.

categorise these strategies on the basis of their empirical, conceptual and political emphases (although these categories are far from watertight, and overlap in practice).

Empirical approaches to legal pluralism seek to provide a more comprehensive account of the actual norms that influence everyday life, and argue that this requires a broader research field than an exclusive focus on State law. This engages with the influential command theory of law, that is, that through people's subservience to law, the State can direct the future shape of society. Legal pluralists argue that if this is what distinguishes State law as law, then it frequently fails to live up to this ideal. Moreover, other forms of normative order often seem better to approximate the special characteristics claimed for State law. In place of the model of (State) law acting upon a passive society, legal pluralists see it as constantly interacting with other legal orders. For example, to return to the example of relations in the family, the limitations of State law in addressing problems such as domestic violence can be attributed to the fact that it does not wholly displace the (often patriarchal) norms of domestic law. The objective here is to understand better how the interaction between these different forms of law may facilitate or impede different policy objectives.

While empirical approaches may lead to a more nuanced account of State law, with more feasible expectations, it could still be objected that we lose conceptual clarity if the category of law becomes overbroad. Conceptual approaches to legal pluralism respond by arguing that the singularity associated with State-centered views provides a distorted basis for legal study, and necessarily gives way, once we accept that law reflects the society within which it is embedded. This approach is grounded in a pluralistic social theory, which views social life in terms of a disorganised struggle between different groups. Seeing law as one part of a larger web of varied and complex social relations, it is argued that legal relations must also be asymmetrical (Sampford 1991). This goes further than some empirical approaches: not only is law decoupled from the state, but also all forms of law tend towards disorder and incoherence. From this perspective, even if our focus is on State law, this has to be recast as inherently plural, with full account taken of its crosscurrents and contradictions (and so the difference between strong and weak legal pluralism may not be as pronounced as has been suggested).

One might accept that the empirical and conceptual approaches present important challenges to traditional legal thought, but still insist there is value in maintaining the distinction between law and other social norms. This brings us to the political dimension of legal pluralism, which reverses the inquiry so far conducted, and asks what purposes are served by presenting State law as the sole category for legal study. For Santos, this reflects less an analytical imperative, and more the operation of a politics of definition designed to portray the State as the only form of political authority in society. He argues that the main consequence of this politics of definition is to mask other sites of social power, and their attendant forms of law, such as the market.[3] Thus the political purpose of pluralising law is not to suggest a moral equivalence, say, between norms produced by States and multinational corporations; rather, it seeks to expand questions about the legitimate use of power across all those institutions (State and non-State) which exercise coercive power.

2.1.5 Future directions in legal pluralism

Ideas of legal pluralism now occupy a more prominent place in legal scholarship than was historically the case, and have recently been employed to address mainstream subjects such as constitutional law (Anderson 2005) and international law (Koskenniemi 2007). With this expanded interest, debates within and about legal pluralism have continued to adapt, and we conclude by briefly discussing three key innovations in the literature. The first, variously termed 'governmentality' or 'governance', can be considered less an elaboration of legal pluralism than a cognate development within a different intellectual tradition. This school of thought emerged from Michel Foucault's social theory, and focuses on the various agencies, techniques and forms of knowledge that seek to govern human behaviour (see Part III, 2.4 below; see, also, Dean 1999). There are strong affinities with legal pluralism to the extent that it is concerned with normative regimes beyond the State: for example, a major strand of research considers the extent to which the governance of security is now located beyond the State (Shearing and Wood 2003, pp 402–3). There are, though, important differences of emphasis, with governance more interested in how social problems are created in the first place, than necessarily with the interaction between different normative systems (Rose and Valverde 1998).

A second approach follows the 'linguistic turn' in political philosophy, and seeks to develop a form of legal pluralism that is both sensitive to the limitations of the State-centered conception, and retains a distinction between law and social norms. The solution, it suggests, lies in a conventionalist approach under which law is what people generally designate as law. Gunther Teubner, one of the leading exponents of this view, argues, for example, that global commercial practices should be seen as a form of law (*lex mercatoria* discussed above), as the binary coding 'legal/illegal' is used by key actors, such as international arbitrators (Teubner 1997, p 4). While this approach may provide a relatively straightforward threshold test for the existence of law, it has been criticised on the grounds that it retains the view that certain functions are essential to law – on Teubner's terms, the controlling and co-ordinating

---

3 For discussion of the operation of the politics of definition in the context of globalisation, see Part III, 1.4 above.

behaviour – which are ultimately derived from the State-based understanding (Tamanaha 2000, pp 308, 312–21).

An approach that seeks to avoid any preconceived notion of how law should be defined comes under the rubric of critical legal pluralism (Kleinhans and Macdonald 1997). This departs from empirically based scholarship, arguing that techniques of mapping tend to see law in positivist terms as something that can be measured 'out there', apart from the human agents who created it. Critical legal pluralists reject this view of law as external knowledge, and instead highlight the role of knowledge in creating our perception of reality. This results in a different test for legal order. The focus is no longer simply on which external legal order exercises normative authority over individuals: we also have to ask within which legal order do individuals regard themselves as acting. This places more emphasis on the legal subject, who is not just a passive recipient of law, but has an active role in producing and shaping legal knowledge. As we perceive ourselves to be working within different legal orders at different times, the legal knowledge produced, and as perhaps the various views canvassed in this section affirms will be necessarily and irretrievably plural.

Reading

A helpful overview of the principal differences between legal pluralism and State-centered accounts of law is found in Arthurs (1985, ch 1). For a discussion of the shift from 'classical' to 'new' legal pluralism, see Merry (1988, pp 872–4), and for the application of ideas of legal pluralism in the context of globalisation, see Santos (2002, pp 194–200). For a review of the debate concerning the utility of the distinction between strong and weak legal pluralism, see Woodman (1998). Davies (2005) highlights the various empirical and conceptual strands within legal pluralist scholarship, and for an elaboration of the 'politics of definition' see Santos (2002, pp 89–91). For a discussion of critical legal pluralism, and its responses to some of Tamanaha's criticisms, see Kleinhans and Macdonald (1997, pp 30–43).

References

Abel, R (ed), 1982, *The Politics of Informal Justice, Vols. 1 and 2*, New York: Academic Press.
Anderson, GW, 2005, *Constitutional Rights after Globalization*, Oxford and Portland, OR: Hart.

Arthurs, HW, 1985a, *Without the Law*, Toronto and Buffalo: University of Toronto Press.

Arthurs, HW, 1985b, 'Understanding Labour Law: The Debate over "Industrial Pluralism" ', 38 *Current Legal Problems* 83.

Asch, M, (ed), 1997, *Aboriginal and Treaty Rights in Canada: Essays on Law, Equality and Respect for Difference*, Vancouver: University of British Columbia Press.

Chanock, M, 1985, *Law, Custom and Social Order: The Colonial Experience in Malawi and Zambia*, Cambridge: Cambridge University Press.

Davies, M, 2005, 'The Ethos of Pluralism', 27 *Syd Law Rev* 87.

Dean, M, 1999, *Governmentality: Power and Rule in Modern Society*, London: Sage.

Hertz, N, 2001, *The Silent Takeover: Global Capitalism and the Death of Democracy*, London: Heinemann.

Griffiths, J, 1986, 'What is Legal Pluralism?', 24 *J Leg Pluralism* 1.

Kleinhans, M-M and Macdonald RA, 1997, 'What is a Critical Legal Pluralism?', 12 *Canadian Journal of Law and Society* 25.

Koskenniemi, M, 2007, 'Global Legal Pluralism: Multiple Regimes and Multiple Modes of Thought', forthcoming in *Eur J Int Law*.

Merry, SE, 1988, 'Legal Pluralism', 22 *Law & Soc Rev* 869.

Rose, N and Valverde, M, 1998, 'Governed by Law?', 7 *Soc & Leg Stud* 541.

Sampford, C, 1991, *The Disorder of Law*, Oxford: Blackwell.

Santos, B, 2002, *Toward and new common legal sense*, London: Butterworth.

Shearing, C and Wood, J, 2003, 'Nodal Governance, Democracy, and the New "Denizens" ', 30 *Jnl of Law & Soc* 400.

Tamanaha, BZ, 1993, 'The Folly of the "Social Scientific" Concept of Legal Pluralism', 20 *Jnl of Law & Soc* 192.

Tamanaha, BZ, 2000, 'A Non-Essentialist Version of Legal Pluralism', 27 *Jnl of Law & Soc* 296.

Teubner, G (ed), 1997, *Global Law Without a State*, Gateshead: Athenaeum Press.

Woodman, GR, 1998, 'Ideological Combat and Social Observation', 42 *Jnl of Leg Pluralism* 21.

2.2 Juridification

2.2.1 Introductory remarks

A development that has preoccupied many recent theorists of legal modernity has been the growth in the scale and scope of legal regulation in the modern State, a phenomenon that can be described as the *juridification* of social relations. This, indeed, has become a central theme in contemporary political debates over the role of the State, with (broadly speaking) politicians of the right decrying the overregulation of the economy and society, and arguing for a reduction in the amount of legal regulation, and politicians of the left defending the necessity of such regulation as a means of remedying social inequalities produced by the operation of the market. This is a debate that has taken on added significance in the context of globalisation. On the one hand, the emergence of supranational bodies such as the European Union (EU), which seek to regulate the conditions of labour and production at a supra-State level, has led to political clashes over questions of national sovereignty and the 'democratic deficit' in European institutions. On the other, the globalisation of the economy has greatly facilitated the capacity of economic producers, such as multinational corporations, to evade or shape particular regulatory regimes, leading to concerns about the impact of certain practices on the environment, and on the health and working conditions of workers in particular industries. It is not our intention to take sides in this particular debate, though it is important to understand the way that these debates are connected to jurisprudential themes. Our purpose is rather to open a different perspective on these debates by situating them in the context of our understanding of legal modernity.

The central issues here are, first, how to explain the growth of legal regulation, and second, what this can tell us about the place of law in the modern State. Underlying these issues, there is the broader question – a theme that runs through the whole of this part of the book – that of whether the development can be understood and explained within the paradigm of modernity, or whether we need to develop new theoretical resources in order to understand these processes. Before we go on, however, we must set out a basic description of the phenomenon of juridification.

We can imagine juridification as having both horizontal and vertical dimensions. Horizontally, we can observe that in modern society law increasingly spreads its regulatory reach across an increasingly diverse range of social activities – a feature that corresponds to Weber's observations about the instrumentalisation of modern law. It has spread, for example, into areas that were formerly considered private and beyond the proper reach of the law, such as aspects of domestic and family relations; it has spread into the area of what were once considered as matters purely of nature, such as the environment, genetics and life and death (as one recent English Court of Appeal judge recently put it, 'Deciding disputed matters of life and death is surely and pre-eminently a matter for a court of law to judge')[4]; and it has spread increasingly – though incompletely and unevenly – into the political realm. This has led public law theorist, Martin Loughlin, to comment that one of the most important features of this, our 'age of rights', is that the 'politicization of law' goes hand in hand with the 'legalisation of politics' (2000, ch 13). In each realm legal norms gain prominence as a means of organising factual and normative aspects of social relations, which were previously under- or unregulated by law. The vast increase in legislation in recent years (at subnational, national, and supranational levels, for example), as well as more popular perceptions of ours being an increasingly litigious society are both symptomatic of this trend.

In tandem with this, the vertical aspect concerns the ways in which legal norms not only tighten their hold on already or newly regulated areas through increased legislation or judicial activity, but do so by way of increasingly detailed normative standards. That is, rather than legal standards being general principles of reasonably broad coverage, there is an observable tendency for these standards to become more detailed in their specification of the factual circumstances that are being legally regulated. Again, this is observable across a broad range of areas of legal practice, such as administrative, corporate and criminal law: the United Kingdom, for example, has seen the creation of more than 3,000 new criminal offences in the last decade – offences that tend to be concerned with detailing more and more precisely the operative facts, rather than in producing whole swathes of new forms of criminality.

Juridification, then, in the words of Jürgen Habermas, one of the leading analysts of this phenomenon:

> refers quite generally to the tendency toward an increase in formal (or positive, written) law that can be observed in modern society. We can distinguish here between the *expansion* of law, that is the legal regulation of new, hitherto informally regulated social matters, from the *increasing density* of law, that is the specialized breakdown of global statements of the legally relevant facts into more detailed statements.

(1987, p 357)

2.2.2 Habermas on juridification

Habermas argues that the process of juridification can generally be understood as part of a series of processes by which the modern State and economy

4 *Re A* [2000] 4 All ER 961 per Ward, LJ at 987.

developed as distinctive bodies or systems that operate subject to their own distinctive rationalities. While the spheres of politics and the economy are increasingly subject to the instrumental demands to reproduce systems of power and money, the rest of society – which he designates by the term the *lifeworld* – operates according to a noninstrumental, communicative rationality. Juridification, then, is a process by which system and lifeworld, and the relationships between them, are legally structured and regulated. This process facilitates the growth of the capitalist economy but also, and crucially, establishes and guarantees political and social liberty as the State seeks to legitimise its actions through the concession of political rights and freedoms.

He designates four distinctive epochs or thrusts of juridification. These begin in the seventeenth century with the emergence of the bourgeois State and the capitalist market economy. Here law is primarily concerned with regulating relations between individual commodity or property owners, and the authorisation of a 'sovereign state power with a monopoly on coercive force as the sole source of legal authority' (1987, p 358). That is to say that the legal order formally guarantees both the capacity of private individuals to own and alienate commodities in the market, through the laws of contract and property, and the political liberty and security of the individual, to the extent that it does not conflict with the security of the State. What is crucial here is the drawing of the distinction between public (the State) and civil society or the private, which is left unregulated. The succeeding epochs see the expansion of the scope of civil society vis à vis the State, as the lifeworld makes demands on the State for greater political freedoms, but these come at the cost of the increasing legal regulation (juridification) of social relations.

The second and third epochs, then, are the development of the constitutional State and the democratic constitutional State. In both these stages 'the idea of freedom already incipient in the concept of law as developed in the natural law tradition was given constitutional force' (1987, pp 360–1). In general terms, State power was first constitutionalised, giving citizens rights against the State (for example, not to be detained or punished except by due process of law), then democratised, as citizens were given rights to political participation (with, for example, the extension of the suffrage and the freedom to organise political associations and parties). Political power is thus made subject to law and then, with the juridification of the legitimation process, its legitimacy is anchored in the democratic process.

While the first three stages mirror Weber's account of the achievements of legal modernity, as in Weber's account we see a more complex and ambivalent picture emerging in the fourth epoch. Here Habermas suggests that while the welfare state continues the line of freedom-guaranteeing juridification of the earlier epochs by 'the institutionalizing in legal form of a social power relation anchored in class structure' (1987, p 361), it does so in ways that, in fact, restrict freedom. Where the capitalist economy, supported by the laws of contract and property, had permitted the unlimited pursuit of self-interest and tolerated the resultant inequality and social deprivation, the welfare state sought to regulate the economy and intervene in the social sphere (or life-world) to mitigate the worst effects of the capitalist system. Classic examples of the juridification of economic relations would be measures to improve working conditions, the right to unionise and collective bargaining, and so on – all of which seek to protect or enhance the freedom of labour. Other social welfare measures can be described as the 'juridification of life-risks', including measures such as State provision of pensions and benefits, socialised healthcare, public education and so on – measures which seek to secure individuals against economic risks and to improve equality of opportunity. While these measures aim to guarantee freedom, Habermas contends that bureaucratic interventions in the lifeworld may also limit freedom by creating new forms of dependency. This occurs because bureaucracies must, of necessity, intervene in ways that require individuals to conform to general legal conditions in return for monetary compensation. This abstracts individuals from their life-situations, obscures the more general social conditions that might have given rise to particular problems, and damages pre-existing networks of social support or communication. Juridical intervention demands a restructuring – or 'colonisation' – of the lifeworlds of those entitled to social security. As he puts it generally:

> The negative effects of this wave of juridification do not appear as side effects; they result *from the very form of juridification itself*. It is now the very means of guaranteeing freedom that endangers the freedom of the beneficiaries.
>
> (1987, p 362)

He thus concludes by pointing to the *dilemmatic* structure of this type of juridification:

> [W]hile the welfare-state guarantees are intended to serve the goal of social integration, they nevertheless promote the disintegration of life-relations when these are separated, through legalized social intervention, from the consensual mechanisms that coordinate action and are transferred over to media such as power and money.
>
> (1987, p 364)

2.2.3 Juridification and the 'regulatory trilemma'

Where Habermas sees the problem of juridification in the dilemma of under- or overregulation, Gunther Teubner's analysis of juridification suggests that it should rather be understood in terms of a 'trilemma'.

Teubner begins by asking why it is that many regulatory initiatives, such as attempts to limit polluting emissions, fail. He suggests that among the many reasons why such a measure might fail – expensive and inaccurate means to detect marginal violations, corruption, excessive budgetary costs on industry due to enforced slowdowns, and so on – is a response that we might even deem, expected. Industry's typical response will be to deal with the penalties of breaching the law as an added cost. And, more often than not, such costs enter the balance sheets and are returned to consumers in terms of higher prices for the products without any effect on environmental damage. Or, to take another perhaps more complex problem, a government committed to fair housing policies may introduce measures to prevent landlords from raising rents. As a direct economic result of such a policy, capital is redirected away from the housing industry towards more lucrative ventures. As a result, tenants find themselves in a housing market where the rents are manageable, but there is very little supply of rented accommodation.

Note that in these scenarios we have crossings of boundaries between the political, legal and economic systems. A political demand (for cleaner environment, for cheaper housing) is *translated* into a legal measure, operating a distinction between what is legal and illegal (penalties, fixity of rents), which is then *re-translated* by the economy into a language of prices and costs. Teubner identifies the problem of regulatory failure as the mistranslations that have occurred from each system using a different register to translate the 'stimulus' they receive: in the political system in which the demand is generated it is about the use of power; the legal system 'picks up' that demand as one that has to do with acting legally or illegally; the economic system picks it up in terms of what makes good economic sense. In this process the systems (political, legal, economic) do not operate causally on each other, but through what Teubner, following Niklas Luhmann, calls 'structural coupling'. It is a moment of reciprocal interference that sends each of the 'interacting' systems in the direction that the limited range of its own possible responses preordains. Regulatory failures are a direct result of this inevitable mismanagement, inevitable because of the change of register that any 'structural coupling' between systems involves.

Teubner thus invites us to think about 'juridification' in the context of the increased instrumentalisation of law in the regulatory State. This use of law stumbles, he argues, on a 'regulatory trilemma', which confronts it with three possibilities – all three detrimental: 'either [to be] irrelevant, or produce disintegrating effects on the social area of life or else disintegrating effects on regulatory law itself' (1987, p 21). What do these three options mean? The first – indifference – denotes an absence of impact: the law has failed to make its demands felt at all and has had no regulatory effect. In the second case, regulation has a disintegrating effect on the field it attempts to regulate: under the bombardment of regulation the field loses its distinctive character, and becomes in a sense, 'colonised' by the legal medium. Examples of this kind of failure abound: think of the family and the way the legalisation of reciprocity within it in terms of rights and duties erodes what we value most about it; or systems of childcare, where bureaucratic–legal criteria come to colonise and substitute for what are hugely nuanced and difficult judgements over what is in the best interests of the child in any concrete case. In the final horn of the trilemma it is law itself, the regulatory mechanism, that in a sense becomes 'colonised' by its object. If the law, in order to avoid riding roughshod through the societal field it is called to regulate, attempts instead to introduce too much complexity in order to respond more sensitively to its object, it runs the risk of undermining itself as a system. That is because the law draws its identity from introducing *general* standards and subsuming individual cases under them. If it is responding on an ad hoc, case-to-case, basis, readjusting itself as it goes, then it no longer provides that certainty and stability of expectations that it must produce and guarantee, leading to the disintegration of what was distinctive about law.

In locating the problem in the specific context of regulatory law, Teubner (unlike Habermas) invites us to understand juridification as a pathology associated with this type of law. Juridification becomes an umbrella term to cover questions of the function, legitimacy, structure and success of this 'managerial' type of law. Teubner pursues the explanation as a question of 'structural coupling' between the political system, where regulatory strategies are hammered out, the legal system, which is the former's means of implementing that policy, and the social field to be regulated, each with its own autonomous logic that defies direct manipulation. Problems of juridification then appear as failures to respect the boundaries and logics of the systems involved. It is all too easy to overstep boundaries on all sides in this delicate process; the result of such overstepping is experienced as juridification.

From within this theoretical framework, only two options remain open in respect of our ability to act through law to fashion our own future. The first is a conservative, laissez-faire option, espoused by Hayek and renewed by Luhmann, which calls us to respect differentiation and the autonomy and integrity of different systems. A functionally differentiated society is one that has no 'centre' remaining from which social demands can be articulated and directed to other systems. If we do not, however, want to give up on the possibilities of intervention, Teubner's social democratic alternative attempts to base such possibilities in the concept of 'reflexive' law – a procedural alternative to substantive intervention. This circumvents the regulatory trilemma by avoiding direct intervention and instead seeking to guarantee the conditions for autonomy and self-reproduction in the system under regulation.

2.2.4 Juridification as depoliticisation

These two approaches to juridification identify it as a crisis of the legal system, a problem that emerges with the growth of regulatory law in the welfare state. The instrumentalisation of law damages social relations (Habermas) or undermines the function of the legal system (Teubner); the response to this must be to limit the function of law by respecting the autonomy of the legal system. An alternative approach, however, sees juridification as a political problem – that is to say a problem that arises as a result of the legal system appropriating, or juridifying, conflicts that should more properly be dealt with politically. On this view, political disputes or problems are distorted by being made to fit legal categories; legal reasoning (which is oriented towards fitting particular cases within pre-existing general rules) excludes the possibility of a consensual or future-oriented resolution. This view does not start from an assumption of the autonomy of the legal system, but sees law as a tool (or strategy) that might be used by the state for the control or management of social relations. The crisis, then, is not one of law, but one that legal regulation brings about in the social field to be regulated (Santos 2002, pp 55–61).

Perhaps the most revealing historical examples of this kind of expropriation are in the area of labour law and industrial relations. It is in fact in this context that the term itself originates, in the polemical writings of early labour lawyers in Germany for whom 'juridification' was explicitly a moment of depoliticisation of industrial conflict, which could only properly be conceived and played out in political, class-conflictual terms. To use legal categories instead of political ones in the workplace not only alienates workers from a conflict that is vital to their sense of identity and their plight, but also hands it over to legal experts and disempowers them further.

The idea that juridification involves 'depoliticisation' is not of course confined to the sphere of industrial relations and labour law. It is in fact possible to establish that the *increasing density* of law can be witnessed in the regulatory modes employed generally by governments, national and supranational. These modes may themselves be more or less public, may themselves exist in regulatory competition, and overall will tend to an increasing specialisation of knowledge and norms in comparison with traditional legal principles. Of greatest importance here is the observation that while a range of legal mechanisms are used to discipline actors and practices, there is no necessary correspondence – in ideal or practice – to furthering goals of political freedom, in particular since the trajectory of freedom-enhancing measures in the pursuit of social or public goods is no longer paramount. Instead, the density of regulation, and the importance of private law mechanisms in this juridical matrix, is geared largely or almost exclusively to economic or efficiency ends.

What are we to take from all this? One response is to see these developments as symptomatic of a general decline in politics, what Isaiah Berlin (1969) saw as the demise of genuine political disagreement and its replacement with debate over means only. Evidence of this is normally of the kind that draws attention to voter apathy, the decline of differences between political parties, and the almost total demise of genuinely influential public political deliberation. However, what is significant is the way that the adherence to particular regulatory regimes or frameworks is used to 'depoliticise' certain issues. So, for example, the augmented and privileged role of private law as an institutional mechanism in public and economic life (in private finance initiatives (PFIs) or the contracting out of government services) acts to signal a decline in political participation in favour of corporate influence and demands.

These changes are not only taking place at a national level, but are replicated at the transnational and global level. The 'constitution of global capital', as Stephen Gill calls it, is made up of institutional mechanisms that discipline markets and States, forcing States, for example, to restructure market and regulatory institutions internally in return for loans or investment. This is done, says Gill, to accord with the 'Three Cs': confidence of investors, consistency of policies and credibility of governments (2000). In this sense, national, but also EU institutions and policies, have to adapt to transnational networks and deregulated markets, such as agreements on competition in services and intellectual property in formerly locally protected markets. Significantly, these forces are locked in through more or less formal legal agreements and conventions, and are implemented by a range of legal institutions – EU, WTO, IMF, central banks – operating at different levels of locality. For these reasons it is appropriate to talk about a 'constitution' of global capitalism.

It is arguable, however, that rather than representing a depoliticisation, these trends could also, or perhaps better, be understood as an immense *repoliticisation* in favour of a certain style of politics. This politics is geared to the naturalisation of unequal distribution of resources and opportunities, to its enforcement through disciplinary mechanisms (including law and the sanctity of contracts and private governance regimes) and in which democratic participation, where it exists at all, tends to be merely formal. Pierre Bourdieu talked insightfully of this 'new' politicisation as:

> a conservative revolution . . . a strange revolution that restores the past but presents itself as progressive, transforming regression itself into a form of progress. It does this so well that those who oppose it are made to appear regressive themselves.
>
> (Bourdieu and Grass 2002, p 65)

2.2.5 A fifth epoch?

The analysis so far has analysed juridification from the perspective of regulatory law in the welfare state, but it could be contended that recent developments, such as those referred to in the last section, require us to develop a new theoretical framework for the analysis of juridification. Should we, in other words, be asking whether we have entered a fifth epoch?

The starting point for this would be the observation that the welfare state is variously seen in many westernised countries as being in decline, under pressure, or, more actively, being dismantled. The postwar ideals and institutions that saw its establishment and development, and around which there existed a broad political consensus, have decayed to a point where the very existence of the welfare state might be in doubt. Such developments, it is important to note, do not signify the triumph of the free market over the State. Rather the State has realigned itself in relation to capital (and in particular corporate capital) in such a way as to demonstrate that the State and the market are not in competition. We can thus identify an increased 'marketisation' of social life in areas formerly considered public. This takes many forms, but is most commonly carried through by the privatisation of the delivery of public goods and services (and in some cases the privatisation of these as public goods themselves). The UK in particular has successfully pioneered and exported models of 'private finance initiative' (rechristened 'public private partnerships (PPP)' by New Labour) where companies pursue profit through the provision of public services, such as schools and hospitals, both in terms of investment capital and ongoing management and delivery. The processes of individualisation and moneterisation established in the fourth epoch continue, but no longer simply in the guise of public-welfare entitlements, but rather as part of a complex web of private or 'public–private' economic relations.

Central to this process is the re-embedding of private law mechanisms – contract and property law in particular – within formerly public, state-owned areas. These carry with them techniques (such as commercial confidentiality clauses, etc.) that exclude more conventional public supervision. In addition, these mechanisms themselves are structured within competition law frameworks, which draw on supranational legal sources, and which at the academic level have seen demands for the convergence of private law at a conceptual level: the development of European private law codes, harmonisation of trade and contract laws, UNIDROIT, etc. Together, these signal a decentralisation of power in contrast to the welfare state model, but also a reconfiguration of power at the supranational level. As MacNeil has put it:

> These 'private' institutions [such as corporations] are delocalized, being almost totally mobile. Many dwarf half the 'sovereign' countries of the world. By their power over money, information and communication they can and do manipulate and control even the largest of 'sovereigns'.
>
> (MacNeil 2000, p 431)

One could say more about these processes, but together they might suggest that a new epoch of juridification is upon us. If we map these changes onto Habermas's definitions we may note the following. First, there can be little doubt about the increased volume of formal law within particular states and in the EU more generally. This might best be seen as part of a longer trajectory, that in itself does not amount to a new epoch. However, when we consider that aspect, which identifies the *expansion* of law, we find that regulatory activity has in fact expanded into new areas. To take only one, emblematic example: the regulation of biomedical sciences and, in particular, those relating to genetics – human, animal and plant – exemplifies a rethinking of the very means and modes of the reproduction of basic social and material life.

Crucially, however, regulation in this and other areas is driven by private enterprise and the desire for commodification, and only secondarily as a public welfare concern. It is for this reason that we can speculate whether the fourth epoch of juridification identified by Habermas is giving way to a fifth.

Reading

For a general account of the epochs of juridification and the problems encountered by law in the fourth epoch, see Habermas (1987, pp 357–73). Teubner (1987) presents a challenge to this interpretation of the problems of juridification. There is some useful background discussion in Cotterrell (1992, pp 65–70 and ch 9), and the debate between Rottleuthner (1989) and Smith (1991), and the further response in Teubner (1992) provides further illustration of the issues here.

For historical accounts linking juridification to the development of the welfare state see Kamenka and Tay (1975) and Unger (1976, pp 58–66, 192–223), and for a critical dismissal of the whole debate, see Santos (2002, pp 55–61).

The question of whether we have entered a fifth epoch of juridification is addressed in Veitch (2004).

References

Berlin, I, 1969, 'Political Ideas in the Twentieth Century', in *Four Essays on Liberty*, Oxford: Oxford University Press.

Bourdieu, P and Grass, G, 2002, 'The "Progressive" Restoration: A Franco–German Dialogue', *New Left Review* (Mar/Apr) 62–77.

Cotterrell, R, 1992, *The Sociology of Law. An Introduction*, 2nd edn, London: Butterworths.

Gill, S, 2000, 'The Constitution of Global Capitalism' at www.theglobalsite.ac.uk/press/010gill.pdf

Habermas, J, 1987, *The Theory of Communicative Action. Vol. 2 Lifeworld and System*, Cambridge: Polity Press.

Kamenka, E and Tay, AE, 1975, 'Beyond Bourgeois Individualism: The Contemporary Crisis in Law and Legal Ideology', in E Kamenka and RS Neale (eds), *Feudalism, Capitalism and Beyond*, London: Edward Arnold, pp 127–44.

Loughlin, M, 2000, *Sword and Scales*, Oxford: Hart Publishing.

MacNeil, I, 2000, 'Contracting Worlds and Essential Contract Theory', *Social & Legal Studies* p 431.

Rottleuthner, H, 1989, 'The Limits of the Law: The Myth of a Regulatory Crisis', 17 *Intnl Jnl of Soc of Law* 273–85.

Santos, B de Sousa, 2002, *Toward a New Legal Common Sense*, 2nd edn, London: Butterworths.

Smith, SC, 1991, 'Beyond "Mega-Theory" and "Multiple Sociology": A Reply to Rottleuthner', 19 *Intnl Jnl of Soc of Law* 321–40.

Teubner, G, 1987, 'Juridification: Concepts, Aspects, Limits, Solutions', in G Teubner (ed), *Juridification of Social Spheres*, Berlin: de Gruyter.

Teubner, G, 1992, 'Regulatory Law: Chronicle of a Death Foretold', 1 *Soc & Leg Stud* 451–75.

Unger, RM, 1976, *Law in Modern Society*, New York: The Free Press.

Veitch, S, 2004, 'Legal Right and Political Amnesia', in K Nuotio (ed), *Europe in search of 'meaning and purpose'*, Helsinki: Faculty of Law, University of Helsinki, pp 89–106.

2.3 Law, ideology and legitimation: the Marxist critique

2.3.1 Introduction

While there is very little direct engagement in Marx's writings with law, there can be little doubt that as the institution in which coercive power is organised and through which the power of the State is exercised, the institution of law is at the centre of the Marxist denunciation of exploitation and oppression under conditions of capitalist production.

Marxism offers a theory of society in which the key determinant of its organisation is its mode of production. The primacy of the economy as determining in the last instance the shape and function of all institutions in society has led some Marxists to underestimate the significance of law in the working of capitalism. As we saw earlier, Marx used the metaphor of the 'base' and 'superstructure' to describe social structure (see Part III, 1.1 above). The mode of production forms the base of every society, determining its shape and the nature of its institutions, in the same way as the foundations determine and delimit the shape of whatever building rests upon them. The economy thus acts upon the institutions of civil society in a way that can be described as broadly causal. The organisation of our economic activity will determine the type of political, legal, religious, educational, cultural and so on, institutions that we have. Law, which is thus located among the institutions of the superstructure, is also in keeping with the conditions of the mode of production. Its operation broadly reflects the necessities of the mode of production and its function is to maintain and consolidate these economic relations.

Why is this function of maintaining and reproducing the relations of production – as performed by the institutions of the 'superstructure' – so important? To see this we must take a few steps back. Marx's point of departure is the image of the productive man, who only realises the true nature of the 'species-being' through creative labour. As history, for Marx, is conceived in terms of a continuing process of creation, satisfaction and reproduction of needs (as opposed to animals whose needs are fixed), man's interchange with the material world to create the means to satisfy those needs becomes the very foundation of society. Labour underlies man's relation to the material world and his relations to others: since production requires co-operation and interdependence between people, at the basis of social life there is a co-ordination of individual labour, and thus there is no society that is not founded on a definitive set of relations of production (Giddens 1971, chs 1–4). The social nature of the individual is a fundamental premise in Marxist theory, because one only realises one's own creative self through collective action and social interdependence. Marx goes on to examine and denounce the exploitative nature of that interdependence in societies which are organised in class terms. In capitalism the classes polarise around the ownership of the means of production. There is the class of those who own the means of production – the factories, the land, the technology, the raw materials – and then there are those who own nothing except their ability to work, an ability that remains an abstraction if denied the means of its realisation. Those who own the means of production and those who 'own' their labour power, employers and workers, meet in the contract of employment, understood as a 'free agreement' entered into by both sides to exchange work for a wage. The crux of what Marx denounces is that under capitalist conditions of production, a minority grouping (the bourgeois ruling class), by virtue of the ownership of the means of production is able to appropriate the accumulated surplus production. 'Surplus value' is the difference between the value of what the product fetches in the market and the value that those who produce the goods (workers) are recompensed for at subsistence level. Under capitalist conditions, surplus value is skimmed off, capital 'accumulates', powerful market players become increasingly powerful at the expense of weaker market players and workers, and classes polarise. Thus two fundamental classes are created: a subordinate class that labours and a ruling class that appropriates surplus value. This creates a potentially explosive antagonism between an ever-shrinking minority of property holders and an increasingly pauperised working class. Capitalism contains the seeds of its destruction because it harbours a 'contradiction' at its very core. The function of the institutions of the superstructure is to manage, alleviate and diffuse the potentially destructive class conflict. Its institutions are thus crucially implicated in providing legitimation of the capitalist mode of production, and the legitimation they provide is in turn linked to ideology. Ideology works to alleviate contradictions and render the society coherent and seamless.

2.3.2 Law in capitalist society

This brings us to the heart of the question of ideology, though we should note that in discussing this there are certain important issues that cannot be addressed at any length. The first is to point out that it is, of course, *not only* law among the institutions of the superstructure that performs the ideological function. When Marxists, for example, call (the Christian) religion the 'opium of the people', their argument is that the religious teaching to 'turn the other cheek' to your aggressor, or the promise that it is the meek that will inherit the earth, serves to disarm the dispossessed from a claim to justice in the here and now. Or when Marxists denounce the parliamentary system as a 'talking shop', their argument is that the populace is duped into thinking that they are represented in the processes of democratic will-formation in the legislature, while the real decisions that affect (and devastate) lives are taken behind the closed doors of the boardrooms of the bourgeoisie, or (to update Lenin's dictum) of the institutions of global capital, such as the World Bank (WB), the IMF, the WTO and the G8.

Second, we should note that while it is not only law that performs the ideological function, it is also not *only* an ideological function that is performed by law. The great Soviet jurist Pashukanis (1978) argued powerfully that law was not merely an institution in the superstructure reflecting economic relations, but was instead crucially implicated in constituting them. If capitalist relations were structured around ownership and the wage relation, it was the legal categories of property (ownership of means of production) and contract (the labour contract) that gave shape to the economic forms and allowed the economic system to function as it did. Law was also centrally implicated in the commodification of social life, not merely by extending the category of property right to cover one's very ability to work – the most human activity – but also by constituting the nodal points of social interaction in terms of contracts, rents, interests, fundamentals etc. In a capitalist society these were all legally sanctioned and policed. This is where the notion of *commodification* also becomes important. For the market mechanism to operate, there needs to be an equation of goods in exchange, and thus a common denominator, which would allow comparisons, needs to be introduced. The 'cash nexus' undergirds the market by making all things commensurable. Money introduces a measure of all things in exchange. There is a loss in this, says Marx: things are no longer of value for what they are (use value), but for what they are worth in exchange (exchange value) (Marx 1849). All things marketable acquire a commodity form including, notoriously, our capacity to work. In the process of its subjection to exchange value, the worker's creative labour becomes expendable energy that can be sold by the worker and bought by the capitalist.

The law thus enables the market to operate by establishing what it means to own a commodity and the conditions of its exchange. The legal concepts of property and contract are fundamental conditions for giving form to the economic relations of production. What is also of paramount importance is our identity in law as legal subjects. While for Marx our very sense of identity depends on our interaction with others, as legal subjects what ties us together is money and our ability to buy and sell. Law *abstracts* from social identity those features that are relevant to relations of commodity owners in the market. The legal subject is thus an abstraction from our social situation. We become in law merely bearers of rights and duties which, in liberal law, means that we are commodity owners, *free to* exchange commodities in the market and *free from* any interference (from the State primarily). (See, also, Habermas' account of the first epoch of juridification, Part III, 2.2 above.) These form part of what Marx identifies as the processes of *alienation*, which take hold in capitalist societies. Co-operative productive activity is crucially undercut when exchange value stands in for what is of intrinsic value. The early Marx spoke passionately of the commodification of labour as 'reduc[ing] the worker into a fragment of a man, destroy[ing] the fruits of his labour . . .' (Marx 1844, pp 77–87). According to Marx, in the communist world that was to succeed the capitalist one this form of alienation would disappear alongside the withering away of the capitalist State and its law. Bourgeois law would be replaced by the technical norm, the regulation of things, not the class subjugation of people. We would then recover our true nature, currently obscured by the legal form, the legal description under which we understand ourselves as property-owners and commodity-exchangers (Marx 1932).

Before we turn more directly to law's ideological function, it should be mentioned that there are a number of strands in the Marxist critique of bourgeois law. These range from an extreme position that denounces law as merely reflecting exploitative economic relations of production, a mere instrument of oppression of the working class, to the acknowledgement of the 'relative autonomy' of law from the economic base. Rather schematically we can identify the following positions:

> A repressive–instrumental view of law views the State and its law as instruments of class rule. This is the Marxist–Leninist line of 'class state – class law'. The rule of law and rights reflect and serve the interests of capitalists. Rights, with their emphasis on individualism, are incompatible with socialist ideals of justice and community; and the rule of law, with its emphasis on due process, merely inhibits the advancement of goals of substantive justice (Lenin 1917).

The argument that law is relatively autonomous of the economic base suggests that it does not merely reflect exploitation in a passive way, but might also develop according to its own logic or in response to other demands. On this view the law might provide opportunities to redress the exploitation, and thus may have a value for the proletariat, strategic or substantive. On this basis one might identify two further strands within the tradition:

> Marxism as 'critical theory' emphasises and tries to expose the law's ideological effects. It is argued that the propounding of rights and the rule of law as the 'natural' expression of freedom sanctions a particular view of the 'natural' order of things in a competitive world of self-interested individuals. The emphasis here is, on the one hand, on what law obscures (exploitation, class conflict), and on the other, on what it presents as necessary (individual right, freedom of contract and property). This is no blanket rejection of the bourgeois law, but a thorough uncovering of the hidden disempowering assumptions that it embodies (Horkheimer 1972; and for how this translates into law and legal theory, see Kelman 1987).

There is a strand of Marxism that acknowledges value in the rule of law and the existence of rights. Edward Thompson characteristically expresses this position (1977, pp 258–69). He suggests that the rule of law 'represents an unqualified human good' and that the existence of legal institutions independent of state manipulation or individual influence is a basic safeguard against arbitrary power and an effective inhibition upon class rule. He writes: 'To deny or belittle this good is . . . a desperate error . . . which encourages us to give up the struggle against bad laws and class-bound procedures and to disarm ourselves against power. It is to throw away a whole inheritance of struggle *about* law' (1977, p 266). This line of argument, in one sense, builds on the critique of ideology for, 'if the law is evidently partial and unjust then it will mask nothing, legitimise nothing, contribute nothing to any class's hegemony' (1977, p 263). An important difference, however, is that it points to the way that the rule of law, or particular laws, can themselves become binding on the ruling classes, and might offer certain forms of protection against the abuses of political or economic power.

2.3.3 Ideology and legitimation

For the remainder of this section let us return to the articulation of law and ideology. While ideology in common parlance usually means a body of ideas and beliefs, in Marxist terminology it defines a function. This function is to sustain relations of domination by a move at the level of representation. Marx invites us to think about the following questions: How are real relations represented and lived? And how is man's relationship to the conditions of his existence understood by him? He locates ideology as that system of representation that mediates his relationship to the material conditions of his life, that is, in simpler terms, the grid or lens through which man perceives the lived reality of his situation in the social world. Ideology here accounts for a certain misrepresentation, a certain misreading of the conditions that allows the continuation of a system of domination that presents itself as free. As John Thompson has put it in an influential piece:

> the concept of ideology calls our attention to the *ways in which meaning is mobilized* in the service of dominant individuals and groups, that is, the ways in which the meaning constructed and conveyed by symbolic forms serves to establish and sustain structured social relations from which some individuals and groups benefit more than others.
>
> (1984, p 73)

Let us have a look at how 'misrepresentation' might work. In the classic example, the superimposition of a framework of general, formal rules upon a sub-terrain of real inequality achieves both the 'mystification' – the cover-up – of the real disparities and also the accentuation of those underlying inequalities. According to the law, it is argued, parties to a bargain (whether this has to do with the buying or selling of goods or of labour) approach it on formally equal terms. Thus while a bargain is struck between parties of unequal bargaining power in real terms, legally it appears as an agreement between equals who are as free to reach agreement as they are to abstain. The realities of the vast disparities of bargaining power, or the threat of advancing unemployment (Marx's 'reserve army' of labour power), are all screened off by the apparition of legal equality. The liberal legal order backs and sanctions individual freedom in the market, but this, as Anatole France put it, is a freedom 'that both rich and poor [have] to sleep under the bridges of Paris' (see also Part I, 1.2 above). Equality before the law hides material inequality, the uneven distribution of power and goods. Also, the market operates to give power to the most powerful market-player (economies of scale, etc.). And yet this privileging of the powerful party is hidden behind a guise of formal equivalence. This concealment is what in Marxist terms is understood as ideology. At the same time as it conceals and abstains from interference, formality boosts capitalist activity that further increases the disparity of wealth and power in society.

Marxists will not deny that coercion to support dominant economic interests often operates 'unmasked', especially when it is 'threatened' by subversive activity. However, such cynical instrumental accounts of law have a limited explanatory power and fail to take account of the vital dimension of legitimation, that is, the importance that power is presented not as brute power but as authority, justified, fair and creating obligation rather than obliging through force. No order, and in particular not one as unjust as the capitalist order, would be able to sustain itself over time if it did not appear as legitimate. Take an example that Hugh Collins uses in his important study of law and Marxism (1982, pp 41–2). Laws that criminalised 'combination' among workers were vital to an early capitalist system that felt the urgent need to protect itself from trade union activity. But such banning needed to present itself as legitimate and the ideological moment comes with its justification as upholding the equality of the parties to the labour contract; any combination that might allow workers to push for higher wages was thus made to appear unjust, a ganging-up of sorts of one party against the other, irrespective of the fact that the bargaining positions were vastly uneven to begin with. It is in examples like this that we see clearly how a system seeks its justification in justice and equality, and is reluctant to rely on brute coercion alone to see through the reproduction of the relations of production.

There are multiple forms through which the ideological 'obscuring' works. Law, argue Marxists, operates ideologically to 'naturalise' concepts like private property and exchange through contract, as if they were essential to our constitution as human beings; to 'mystify' or cover up substantive inequality through formal equality, and powerlessness through equal rights; to 'depoliticise' social struggles, that is, remove their political dimension and make them appear as merely criminal; present them in a form that depletes them and renders them controllable. Here is Marx in *The German Ideology*:

> The class which has the means of material production at its disposal, has the control at the same time over the means of intellectual (geistig) production, so that thereby, generally speaking, the ideas of those who lack the means of intellectual production are subject to it
>
> (1932: 176)

There is a connection here between material production and the control of intellectual production, but that is not all. From the time of his earliest writings, Marx was keen to expose the subtle ways in which capitalism diffuses resistance and critique through subtle moves and strategies at the level of representation. One of his most famous denunciations is in 'On the Jewish Question' (1843), where he famously draws a distinction between political and human emancipation. He argues that the great political revolutions of the eighteenth century – the French and American – declared political emancipation while leaving the structures of 'private right' intact, notably the regime of property rights, including them as 'rights of man' in the name of which the revolutions were fought. But 'who is "man"' asks Marx, and 'why are his rights called the rights of man?' He answers: 'No one but the member of civil society, i.e. egoistic man, man separated from other men and the community . . . who sees in other men not the realisation but the limitation of his own freedom' (1843, pp 52, 53). In proclaiming and entrenching the rights of 'egoistical' man as the rights of the citizen, the revolutions in fact served to install a system of bourgeois property relations in the name of freedom, and despite the universalism of their declarations and the extension of political rights, left citizens powerless before owners. For Marx this is 'revolutionary practice in flagrant contradistinction with its theory' (1843, p 54).

It is precisely this that 'ideology' is about: identifying modes in which systems and practices that oppress are presented in an emancipatory idiom and redeemed in the process. 'We find ourselves' says Antonio Negri, possibly the most influential Marxist philosopher writing today, 'with a revolutionary tradition that has pulled the flags of the bourgeoisie out of the mud.' (2001, p xx). So when Marx in the 'Eighteenth Brumaire' famously issued his call to 'let the dead bury the dead', it was a call to leave behind those modes of thinking about emancipation that in fact perpetuate systems of domination.

In possibly the most discussed text on ideology in the Marxist canon, the French communist Louis Althusser (1971) argued that ideology is embodied in material institutions and practices; and that it is in fact nothing short of constitutive of the way we understand ourselves as subjects. The first part of this famous text explores what Althusser calls Ideological State Apparatuses (ISAs), by which he meant all the institutions (church, family, educational institutions, etc.) that were in effect for him continuous with the coercive apparatuses of the State (police, courts, army) in keeping the population docile. The crucial link between the two is seen in terms of 'material' practices. Here, Althusser takes Pascal's statement, 'act as if you believe, pray, kneel and you *shall* believe', and generalises it to rituals and practices that serve to inculcate beliefs in populations that sustain institutions as legitimate. Note that the inculcation is radical: what Althusser is adding to Pascal is that 'you shall believe that you knelt down because you are a believer', and this introduces a crucial further step in the logic of how ideology works. There is, in other words, here introduced what Althusser refers to as a 'toujours-deja' – an 'always-already'. The material practice (kneeling down) does not merely create a belief, it also justifies itself in terms of it. Althusser pursues this further to the constitution of subjectivity in the famous theory of 'interpellation'. Ideology is 'materialised' in everyday life, and the material–symbolic order creates 'subject positions' into which we are 'hailed' (interpellated): that is to say that we come to recognise ourselves in their terms. Legitimation is thus secured unquestionably and ideology has been effective at the deepest level, because if capitalism controls the conditions of our recognition as subjects it becomes impossible to step behind the starting line to hold that constitution to question.

These are complex analyses and to appreciate their significance fully would involve us in debates that would take us beyond this introductory exposition. Suffice it for now to reiterate the main point about ideology. To reproduce itself over time capitalism must secure that relations of production are reproduced in their current form; and that class struggle be prevented from erupting in a way that might challenge the capitalist distribution of advantage through ownership of the means of production. To generate legitimation for the system, the law acts ideologically in a range of ways outlined here. Thus the Marxist analysis of ideology is far-reaching and has informed many critical stances today beyond strictly Marxist positions.

Reading

For a concise introduction to Marx see Giddens (1971: chs 1–4). For a short, classic, account of Law and Marxism see Pashukanis (1978). There is also a useful introduction in Collins (1982) and Cotterrell (1992: 106–18).

The concept of Ideology is discussed in a number of works by Marx and for one of its most interesting manifestations see 'On the Jewish Question' (Marx 1843). In connection to the materialist conception of history see the first section of 'The German Ideology' (Marx 1932). For a recent work discussing the conception of ideology in relation to international law see Marks (2000; ch 1) and more generally to law Hirst (1979).

In his edited volume, Zizek (1994, especially chs 1, 6, 9, 12 and 13) has compiled one of the best collections of writings in the Marxist tradition of ideology.

References

Althusser, L, 1971, 'Ideology and Ideological State Apparatuses', in L Althusser (ed), *Lenin and Philosophy, and other essays*, London: New Left Books.

Collins, H, 1982, *Marxism and Law*, Oxford: Oxford University Press.

Cotterrell, R, 1992, *The Sociology of Law. An Introduction*, 2nd edn, London: Butterworths.

Giddens, A, 1971, *Capitalism and Modern Social Theory: An analysis of the writings of Marx, Durkheim and Weber*, Cambridge; Cambridge University Press.

Hirst, PQ, 1979, *On Law and Ideology*, London: Macmillan.

Horkheimer, M, 1972, *Critical Theory*, New York: Herder & Herder.

Kelman, M, 1987, *A Guide to Critical Legal Studies*, Cambridge, MA: Harvard University Press.

Lenin, VI, 1917, *The State and Revolution*, various editions.

Marks, S, 2000, *The Riddle of All Constitutions*, Oxford: Oxford University Press.

Marx, K, 1843, 'On the Jewish Question', in D McLellan (ed), *Karl Marx. Selected Writings*, 1977, Oxford: Oxford University Press, pp 39–62.

Marx, K, 1844, 'Economic and Philosophical Manuscripts' in D McLellan (ed), *Karl Marx. Selected Writings* 1977, Oxford: Oxford University Press, pp 75–112.

Marx, K, 1849, 'Wage labour and Capital' in D McLellan (ed), *Karl Marx: Selected Writings*, 1977, Oxford: Oxford University Press, pp 248–68.

Marx, K, 1851, 'The Eighteenth Brumaire of Louis Bonaparte', in D McLellan (ed), *Karl Marx. Selected Writings*, 1977, Oxford: Oxford University Press.

Marx, K, 1932, 'The German Ideology' in D McLellan (ed), *Karl Marx. Selected Writings*, Oxford: Oxford University Press, pp 159–91.

Negri, A, 2001, *The Savage Anomaly*, Minneapolis: University of Minnesota Press.

Pashukanis, EB, 1978, *Law and Marxism. A General Theory*, London: Pluto Press.

Thompson, EP, 1977, *Whigs and Hunters*, Harmondsworth: Penguin.

Thompson, J, 1984, *Studies in the Theory of Ideology*, Cambridge: Polity Press.

Zizek, S, 1994, *Mapping Ideology*, London: Verso.

2.4 Displacing the juridical: Foucault on power and discipline

2.4.1 Introductory remarks

Our discussions of legal modernity up to this point have accorded a central role to the law. In analyses such as Weber's, for example, the development of modernity is linked to the law playing an evermore central role in the constitution of political power, in the regulation of economic transactions and in the government of social life. These replicate the arguments in, say, liberal political theory that emphasise the role of the law in developing human rights and democracy and protecting the autonomy of the individual. This is challenged by theoretical approaches which seek to displace the centrality of the law in the development or analysis of modernity. These approaches go beyond merely attempting to displace the centrality of State law, such as we see in Santos' discussion of globalisation and legal pluralism, to the argument that in the development of modernity law is transformed in such a way as to reduce the significance of juridical categories. It is argued that law is no longer a category through which we can understand or analyse the operation of power in modernity (see Part III, 2.1 above). We shall examine these types of claims through an examination of the work of the French philosopher and social theorist Michel Foucault (1926–1984).

Foucault famously, and controversially, contended that the period of modernity is a 'phase of juridical regression', and that a focus on the constitutions and legislation that had been passed since the eighteenth century would prevent us from understanding fundamentally important shifts in the nature of the operation of power in modernity (1979, p 144). He argues that new techniques of government that developed in the modern period were distinct from the traditional juridical forms of sovereignty. The juridical, he suggests, has been displaced as a principle of power, and modern society should be analysed in terms of the development of a 'governmentality', which constitutes both 'society' and the individual as effects of the operation of power.

Foucault's work has been important and influential, and though it rarely focuses on the law directly, it raises radical questions about the social role and function of law in modern society. In this section we will first of all examine the key terms of discipline and biopower, and their place in the complex of techniques that Foucault called 'governmentality'. We will then look at the concept of power in Foucault's work before addressing the question of how his work can contribute to our understanding of law in modern society.

2.4.2 Discipline and biopower

Some of Foucault's most intriguing and important remarks on power and the law are contained in the short section, entitled, 'The Right of Death and the Power over Life', which concludes volume I of the *History of Sexuality* (1979, pp 135–59). Here, Foucault sets out two models of political power: the pre-modern, or classical, model of *juridical* power, and the modern *normalising* power. In the juridical model, the sovereign had the right to take the life of those who threatened the internal or external order of the State, or to demand that his subjects give up their lives in the defence of the State. This power could be characterised as a right of seizure (of things, time, bodies, even life itself): a power of life and death exercised by a sovereign over their subjects. The normalising model, by contrast, is characterised by its power over life: to administer, sustain, develop and multiply the life of the population of a particular territory. This did not necessarily exclude the right to take life, but to the extent that it remained, it was part of a complex of forces that were aimed primarily at the fostering or production of life – the administration of bodies – rather than its seizure or negation. Thus if juridical power was characterised by negativity (the prohibition), exemplified in the use of the death penalty, this new form of power was productive or positive in its effects, and subtle and diverse in the techniques and strategies that it employed. Where juridical power relied on the single intervention, these new powers were continuous and regulatory in their effect. Most important of all, he claims that these new apparatuses of power increasingly incorporated and transformed the judicial institution, leading to the decline, or regression, of the juridical.

The normalising power:

> evolved in two basic forms . . . two poles of development linked together by a whole intermediary cluster of relations. One of these poles . . . centered on the body as a machine: its disciplining, the optimization of its capabilities, the extortion of its forces, the parallel increase of its usefulness and its docility . . . [A]ll this was ensured by the procedures of power that characterised the *disciplines*: an *anatomo-politics of the human body*. The second, formed somewhat later, focused on the species body . . . [S]upervision was effected through an entire series of interventions and *regulatory controls: a bio-politics of the population*.

(1979, p 139)

These two forms, then, are discipline and biopower. While the former operates on individuals located in institutions such as prisons, factories, schools and hospitals by surveillance and control with the constant aim of the more efficient distribution and use of power, the latter is concerned with the management of populations through the science of statistics and techniques of political economy.

2.4.2.1 Discipline

Foucault's analysis of discipline is developed in what is probably his most famous book, *Discipline and Punish*, first published in 1975 (Foucault 1977).[5] Although the primary subject of the book is the birth of the prison, that is to say an analysis of the dramatic shift that took place in the early nineteenth century towards the systematic and large-scale use of incarceration as a form of punishment in its own right, Foucault's main concern is with how institutions such as the prison were based on (and in turn fostered) new techniques for the disciplining or control of the body. He is concerned here with the question of how power operates in institutions such as the prison, for he observed that the modern prison did not seek simply to segregate the prisoner from society. The prison, he argued, developed techniques that sought to operate on the mind or soul of the prisoner, placing them in a network of power relations aimed at creating a new kind of individual. It was, in short, a form of discipline. This, he argued was comprised of three techniques or modalities of power: hierarchical observation, normalising judgment and the examination (1977, pp 170–94).

Hierarchical observation enabled coercion through the means of surveillance or monitoring. While observation, of course, was not new, what was distinctive about the modern period was the way that it became embedded in the architecture and design of certain institutions. Prisons were designed in such a way as to make the prisoner physically visible to other inmates or officers, who were themselves being watched and supervised. At the same time, the network or hierarchy of management was an apparatus that placed individuals in a field of relations in which all were continuously supervised by their superiors and inferiors. These institutions and networks made possible the exercise of a continuous control over conduct. *Normalising judgment*, by contrast, refers to the breaking down of actions and behaviours into evermore distinct elements, the normal (or average) way of behaving or performing an action, the departure from which is corrected by discipline aimed at training or instilling in the individual the proper way of acting. Corresponding to the deviations from the norm, there was a new microeconomy of penality, of rewards and punishments, according to which individuals could be compared, differentiated, hierarchised, homogenised and excluded (1977, p 183). Last, Foucault suggests that these first two techniques are combined in the *examination*. The importance of the examination (the physical examination of the patient or prisoner, the assessment of the student and so on) lies in the fact that it constitutes the object of the examination as a field of knowledge, something that is to be known. The examination, then, made possible the gathering of a certain kind of knowledge (of individuals, of cases), that could be systematised, made more scientific, and which would in

---

5 The French title is *Surveillir et Punir*, but see the translator's note to the English edition.

turn enable more effective future examination and control. The examination thus 'linked to a certain type of the formation of knowledge a certain form of the exercise of power' (1977, p 187). The aim of all these techniques was the production of more efficient distributions of power or mechanisms of control, but central to them was the constitution of the individual as both the object of power and the instrument of its exercise.

The importance of these 'modest' techniques goes well beyond the analysis of the prison, for Foucault argues that these represent a new political technology of the body, that is to say, a set of techniques and forces that aimed at maximising the productivity and obedience of the individual. Indeed, he took Jeremy Bentham's model of the *panopticon* – the prison in which the prisoners are continually visible to their jailer, and must believe themselves to be observed even when they are not – as a model for the operation of this form of power throughout the social body (1977, pp 200–9; Bentham 1995). The mechanism could be used for the surveillance of prisoners and patients, but also on workers in a factory to increase their productivity. This form of constant observation was more effective, inducing people to act as though they were always being observed, and thus to internalise the operation of discipline. It was a form of police power, systematic, far-reaching and intense that allowed the government of society as a whole without the need of recourse to repression or the outward display of force. The panopticon internalised the operation of disciplinary power, while maximising the numbers of people on whom it could be exercised. Most important of all, it was capable of being transferred between different contexts or institutions, making possible a generalised surveillance. It was, in this sense, 'the diagram of a mechanism of power reduced to its ideal form' (1977, p 205).

2.4.2.2 Biopower

Where discipline works on the individual, 'biopower' is aimed at the administration and production of life. This Foucault proclaims rather grandly, was 'nothing less than the entry of life into history' (1979, p 141), by which he meant that the conditions of biological existence became the concern of politics.

Foucault remarks here that the modern period sees the development of a new kind of concern with public health. States and sovereigns had had to contend throughout history with disease and epidemics, and their damaging consequences. Famine and natural disaster had caused economic slumps. However, he noted that the eighteenth century saw the beginning of attempts to regulate or manage public health, and to adjust the life and wellbeing of the population to the needs of economic production. This was made possible by the development of three techniques. First, the collection of social statistics allowed the monitoring of the size and wellbeing of the population, the recording of birth and death rates, and the measuring of the incidence of disease. It was observed that there are regularities or patterns in these figures at the level of the population – in birth or mortality rates, or the incidence of certain illnesses – and that the social body has a life that can be studied and regulated. Second, interventions in public health could improve collective welfare or security at the level of the population. Thus for example, improvements in drinking water and sewage disposal eradicated certain diseases; mass vaccination programmes led to dramatic improvements in health and mortality rates; the provision of public housing led to improvement of the collective health of the working classes; and the regulation of sex and the family, through programmes of contraception and sex education, could alter birth rates and infant mortality. Third, population dynamics have economic effects – the size, health, level of education and wealth of the population are all, more or less, directly linked to the economic capacity of the State. The new science of political economy arose out of the perception of these links between population, territory and wealth, and was accompanied by new forms of intervention: managing economic production through the provision of social infrastructure such as roads or housing; establishing systems of public education for an educated workforce; the provision of benefits to workers to sustain the workforce even during economic slumps, and so on.

We can thus see how this biopower was central to the development of capitalism: inserting bodies into the machinery of production and adjusting the phenomena of population to economic processes. However, Foucault wants to contend that this was neither the outcome of the process of economic development nor a process that was directed by the State. It was, he argued, a new rationality of government, or *governmentality*, based around techniques for the management of individuals and populations, but which was not reducible to changes in the form of state institutions.

2.4.3 Governmentality

Governmentality, he argued, is a specific and complex form of power (institutions, procedures, analyses, tactics), which 'has as its target population, as its principal form of knowledge political economy, and as its essential technical means apparatuses of security' (2000, p 220). There were thus certain techniques of individualisation and totalisation that characterise the operation of power in modern society: the production of knowledge through statistics as a means of establishing the social as a field of intervention; the production of collective welfare, health, wealth; the production of the citizen through discipline as a certain way of relating inner being and outer behaviour; and the production of new apparatuses of security and surveillance (the prison, the hospital, the asylum, police) that created and regulated social space.

The importance of these forms of power is that they do not necessarily emanate from the state, nor are they employed exclusively in State institutions. Indeed, he is at pains to contrast governmentality with traditional juridical forms of sovereignty centred on the State. There are three important differences between the two forms of power. First, while juridical power is repressive and negative, Foucault argues that normalising power is productive. It is an action upon an action, not upon a thing, and through action it produces or constructs knowledge about its object and the processes of its application. It thus constructs society and the individual as the targets of power. Second, it is not a property, but a strategy. Power is not located at a particular point in the social body (the sovereign, the constitution), and it cannot be possessed, either in itself (as a right) or as a consequence of the ownership of something else (such as the means of production). Power is a relation and it operates through clusters of individual relations or nodal points in the social body. And third, then, its operation is always localised rather than centralised. Power is not handed down from the great institutions of State, but operates through diverse and multiple networks. Thus in his radical formulation, the State and the rights-bearing individual appear as an *effect* of power rather than as its source.

However, while this analysis does not take the State and State institutions as its starting point, it is also important to note that Foucault sees the State as having been 'governmentalised' in the sense that problems of sovereignty, such as the competences of the State, come to be thought of within the matrix of powers and knowledges that have been produced by governmentality (2000, p 221). In a more specific sense, governmentality goes hand in hand with the modern liberal State and capitalist economy as the means by which population and individuals are managed so that individuals can become the self-governing subjects of the liberal legal order. However, where traditional political theory has interpreted sovereignty in juridical terms – founded on a contract, and structured by rights – the analysis of governmentality argues that political and social relations cannot be reduced to the legal relation, and that we should additionally focus on the governmental practices that shape the subject as the self-governing, rational actor presumed by political theory (Dean 1999, ch 6).

2.4.4 A theory of legal modernity?

Let us now return to the question with which we started: to what extent can Foucault's theory contribute to our understanding of the place of law in modernity? We can now see that Foucault is making two claims about the law. First, that with the development of governmentality the law is transformed by normalising power. Second, that the basis of sovereignty, which before the modern period was constituted in juridical terms, requires to be rethought.[6] Let us look at each of these in a little more detail.

---

6 See Ewald (1991, p 139) for a slightly different formulation.

The characteristic form of modern law, Foucault argues, is not the absolute rule or prohibition, but the norm as 'the judicial institution is increasingly incorporated into a continuum of apparatuses (medical, administrative and so on), whose functions are for the most part regulatory' (1979, p 144). Consider, for example, the end of life. Death no longer merely marks the limit of sovereign authority, but is surrounded by detailed legislation regulating the point of legal death, how a person may die (euthanasia, medical intervention), the responsibility for the wellbeing of the terminally ill patient, and even the disposal of the body so as to protect public health. The norm is not an absolute rule, referable to an external source of authority, but is produced through the logics of discipline and government; a norm of behaviour is established through observation and then applied to the same objects that it seeks to govern. The norm as a standard of behaviour is thus strictly self-referential, not emanating from a sovereign power. The strengths of the norm, however, are that it is a common, even objective, standard of measurement, and that it can measure and adjust the behaviour of different individuals. Modern law thus operates as a series of continuous regulatory and corrective mechanisms, rather than on the basis of the sovereign prohibition. It is constituted with reference to the object of regulation rather than according to a set of universal principles. And the sources, objects, institutions and practices of law are necessarily plural. Law in this sense must be understood as a medium rather than a principle of power.

We can now see that claim about modernity as a phase of juridical regression is not necessarily a claim about the declining importance of law so much as a claim about the declining significance of a particular form of sovereignty. The juridical should thus be taken as a way of describing a particular historical form of monarchical sovereignty. However, this is important because this conception of sovereignty has been of importance in shaping our theoretical understanding of the concept. On this view, law is increasingly sidelined, as it is no longer the principle of power: real power is neither constituted nor defined in legal terms, but operates through non-legal strategies and mechanisms. The importance of law may be merely that of legitimising certain actions of the State; indeed, Foucault suggests at various points that formal legal liberties are founded on the corporal disciplines, and that these were the forms that made normalising power acceptable (1977, p 222; 1979, p 144). We believe power is constituted in legal terms (rights, constitutions, etc.) and so are distracted from the real operation of power in society.

The claim of juridical regression is, however, significant in two further and closely linked senses. On the one hand it is a claim about the declining capacity of the categories of the law to capture or define the nature of social (Murphy 1991). On this view law is neither a measure of rationality nor an index of social solidarity; the study of law can reveal nothing essential or fundamental about the nature of society. On the other hand it raises a question about how sovereignty is to be constituted in the absence of an external source of power such as the monarchical sovereign, for we cannot start from any assumptions about the nature or proper function of law as distinct from its actual operations. How, that is to say, can we theorise a sovereignty that is referable only to its own practices? How do we theorise law if it possesses no fundamental characteristics? And how, as a question of politics, can law limit the operation of power in the knowledge that there is no space 'outside' in which law can stand against power?

These questions are not easily answered, but the importance of Foucault's theory is that he raises them in particularly acute form.

Reading

The starting point for any understanding of Foucault must be the original texts, because of his distinctive style. The most accessible are probably *Discipline and Punish* (1977) and Volume I of the *History of Sexuality* (1979). It is also worth bearing in mind that Foucault published a number of interviews, which also provide short, accessible introductions to his work. Many of these have now been reproduced in the three-volume *Essential Works*. You will also find a selection in Foucault (1980). Gordon (1987) is a useful comparison with the work of Max Weber. There is little secondary literature directly on Foucault and law, but Ewald (1991) and Murphy (1991) are most useful.

On governmentality, you should begin with Foucault (2000), while Dean (1999) provides a very useful summary and discussion of the ideas and of the literature spawned by the lecture. The lecture is also published in Burchell *et al.* (1991), together with a number of other essays discussing and applying the ideas.

Finally, it is worth reading some of the more recent attempts to extend and apply Foucault's thought. The themes of governmentality and police are explored in the essays in Dubber and Valverde (2006), and the legal construction of categories of gender in medicine and law in Sheldon (1997). Hardt and Negri (2000), and Agamben (1998) are stunning and important attempts to address the questions of sovereignty and biopower in a globalised world.

References

Agamben, G, 1998, *Homo Sacer. Sovereign Power and Bare Life*, Stanford: Stanford University Press.

Bentham, J, 1995, *The Panopticon Writings*, M Bozovic (ed), London: Verso.

Burchell, G, Gordon, C and Miller, P (eds), 1991, *The Foucault Effect: Studies in Governmentality*, London: Harvester Wheatsheaf.

Dean, M, 1999, *Governmentality: Power and Rule in Modern Society*, London: Sage.

Dubber, MD and Valverde, M (eds), 2006, *The New Police Power*, Stanford: Stanford University Press.

Ewald, F, 1991, 'Norms, Discipline and the Law', in R Post (ed), *Law and the Order of Culture*, Berkeley: California University Press.

Foucault, M, 1977, *Discipline and Punish. The Birth of the Prison*, Harmondsworth: Penguin.

Foucault, M, 1979, *The History of Sexuality. Vol.I. The Will to Knowledge*, Harmondsworth: Penguin, 1978.

Foucault, M, 1980, *Power/Knowledge. Selected Interviews and Other Writings 1972–77*, C Gordon (ed), Brighton: Harvester.

Foucault, M, 2000, 'Governmentality', in *Essential Works of Foucault 1954–1984. Vol.III Power*, New York: New Press.

Gordon, C, 1987, 'The Soul of the Citizen: Max Weber and Michel Foucault on Rationality and Government', in S Whimster and S Lash (eds), *Max Weber, Rationality and Modernity*, London: Allen & Unwin.

Hardt, M and Negri, A, 2000, *Empire*, Cambridge MA: Harvard University Press.

Murphy, WT, 1991, 'The Oldest Social Science? The Epistemic Properties of the Common Law Tradition', 54 *Mod LR* 182–215.

Sheldon, S, 1997, *Beyond Control: Medical Power, Women and Abortion Law*, London: Pluto Press.

2.5 Law in the risk society

2.5.1 Introduction

We might think, plausibly enough, that law and legal institutions are centrally concerned with the organisation of risk. This might be in the private law of delict (or tort), where legal rules and principles are employed to govern the allocation of benefits and burdens, consequent on negligently or intentionally caused harms; or in contract law, which organises the formation and consequences of consensually reached bargains in the market; or in public or international law, where rights and responsibilities are set out in legal norms as a means of addressing and trying to plan around the uncertainties of events and the practices of power associated with particular spheres of action. In all these areas, risks and the way they are dealt with are an indispensable element of the legal world. We might believe that this observation merely acknowledges the fact that the world is an inherently 'risky' place, and that legal mechanisms, particularly of the type associated earlier with the formal rationality of Weber's analysis, provide ways of organising these risks in a relatively predictable way in order to secure some kind of human control over an inevitably unpredictable future. While we might be tempted to see risk in that sense as a negative feature of social life, we should also acknowledge that it is absolutely fundamental to social life, including of course the fact that risks are crucial to the capitalist form of economic organisation.

But our concern with risk in this section has a different emphasis. Here we will concentrate on what the German sociologist, Ulrich Beck, has labelled 'Risk Society', and by which he means something much more specific. In what follows we will outline its main features and some of the challenges it poses to legal order. It is important to analyse these for a number of reasons. First, the social and environmental conditions that mark the emergence of risk society in Beck's terms are of great and potentially enduring significance to human communities on a global scale. Second, these conditions arguably work to undermine the effectiveness of the rationalities associated with modernity, but – and this is the key point – such undermining is a consequence of these very rationalities themselves. Finally, as a crucial component of this, the legal rationality associated with modernity is itself threatened in ways that put in question its ability to deal with the kinds of risks that have emerged. All together then, the question of risk society is a question of the very future viability of law in, indeed of law *and*, modern society.

2.5.2 Features of the 'risk society'

Risk society, according to Beck, is a catastrophic society. It is one in which the technological developments of modernity produce risks of such magnitude and such potentially vast environmental devastation that they threaten human, animal and plant life on the planet. Progress in terms of chemical, nuclear and biological science may have led, in the West at any rate, away from a society of scarcity, but it is now precisely in terms of wealth and *over*production that risks appear most prevalently. Environmental pollution, nuclear radiation, toxins in food, and genetic engineering, for example, stem directly from the practices of modern society, but all arise from or produce hazards that put in jeopardy the very successes of modernity. As Beck puts it, 'at the turn of the twenty-first century the unleashed process of modernisation is overrunning and overcoming its own coordinate system' (Beck 1992, p 87), and it is this, he argues, which signals that we have now entered a period of 'reflexive modernity' in which modernity itself 'is becoming its own theme' (1992, p 19).

In comparison with earlier phases, what is so specifically dangerous and novel about the nature of the hazards associated with reflexive modernity is that they are irreversible and incalculable. Such risks are often difficult to detect, both spatially and temporally, until they result in harms and hence they affect the future in ways that are highly unpredictable. They tend to render traditional calculations about cause and effect problematic, as hazards become not only potentially uncontrollable, but perpetrators (where they can be singled out at all) are identifiable only once irremediable damage has occurred. Moreover, risks such as those associated with environmental devastation or global warming respect no national boundaries and, while they are not dissociable from existing structures of wealth, they no longer conform to these in traditional ways – as Beck puts it succinctly, 'poverty is hierarchic, smog is democratic' (1992, p 36). Finally, given the global nature of the dangers these processes produce, action in response to them can no longer be plausibly understood in modernity's traditional terms; for example, actions undertaken by States acting alone to defend their own populations will not be able to combat the effects of global warming, no matter how 'environmentally friendly' their own political programmes. As such, the State's sovereign powers are diminished under threats that they can no longer directly or unilaterally control, and risk society thus renders the effectiveness of the Nation-State system highly problematic. In these respects, and others, the hazards of risk society come to undermine many of the basic elements we have seen associated with modernity. Beck describes the effects of these developments in stark terms:

> The dangers of highly developed nuclear and chemical productive forces abolish the foundations and categories according to which we have thought and acted to this point, such as space and time, work and leisure time, factory and nation state, indeed even the borders between continents.
>
> (Beck 1992, p 22)

As part of this process, Beck identifies what he terms the 'boomerang effect' of risks under conditions of globalisation. According to this, even those who might think themselves safe from the disastrous effects of socially harmful activities – the rich and the powerful – cannot escape these risks. At its most extreme, for example, the physical effects of a nuclear war perpetrated by a powerful nuclear State, would be such that the damage caused could not be confined to the 'enemy' State (and would affect third-party countries not part of the conflict); the perpetrator itself would not be able to immunise its *own* population from the effects of radiation carried back on the winds or in the food chain. Such modernisation risks, says Beck, mean that 'perpetrator and victim sooner or later become identical' (1992, p 38).

This boomerang effect, moreover, does not apply only to human life, but also to central elements of the dominant world order, such as 'money, property, and legitimation. It does not just strike back directly at the individual source; in a wholesale, egalitarian way it impairs everyone' (1992, p 38). Environmental devastation, for example, will return at some point to have an impact on those who might be thought to have been most culpable in permitting or committing the original wrong, such as powerful states or economic actors. Unable to escape from the effects of the interdependency of global financial, productive and consumer activity, the very successes of these actors – in political or economic terms – will themselves be put in danger by the hazards they have been involved in creating. Thus the 'boomerang effect' impacts on all levels of social interaction, including the security and stability of property relations subject to its impact. Beck sums up this point in the following terms:

> Everything which threatens life on Earth also threatens the property and commercial interests of those who live *from* the commodification of life and its requisites. In this way a . . . *contradiction* arises between the profit and property of interests that advance the industrialization process and its frequently threatening consequences, which endanger and expropriate possessions and profits (not to mention the possession and profit of life).
>
> (1992, p 39)

States and economic actors have acknowledged these features only slowly, and many are still in denial about them (as the refusal of the US government to sign up to the Kyoto agreement confirms; see also the UK's Stern Review of 2006.) Ironically, of course, as Beck points out, it is often the case that where proposed solutions to these problems are sought within the terms of capitalist development itself; one effect is to commodify these risks themselves, turning them into business. (Carbon emissions trading, for example, involves making a market out of pollution.) As such, the 'diffusion and commercialisation of risks do not break with the logic of capitalist development completely, but instead they raise the latter to a new stage' (1992, p 23). But for how long, it might be asked, will such development remain *development*, when the very conditions of the reproduction of life may be put at risk by such activities? This is precisely the problem Beck identifies for reflexive modernity.

2.5.3 Law in risk society

The issue of property returns us to questions about the impact of risk society on law and legal regulation. There are two aspects to this that we should consider. First, in line with the earlier observations, it would seem that trad- itional legal categories are threatened by the consequences associated with the large-scale hazards produced under conditions of reflexive modernisa- tion. Thus as we have already seen, the legal powers of States to have a monopoly on determining internally the conditions of their citizens' life and opportunities may be threatened by global risks that cannot adequately be dealt with by national legislation. Even regional regulation (such as within the EU) may be insufficient to stem the production of hazards on a global scale. Moreover, where the environmental costs of production might be thought to be locatable elsewhere (in terms of industrial production being displaced from one region to another for the sake of increasing profit) these costs will not remain in the place they are generated where the boomerang effect cannot be avoided.

At a more theoretical level, however, given the extensive nature of the hazards that have emerged, it is also the case that traditional legal concepts and categories may themselves become redundant in the face of global ecological threats. Thus conventional legal categories of causation, individual liability and forseeability of harm are no longer adequate conceptual means of redressing the harms of risk society. In the face of incalculable threats and in situations where the identities of victims and perpetrators merge, modernity's legal mechanisms for dealing with risk allocation might be thought to provide inadequate resources. We will return to this point again in a moment.

Finally, the relation between law, politics and science is reconfigured in risk society in ways that challenge the very ability of legal and democratic accountability to organise regarding the dangers faced and ways of dealing with them. Because risks tend to be 'knowledge based', they are 'open to social definition and construction'; consequently they can, says Beck, 'be changed, magnified, dramatized or minimized within knowledge' (1992, p 23). What this means is that they are open to conflictual understandings in such a way that the *politics* of the definition of risks becomes a crucial feature of attempts to acknowledge or alleviate them. One of the central problems here is the emergence of an asymmetry between, on the one hand, the production of, and knowledge about, risks, and on the other, the responsibility for them.

This plays out directly in the context of the relationship between law, politics, science and business. As Beck maintains, 'The structuring of the future is taking place indirectly and unrecognisably in research laboratories and executive suites, not in the parliament or in political parties', adding that the potential is that 'politics is becoming a publicly financed advertising agency for the sunny sides of a development it does not know, and one that is removed from its active influence' (1992, pp 223–4). This asymmetry is compounded by the fact that, at the level of social expectations, governments and States are still seen as the key players in legitimating the practices and consequences of scientific 'progress', even when in fact they are ill-equipped to do so. Government is still perceived as the main port of call in terms of trying to alleviate or compensate for harms caused by business. However, business sees these harms as side effects, which are not their responsibility. The consequence is that 'business is not responsible for something it causes, and politics is responsible for something over which it has no control' (1992, p 227).

This leads us to our second observation about the role of law in risk society. This is to suggest that law and legal institutions may themselves be complicit in the ongoing production and normalisation of global risks. If this is so, then we are confronted by the possibility, not only of law's inability to confront global hazards, but by the fact that it actually promotes them. This is a far more devastating critique of law's role than merely pointing to its inadequacy. Let us see how Beck argues this point.

If modern industrial society was centrally concerned with the distribution of goods, says Beck, then risk society is concerned with the distribution of 'bads'. But such distribution takes place according to certain dynamics, including importantly, that of legal regulation. But here, law, instead of operating to regulate responsible behaviour and impose consequences for irresponsible behaviour – that is, to set standards and impose sanctions consequent on their breach – it actually operates as a way of organising *irresponsible* behaviour. In other words, dangerous actors – be they States or corporations – carry out activities that contribute to global risk, but these harmful activities are legalised through a regime that claims still to be there to protect people and the environment from such harms. The reason this happens is because the principles law has for organising responsibility – in particular those regarding causation, individual liability, and proof – are rooted in an earlier form of modernity and have not caught up with the nature and extent of the dangers now being faced. Thus their operation is not only inadequate, but contributes to the problem. This, says Beck, is the 'concealed gap of the century', and in the context of ecological harms, in fact legalises universal pollution:

> [D]angers worldwide make it harder to prove that a single substance is the cause; the international production of harmful substances works against proving the culpability of a single company or perpetrator; the

individual character of criminal law contradicts the collective danger; and the global character of the danger has abolished 'causes' as our industrial forefathers understood them.

(Beck 1995, pp 131–2)

By assigning responsibilities only under certain well-established legal categories, what modern law and legal institutions do is to organise a system of *non*-liability, a regime of unaccountability: environmental harms continue at an alarming rate, and yet either no one at all can be or is held responsible for them (or everyone and thus no one is responsible for causing them), or responsibility is massively asymmetrical to the harms caused (small fines, say, for massive damage caused). Here then is how Beck sums up the overall effect:

If one wanted to think up a system for turning guilt into innocence, one could take this collaboration between justice, universal culpability, acquittal and pollution as one's model. Nothing criminal is happening here, nothing demonstrably criminal anyway. Its undemonstrability is guaranteed precisely by compliance with, and strict application of, the fundamental rule of justice – the principle of individual culpability, whereby both pollution and non-pollution, justice and (coughing) injustice, are guaranteed.

(1995, p 135)

In this way modern law is not simply inadequate to the task of combating the dangers of risk society, but is rather directly involved in *perpetuating* their ongoing development. This, says Beck, shows how law in risk society engineers a global system of *organised irresponsibility*.

2.5.4 Individualisation

There is one further aspect to Beck's analysis that is worth paying attention to here, since it returns us to certain themes covered earlier. In his work, Beck includes an important discussion of the notion of 'individualisation', which he sees as central to an understanding of risk society. Under conditions of reflexive modernisation, even though patterns of inequality remain, traditional categories of family, work, class and gender tend to break down. For Beck, in contemporary Western capitalist societies, it is instead, increasingly, the case that the individual becomes the reproduction unit for the social in the lifeworld. But the 'individual' is not to be understood in a natural or pre-social way. In ways reminiscent of Foucault's work (see Part III, 2.4 above), the individual should be thought of as something produced, not something pre-existing, the *result* or gathering point of the effects of external social forces. As such, the 'individual' is something whose characteristics, expectations and sensibilities change over time. Of course there is a paradoxical aspect to this: if individuals are products, then they are not truly individual precisely to the extent that they are produced, and, more decisively, produced as *similar* individuals. But this is what in fact is happening: the process of individualisation is also one of *standardisation*, through which the characteristics of the individual are formed with reference to a range of social and bureaucratic institutions and demands, be they financial, educational, or legal systems. This paradoxical situation is described by Beck as:

> [T]he contradictory double face of institutionally dependent individual situations. The apparent outside of the institutions becomes the inside of individual biography. The design of life situations spanning institutional boundaries results from their institutional dependency (in the broadest sense). The liberated individuals become dependent on the labour market and *because of that*, dependent on education, consumption, welfare state regulations and support, traffic planning, consumer supplies, and on possibilities and fashions in medical, psychological and pedagogical counselling and care. This all points to the *institution-dependent control structure* of individual situations. Individualization becomes the *most advanced* form of socialization dependent on the market, law, education and so on.
>
> (1992, pp 130–1, emphasis in original)

But if this is so then it follows that the individual becomes 'emphatically dependent on situations and conditions that completely escape its reach' (1992, p 130–1). That is, to the extent that individuals are the *deposit* of social institutions, and that individuals as individuals do not themselves control these institutions or the logics according to which they operate, then they are therefore condemned to live out their lives according to demands and *risks* that these institutions generate. As Beck therefore points out, 'under these conditions, how one lives becomes the biographical solution to systemic contradictions' (1992, p 137).

This point signals one further aspect to this situation that compounds the problem. For it is of the utmost importance that these are processes of individualisation; that what is produced are individuals who are thereby deemed themselves to be responsible for their own destinies and treated as if they were in fact able to manage these external forces. The individual is thus valorised as a key achievement of modern society – a key focal point of work responsibilities, leisure and consumption activities, financial and legal decisions, etc. – and yet they are in fact at the mercy of external forces over which they have little control for the very reason that these systems are what produce the sense of individuality in the first place. Hence the full force of the paradox: 'At the same moment as he or she sinks into insignificance, he or she is elevated to the apparent throne of world-shaper' (1992, p 137).

In some ways, the liberal mind-set – the liberal personality of capitalist society – is the most problematic of all versions of individuality, since it fulfils this paradoxical condition expertly, by *internalising choices given from outside but making them their own*. And where this is so, individuals are subject to the power and risks of social systems in ways that are not at all persuasively captured by the stereotypical claims of modern society being 'individualist'. In many respects this was also the insight that Foucault's technologies of the self provided in such a nuanced but cogent manner, for it exemplifies his apparently counterintuitive claim that we are 'governed through our freedoms'. To the extent that Beck's analysis is accurate then, it is precisely these processes of individualisation that unsettle an optimistic account of modernity as releasing the individual from the bonds of conventional forms of power. To the extent that individuals were released from, for example, religious or mystical forms of domination, they are reinserted far more thoroughly – because far more invisibly – within other forms of systemic control, whether economic, bureaucratic, or governmental. For as we are increasingly aware, through techniques such as biometric testing, DNA profiling and identity surveillance, under legal authority, governments (as well as some corporate actors) are able to set in motion powers that are not properly understandable or made accountable through conventional forms of legal regulation. It is this that leads one commentator on Foucault to observe that, 'the modern Western state has integrated techniques of subjective individualisation with procedures of objective totalization to an unprecedented degree' (Agamben 1998, p 5).

Reading

Beck's most famous work (Beck 1992) remains the best starting point for research on risk society. The question of 'organised irresponsibility' is pursued most thoroughly in Beck 1995. For his latest treatment of ways to think about addressing the problems of risk society, and which also connects directly with themes of globalisation, see Beck 2005.

There is a burgeoning secondary literature on risk society; see, indicatively, Adam (2000). For a concise treatment of risk and law, though one that tends to focus on the traditional ways in which law has managed risk, see Steele (2004).

References

Adam, B *et al.* (eds), 2000, *The Risk Society and Beyond*, London: Sage.

Agamben, G, 1998, *Homo Sacer: Sovereign Power and Bare Life*, Stanford: Stanford University Press.

Beck, U, 1992, *Risk Society: Towards a New Modernity*, Ritter, M (trans), London: Sage.

Beck, U, 1995, *Ecological Politics in an Age of Risk*, Weisz, A (trans), Cambridge: Polity Press.

Beck, U, 2005, *Power in the Global Age*, Cambridge: Polity Press.

Power, M, 1997, 'From risk society to audit society', 3 *Soziale Systeme* 3–21.

Steele, J, 2004, *Risks and Legal Theory*, Oxford: Hart.

TUTORIALS

TUTORIAL I

Understanding legal modernity

Responding to pressure from the trade union movement and left wing political parties, the Ukanian Parliament passed legislation in 1930 to require employers to continue to pay workers who were sick when they were unable to work, for a period of up to two months. The legislation came into force on January 1st 1931.

In February 1931 a dispute arose at the factory of United Washers Ltd., a company that produced components that were essential to the manufacture of domestic appliances. Six workers were sacked after failing to turn up to work for three consecutive days, a situation which the company argued had led to a significant reduction in output. The men argued that they had been sick and unable to work and that they should have received sick pay during their absence. The company responded that the men had been paid for days that they were absent before they were sacked. The case was taken up by the men's trade union who brought a legal action against the company, requiring that the men be reinstated. The court of first instance held that the men should not be reinstated: there was nothing in the legislation that prevented a company from sacking those who were too sick to work, and that they had been paid by the company for the period that they were sick, in accordance with the legislation.

The union appealed the case to the Supreme Court of Ukania, where the five judges delivered the following opinions.

JUDGE ANTONY:

The central issue in this case is the wording of the legislation, which alone expresses the intention of Parliament. The courts cannot and must not go beyond that wording in the determination of a case, for to do so would undermine the very legitimacy of the legal system. In this case the legislation provides for the protection of employees who are sick, but there is nothing in the legislation to prevent a company from terminating the contract of employment at any point, irrespective of the health of the worker.

JUDGE BELINDA:

I am not persuaded by the argument of my brother Judge Antony. The intention of Parliament is expressed in the legislation as a whole and it is very clear that the spirit or intention of this legislation was to protect workers against just these types of actions by their employers. The rights given by the statute become meaningless if they can be avoided so easily, and so the legislation must be interpreted in the light of the intention of Parliament to protect the security and quality of employment. The legitimacy of the law will not survive unless it is interpreted in such a way.

JUDGE CHARLES:

There is much that is of merit in the argument of Judge Belinda. She is right to focus on the question of the legitimacy of the law, but unfortunately her argument is purely speculative. The present case cannot be decided simply on the basis of the narrow interpretation of the legislation. If the courts are to deal with such issues properly they must be provided with more information about the profitability of washer manufacture; time lost through sickness and injury in this sector of the economy; about the income and employability of workers, skilled and unskilled in this sector; about the attitudes to the law of all workers and so on. As we know, such information is central to the management of modern society and the economy, and is the basis for decision making by all other organs of government. If the courts continue to confine themselves to the interpretation of the wording of statutes alone, then they run the risk of becoming increasingly irrelevant.

JUDGE DIANA:

I am not persuaded that this is a question for the courts at all. It is clear to me that the legislation has been poorly drafted, in that it allows employers to act in a way that is clearly contrary to the spirit of the law. Parliament should, as a matter of urgency, revisit and amend this statute to close this loophole. This, however, is a political question, and the courts should not be drawn into such political disputes. The law must stand apart from politics.

JUDGE ERIC:

The issue in this case can best be dealt with by placing it in the context of our existing law concerning the relations between master and servant. This is an important body of law, which has developed over centuries, which both expresses and regulates the nature of the employment relation. New legislation must not be understood as replacing this traditional law but as merely developing and extending it to new situations. According to this traditional law trust is the fundamental basis of the master–servant relation, and the courts should move to prevent any action, by either party, which seeks to undermine this trust. The actions of the employers here do precisely this and so the men should be reinstated.

Questions:

1. How might we categorise these arguments in the light of Weber's typology of legal rationality?

2. Do these different arguments express differing attitudes towards and understandings of legal modernity?

3. The different judgments express different attitudes towards the legitimacy of the legal system. Which of these do you think most accurately expresses the proper basis of legal legitimacy and why?

Corresponding sections: Part III 1.2–1.3.

TUTORIAL 2

Law and modernity

1. Discuss the significance of formal legal rationality to Max Weber's account of the development of modern law.

2. Does law always serve the interests of the ruling class, or has it developed in a way that is independent of particular interests?

3. Why has it been argued that globalisation requires that we reassess our understanding of the nature of modern law?

Corresponding sections: Part III 1.2 and 1.4.

TUTORIAL 3

Legal rights as ideology
** Advanced

1. Read *On the Jewish Question* (Marx 1843) pp 44–7 and 51–7.

Answer the following questions:

- What does Marx mean when he argues (p 44) that through the right to freedom of religious worship 'man liberates himself from an impediment through the medium of the state'? Why should this liberation be only 'limited, abstract and partial'?
- He goes on to argue (p 45) that the political annulment of private property actually presupposes it. Why?
- What is the basis of the distinction he draws (pp 45–6) between 'material' life and 'species' life? How does this correspond to the distinction between public, political, life and private life?
- Consider Marx's analysis of the rights to freedom of conscience, liberty, property and security (pp 52–3). What is the basis for his criticism of these rights?
- What is the basis of the character of the political revolution he discusses at pp 55–6?
- In his conclusion he argues that the 'actual individual man must take the abstract citizen back into himself' (p 57), and that emancipation requires the ending of the separation of between political and social forces: what does this mean?

2. Can a Marxist believe in human rights?

Corresponding sections: Parts II 1.1 and III 2.3.

TUTORIAL 4
**Advanced

Law and discipline

Read M Foucault, *Discipline and Punish* (Foucault 1977) pp 264–85.

1. Answer the following questions:

- Why does Foucault argue that the prison is denounced as a failure, even from the very moment of its adoption as a common and generalised mode of punishment? To what extent do these criticisms correspond to contemporary arguments against imprisonment?
- What does Foucault argue is the invariable response to such criticisms (pp 268–70)?
- Why does he argue (p 271) that the supposed failure is part of the functioning of the prison?
- What does he mean by the terms 'discipline' and 'surveillance'?
- 'It is not so much that they render docile those who are liable to transgress the law, but that they tend to assimilate the transgression of the laws in a general tactics of subjection' (p 272). What does this mean? How does this differ from our normal understanding of the function of the criminal law?
- What does Foucault mean when he argues (p 277) that the prison *produces* delinquency? What, does he suggest, are the 'uses' of delinquency? Think of some contemporary examples of delinquency that are used in this way. What does this tell us about the relationship between power and knowledge?

2. What conclusions, if any, can we draw from this passage about the function of law in modern society?

Corresponding sections: Part III 2.4.

TUTORIAL 5
**Advanced

Globalisation and juridification

Washers Unlimited International PLC (WUI) is a multinational corporation based in Ukania. In 1999 they closed all their manufacturing plants in Ukania and opened factories in Ruritania, an ex-Soviet-bloc country that offered cheap labour and low levels of regulation of health and safety. Ruritania is, however, a member of the Council of Europe and a signatory to the European Convention of Human Rights.

In 2003, the nationalist neoliberal party that had been in power in Ruritania lost the general election and was replaced by the Social Democratic Party, which had campaigned on the basis of improving working conditions and limiting the power of foreign corporations in Ruritania. Their first acts on taking power were to introduce a new tax on the profits of foreign corporations and to introduce a new system of health and safety regulation, which they promised would be actively enforced. WUI immediately declared that this was unduly restrictive and that they would be investigating ways of closing their factories in Ruritania. As an interim measure they immediately sacked 100 employees who had engaged in a public protest against the employment practices of the company, citing the increased costs of conforming to regulation as the reason for this measure.

Consider the following issues arising from this scenario:

1. The Ruritanian government approaches you for advice on how best to modify the proposed regulatory schema. They understand that regulation might be expensive for business, but they are keen to fulfil their democratic mandate. How might theories of juridification help us to analyse this situation?

2. The sacked workers take legal advice. In the absence of any employment rights under Ruritanian law they decide that they want to bring a legal action against WUI for breaching their right to peaceful protest under the ECHR. WUI argue that the ECHR cannot apply against private corporations, and that Ruritanian law is sovereign. The Ruritanian government supports the sacked workers' legal action, arguing that their independence has been undermined by the actions of corporations like WUI.

    (i) What are the different types of legal order that are involved in this dispute?

(ii) How might a theory of globalisation help us to understand the complexities of this dispute?
(iii) Discuss the theoretical basis for the non-application of human rights to private bodies. Why might this exemption be challenged by the process of globalisation of law?

3. Does this scenario confirm or contradict the assertion that we are entering a fifth epoch of juridification (pp. 223–5)?

> **Corresponding sections: Parts III 1.4 and III 2.1–2.2.**

TUTORIAL 6
**Advanced

1. Evaluate the significance of the public/private distinction in thinking about the role of law in contemporary society?

Discuss with reference to either

    a)   theories of legal pluralism, or
    b)   the development of the 'risk society', or
    c)   theories of juridification

2. Is juridification a legal or a political problem?

Corresponding section: Part III 2.

References

Christodoulidis, E, 2004, 'End of history jurisprudence: Dworkin in South Africa', *Acta Juridica* 64–85.

Dworkin, R, 1986, *Law's Empire*, London: Fontana.

Dyzenhaus, D, 1998, 'Law as justification: Etienne Mureinik's conception of legal culture', 14 *SAJHR* 13.

Farmer, L, 1990, 'The genius of our law', *Modern LR* 1.

Foucault, M, 1977, *Discipline and Punish: The Birth of the Prison*, Harmondsworth: Penguin.

Fuller, L, 1949, 'The case of the speluncean explorers', 62 *Harvard LR* 616.

Marx, K, 1843, 'On the Jewish Question', in D McLellan (ed), *Karl Marx: Selected Writings*, Oxford. Oxford University Press.

Unger, R, 1976, *Law in Modern Society*, New York: Free Press.

Waldron, J, 1990, *The Law*, London: Routledge.

Bibliography

Abel, R (ed), 1982, *The Politics of Informal Justice, Vols. 1 and 2*, New York: Academic Press.

Abel, R, 1986, 'The Decline of Professionalism', 49 *Mod LR* 1.

Adam, B *et al.* (eds), 2000, *The Risk Society and Beyond*, London: Sage.

Agamben, G, 1998, *Homo Sacer: Sovereign Power and Bare Life*, Stanford: Stanford University Press.

Alexy, R, 1999, 'In defence of Radbruch's Formula' and Julian Rivers, 'The Interpretation and Invalidity of Unjust Laws', in D Dyzenhaus (ed), *Recrafting the Rule of Law*, Oxford: Hart.

Althusser, L, 1971, 'Ideology and Ideological State Apparatuses', in L Althusser, *Lenin and Philosophy, and other essays*, London: New Left Books.

Altman, A, 1993, *Critical Legal Studies*, University of California Press.

Anderson, GW, 2005, *Constitutional Rights after Globalization*, Oxford and Portland, OR: Hart.

Arendt, H, 1965, *Eichmann in Jerusalem: A report on the banality of evil*, Harmondsworth: Penguin.

Arthurs, HW, 1985a, *Without the Law*, Toronto and Buffalo: University of Toronto Press.

Arthurs, HW, 1985b, 'Understanding Labour Law: The Debate over "Industrial Pluralism" ', 38 *Current Legal Problems* 83.

Asch, M, (ed), 1997, *Aboriginal and Treaty Rights in Canada: Essays on Law, Equality and Respect for Difference*, Vancouver: University of British Columbia Press.

Atiyah, PS, 1986, 'Form and Substance in Legal Reasoning', in DN MacCormick and P Birks (eds), *The Legal Mind*, Oxford: Oxford University Press.

Austin, J, 1954, *The Province of Jurisprudence Determined*, London: Weidenfeld and Nicolson.

Bangkok Declaration, 1993, 'Final Declaration of the Regional Meeting for Asia of the World Conference on Human Rights', available at http://law.hku.hk/lawgovtsociety/Bangkok%20Declaration.htm

Bankowski, Z, 2001, *Living Lawfully: Love in Law and Law in Love*, Dordrecht: Kluwer.

Bankowski, Z and Christodoulidis, E, 1998, 'The European Union as an Essentially Contested Project', *European Law Journal* 341–54.

Bankowski, Z and MacLean, J, 2006 (eds), *The Universal and the Particular in Legal Reasoning*, Aldershot: Ashgate.

Bartlett, K, 1990, 'Feminist Legal Methods', 103(4) *Harvard Law Review* 829.

Bartlett, R, 1993, '*Mabo*: Another triumph for the common law', 15:2 *Sydney Law Review* 178–86.

Baxi, U, 2002, *The Future of Human* Rights, New Delhi: Oxford University Press.

Beck, U, 1992, *Risk Society: Towards a New Modernity*, Ritter, M (trans), London: Sage.

Beck, U, 1995, *Ecological Politics in an Age of Risk*, Weisz, A (trans), Cambridge: Polity Press.

Beck, U, 2005, *Power in the Global Age*, Cambridge: Polity Press.

Bennett, W and Feldman, M, 1981, *Reconstructing Reality in the Courtroom*, New Brunswick: Rutgers University Press.

Bennion, F, 2001, *Understanding Common Law Legislation*, Oxford: Oxford University Press.

Bennion, F, 2002, *Statutory Interpretation*, 4th edn, London: Butterworths.

Bentham, J, 1995, *The Panopticon Writings*, M Bozovic (ed), London: Verso.

Berlin, I, 1969, *Four Essays on Liberty*, Oxford and New York: Oxford University Press.

Bernstein, B, 1971, *Class, Codes and Control*, London: Routledge and Kegan Paul.

Bickel, A, 1962, *The Least Dangerous Branch: The Supreme Court as the Bar of Politics*, Cambridge, MA: Harvard University Press.

Bilsky, L, 2001, 'Justice or Reconciliation? The Politicisation of the Holocaust in the Kastner Trial', in E Christodoulidis and S Veitch (eds), *Lethe's Law*, Oxford: Hart.

Bourdieu, P and Grass, G, 2002, 'The "Progressive" Restoration: A Franco–German Dialogue', *New Left Review* (Mar/Apr) 62–77.

Buijs, G, 2003, '*Que les Latins appelland maiestatem*': An exploration into the theological background of the concept of sovereignty', in N Walker (ed).

Burchell, G, Gordon, C and Miller, P (eds), 1991, *The Foucault Effect: Studies in Governmentality*, London: Harvester Wheatsheaf.

Buss, D and Manji, A (eds), 2005, *International law: Modern Feminist Approaches*, Oxford: Hart.

Chanock, M 1985, *Law, Custom and Social Order: The Colonial Experience in Malawi and Zambia*, Cambridge: Cambridge University Press.

Christodoulidis, E, 1996, 'The Inertia of Institutional Imagination: A Reply to Roberto Unger', 59 *Modern Law Review* 377.

Christodoulidis, E, 2004, 'End of history jurisprudence: Dworkin in South Africa', *Acta Juridica* 64–85.

Christodoulidis, E and Finnie, W, 1995, 'How the Ace of trumps failed to Win the Trick', *Res Publica*, 131.

Christodoulidis, E and Veitch, S, 2001 (eds), *Lethe's Law: Justice, Law, and Ethics in Reconciliation*, Oxford: Hart.

Cohen, LJ, 1977, *The Probable and the Provable*, Oxford: Clarendon.

Collins, H, 1982, *Marxism and Law*, Oxford: Oxford University Press.

Collins, H, 1986, *The Law of Contract*, London: Weidenfield and Nicholson.

Collins, H, 1987a, 'The decline of privacy in private law', 14 *JLS* 91.

Collins, H, 1987b, 'Roberto Unger and the Critical Legal Studies Movement', 14 *JLS* 387.

Cotterrell, R, 1992, *The Sociology of Law. An Introduction*, 2nd edn, London: Butterworths.

Cotterrell, R, 1995, 'Legality and Legitimacy: The Sociology of Max Weber', in Cotterrell, *Law's Community*, Oxford: Clarendon.

Craig, P, 1997, 'Formal and Substantive Conceptions of the Rule of Law', *Public Law* 466–487.

Craven, M, 1995, *The International Covenant on Economic, Social and Cultural Rights: A Perspective on its Development*, Oxford: Oxford University Press.

Cross, R, 1995, *Statutory Interpretation*, 5th edn, London: Butterworths.

Cross, R and Harris, JW, 1991, *Precedent in English Law*, 4th edn, Oxford: Clarendon.

Cutler, AC, 2003, *Private Power and Global Authority*, Cambridge: Cambridge University Press, ch 2.

Davies, M, 2005, 'The Ethos of Pluralism', 27 *Syd Law Rev* 87.

Dean, M, 1999, *Governmentality: Power and Rule in Modern Society*, London: Sage.

Detmold, M, 1984, *The Unity of Law and Morality*, London: Routledge & Kegan Paul.

Dubber, MD and Valverde, M (eds), 2006, *The New Police Power*, Stanford: Stanford University Press.

Duff A, Farmer L, Marshall S and Tadros, V, 2005 (eds), *The Trial on Trial*, volumes 1 (2004) and 2 (2005), Oxford: Hart.

Duff, A, Farmer, L, Marshall, S and Tadros, V, 2007, *The Theory of the Trial*, Oxford: Hart.

Durkheim, E, 1933, *The Division of Labour in Society*, New York: The Free Press.

Duxbury, N, 1997, *Patterns of American Jurisprudence*, Oxford: Clarendon.

Dworkin, R, 1977 (ed), *The Philosophy of Law*, Oxford: Oxford University Press.

Dworkin, RM, 1977, 'The Model of Rules', extracted in Dworkin (ed) *The Philosophy of Law*, Oxford: Oxford University Press, and expanded in chapters 2 and 3 of *Taking Rights Seriously*.

Dworkin, R, 1985, *A Matter of Principle*, Oxford University Press.

Dworkin, R, 1986, *Law's Empire*, London: Fontana.

Dworkin, R, 1990, 'Law, Philosophy and Interpretation [the Kobe lecture for Legal and social Philosophy]', *ARSP*, 1.

Dyzenhaus, D, 1991, *Hard cases in wicked legal systems: South African law in the perspective of legal philosophy*, Oxford: Clarendon.

Dyzenhaus, D, 1997, *Legality and Legitimacy*, Oxford: Clarendon.

Dyzenhaus, D, 1998, 'Law as justification: Etienne Mureinik's conception of legal culture', 14 *SAJHR* 13.

Dyzenhaus, D, 1998, *Judging the Judges, Judging Ourselves*, Oxford: Hart.

Dyzenhaus, D, 1999 (ed), *Recrafting the Rule of Law*, Oxford: Hart.

Dyzenhaus, D, 2000, 'Form and substance in the Rule of Law', in C Forsyth (ed), *Judicial Review and the Constitution*, Oxford: Hart.

Dyzenhaus, D, 2003, 'Review Essay: Transitional Justice', 1.1 *International Journal of Constitutional Law* 163–75.

Dyzenhaus, D, 2006, *The Constitution of Law: Legality in a Time of Emergency*, Cambridge: Cambridge University Press.

Ely, JH, 1981, *Democracy and Distrust*, Cambridge, MA: Harvard University Press.

Ewald, F, 1991, 'Norms, Discipline and the Law', in R Post (ed), *Law and the Order of Culture*, Berkeley: California University Press.

Ewing, S, 1987, 'Formal Justice and the Spirit of Capitalism: Max Weber's Sociology of Law', 21 *Law and Soc Rev* 487–512.

Farmer, L, 1990, 'The genius of our law', *Modern LR* 1.

Feldman, S, 2001, *Discrimination Law*, Oxford: Oxford University Press.

Finley, L, 1989, 'Breaking Women's Silence in Law: the dilemma of the gendered nature of legal reasoning', 64 *Notre Dame LR* 886.

Finn, JE, 1991, *Constitutions in Crisis*, Oxford: Oxford University Press.

Finnis, J, 1980, *Natural Law and Natural Rights*, Clarendon: Oxford.

Finnis, J, 1993, '*Bland*: Crossing the Rubicon', 109 *LQR* 329.

Finnis, J, 1999, 'Natural law and the ethics of discourse', 12 *Ratio Juris* 354.

Fletcher, G, 1978, *Rethinking Criminal Law*, Boston: Little, Brown & Co.

Foucault, M, 1977, *Discipline and Punish: The Birth of the Prison*, Harmondsworth: Penguin.

Foucault, M, 1979, *The History of Sexuality. Vol.I. The Will to Knowledge*, Harmondsworth: Penguin, 1978.

Foucault, M, 1980, *Power/Knowledge. Selected Interviews and Other Writings 1972–77*, C Gordon (ed), Brighton: Harvester.

Foucault, M, 1984, 'What is Enlightenment?' in P Rabinow (ed), *The Foucault Reader*, Harmondsworth: Penguin.

Foucault, M, 2000, 'Governmentality', in *Essential Works of Foucault 1954–1984. Vol.III Power*, New York: New Press.

Frank, J, 1949a, *Courts on Trial: Myth and Reality in American Justice*. Princeton: Princeton University Press.

Frank, J, 1949b, *Law and the Modern Mind*, London: Stevens.

Frank, J, 1970, *Law and the Modern Mind*, Gloucester, MA: Peter Smith.

Fraser, N, 1995, 'From Redistribution to Recognition? Dilemmas of Justice in a "Post-Socialist" Age', 212 *New Left Review*, 63.

Fuller, L, 1949, 'The case of the speluncean explorers', 62 *Harvard LR* 616.

Fuller, L, 1969, *The Morality of Law*, New Haven: Yale University Press.

Gaita, R, 1999, *A Common Humanity*, Melbourne: Text Publishing.

Gardner, J, 1989, 'Liberals and Unlawful Discrimination', *OJLS* 1.

George, R, 1994 (ed), *Natural Law Theory*, Oxford: Clarendon.

Giddens, A, 1971, *Capitalism and Modern Social Theory: An analysis of the writings of Marx, Durkheim and Weber*, Cambridge; Cambridge University Press.

Gill, S, 2000, 'The Constitution of Global Capitalism' at www.theglobalsite.ac.uk/press/010gill.pdf

Gilligan, C, 1982, *In a Different Voice*, Cambridge, MA: Harvard University Press.

Gordon, C, 1987, 'The Soul of the Citizen: Max Weber and Michel Foucault on Rationality and Government', in S Whimster and S Lash (eds), *Max Weber, Rationality and Modernity*, London: Allen & Unwin.

Griffith, JAG, 1977, *The Politics of the Judiciary*, London: Fontana.

Griffith, JAG, 1979, 'The Political Constitution', 42 *Modern Law Review*, 1.

Griffiths, J, 1986, 'What is Legal Pluralism?', 24 *J Leg Pluralism* 1.

Guest, S, 1997, *Ronald Dworkin* (2nd edn), Edinburgh: Edinburgh University Press.

Habermas, J, 1987, *The Theory of Communicative Action. Vol. 2 Lifeworld and System*, Cambridge: Polity Press.

Habermas, J, 1992, 'Citizenship and National Identity: Some Reflections on the Future of Europe', 12 *Praxis International* 1–19.

Habermas, J, 1996, *Between Facts and Norms*, Cambridge, MA: MIT Press.

Habermas, J, 1999, *The Inclusion of the Other*, Cambridge: Polity.

Habermas, J, 2001, 'Why Europe needs a constitution', 11 *New Left Review* 5–26.

Hardt, M and Negri, A, 2000, *Empire*, Cambridge MA: Harvard University Press.

Hart, HLA, 1961, *The Concept of Law*, Oxford: Clarendon.

Hart, HLA, 1983, 'The Legal Nightmare and the Noble Dream', in ch 4 of *Essays in Jurisprudence and Philosophy*, Oxford: Clarendon.

Hayek, FA, 1944, *The Road to Serfdom*, London: Routledge & Kegan Paul.

Hayner, P, 2002, *Unspeakable Truths: Facing the Challenge of Truth Commissions*, London: Routledge.

Held, D and McGrew, A, 2003, 'The Great Globalization Debate: An Introduction', in D Held and A McGrew (eds), *The Global Transformations Reader*, 2nd edn, Cambridge: Polity Press, pp 1–50.

Henkin, L, 1999, 'The "S" Word: Sovereignty, and Globalization, and Human Rights Et Cetera', 68 *Fordham Law Review* 1–14.

Hertz, N, 2001, *The Silent Takeover: Global Capitalism and the Death of Democracy*, London: Heinemann.

Hirst, PQ, 1979, *On Law and Ideology*, London: Macmillan.

Hobbes, T, 1996, *Leviathan*, Cambridge: Cambridge University Press.

Holmes, OW, 1897, 'The Path of Law', 10 *Harvard Law Review* 457.

Horkheimer, M, 1972, *Critical Theory*, New York: Herder & Herder.

Horwitz, M, 1992, *The transformation of American law, 1870–1960 : the crisis of legal orthodoxy*, New York: Oxford University Press.

Ignatieff, M, 1998, 'The nightmare from which we are trying to awake', in M Ignatieff, *The Warrior's Honor*, London: Chatto & Windus.

Ilgen, TL, 2003, 'Reconfigured Sovereignty in the Age of Globalization', in TL Ilgen (ed) *Reconfigured Sovereignty: Multi-Layered Governance in the Global Age*, p 6, Aldershot: Ashgate.

Jackson, B, 1988, *Law, Fact and Narrative Coherence*, Merseyside: DC Publications.

Jackson, B, 1995, *Making Sense in Law*, Merseyside: DC Publications.

Johnstone, G, 2003, *A Restorative Justice Reader: texts, sources and context*, Cullompton: Willan.

Jones, A and Sergot, M, 1992, 'Deontic logic in the representation of law: towards a methodology', *Artificial Intelligence and Law* 1:1 45–64.

Kamenka, E and Tay, AE, 1975, 'Beyond Bourgeois Individualism: The Contemporary Crisis in Law and Legal Ideology', in E Kamenka and RS Neale (eds), *Feudalism, Capitalism and Beyond*, London: Edward Arnold, pp 127–44.

Kant, I, 1991, 'What is Enlightenment?' in H Reiss (ed), *Political Writings*, Cambridge: Cambridge University Press.

Kelman, M, 1987, *A Guide to Critical Legal Studies*, Cambridge, MA: Harvard University Press.

Kelsen, H, 1992, *Introduction to the problems of Legal Theory*, Oxford: Clarendon.

Kerruish, V and Purdy, J, 1998, 'He "Look" Honest, Big White Thief', 4:1 *Law.Text.Culture* 146–71.

Kleinhans, M-M and Macdonald RA, 1997, 'What is a Critical Legal Pluralism?', 12 *Canadian Journal of Law and Society* 25.

Koskenniemi, M, 2007, 'Global Legal Pluralism: Multiple Regimes and Multiple Modes of Thought', forthcoming in *Eur J Int Law*.

Kritz, N, 1995, *Transitional Justice: How Emerging Democracies deal with former regimes*, Washington, US: Institute of Peace Press, 3 vols.

Kronman, A, 1983, *Max Weber*, London: Edward Arnold.

Lacey, N, 1998, *Unspeakable Subjects: Feminist essays in legal and social theory*, Oxford: Hart.

Larson, SM, 1977, *The Rise of Professionalism: A Sociological Analysis*, Berkeley: California University Press.

Laws, J, 1996, 'The Constitution: Morals and Rights', *Public Law* 622–635.

Lenin, VI, 1917, *The State and Revolution*, various editions.

Levi, E, 1948, 'An Introduction to Legal Reasoning', 15 *University of Chicago LR* 501.

Lindahl, H, 1998, 'The purposiveness of law: two concepts of representation in the European Union', 17 *Law & Philosophy* 481–507.

Locke, J, 1988, The Second Treatise of Government, in P Haslett (ed), *Two Treatises of Government*, Cambridge: Cambridge University Press.

Loughlin, M, 2000, *Sword and Scales: An Examination of the Relationship Between Law and Politics*, Oxford: Hart, ch 10.

Loughlin, M, 2003, 'Ten Tenets of Sovereignty' in N Hart Walker (ed), *Sovereignty in Transition*, pp 55–86.

Loughlin, M, 2004, *The Idea of Public Law*, Oxford: Oxford University Press, ch 5.

Macaulay, S, 1963, 'Non-contractual Relations in Business: A Preliminary Study', 28 *Am Soc Rev* 55–67.

MacCormick, DN, 1994, 'On the Separation of Law and Morality', in George, 1994.

MacCormick, N, 1978, *Legal Reasoning and Legal Theory*, Oxford: Clarendon.

MacCormick, N, 1979, 'The Artificial Reason and Judgement of Law', *Rechtstheorie* 105.

MacCormick, N, 1981, *H.L.A. Hart*, London: Arnold.

MacCormick, N, 1982, 'Law, Obligation and Consent: Reflections on Stair and Locke', in N MacCormick, *Legal Right and Social Democracy*, Oxford: Clarendon.

MacCormick, N, 1989, 'The Ethics of Legalism', 2 *Ratio Juris* 184–93.

MacCormick, N, 1992, 'Law and the Separation of Law and Morals', in RP George (ed), *Natural Law Theory*, Oxford: Clarendon.

MacCormick, N, 1993, 'Argument and Interpretation in Law', *Ratio Juris* 16.

MacCormick, N, 1993, 'Constitutionalism and democracy' in R Bellamy (ed), *Theories and Concepts of Politics*, Manchester: Manchester University Press, 124–47.

MacCormick, N, 1994, *Legal Reasoning and Legal Theory*, 2nd edn, Oxford: Clarendon.

MacCormick, N, 1999, *Questioning Sovereignty*, Oxford: Oxford University Press.

MacCormick, N, 2004, 'Questioning Post-Sovereignty', 29 *Eur L Rev* 852.

MacCormick, N, 2005, *Rhetoric and the Rule of Law*, Oxford: Oxford University Press.

MacCormick, N, 2007, *Institutions of Law*, Oxford: Oxford University Press.

MacCormick, N and Summers, R, 1991, *Interpreting Statutes*, Aldershot: Dartmouth.

MacKinnon, CA, 1987, *Feminism Unmodified: Discourses on Life and Law*, Cambridge, MA: Harvard University Press.

MacKinnon, CA, 1989, *Toward a Feminist Theory of the State*, Cambridge, MA: Harvard University Press.

MacNeil, I, 2000, 'Contracting Worlds and Essential Contract Theory', *Social & Legal Studies* p 431.

Marks, S, 2000, *The Riddle of All Constitutions: International Law, Democracy and the Critique of Ideology*, Oxford: Oxford University Press.

Marshall, TH, 1992, *Citizenship and Social Class*, London: Pluto Press.

Marx, K, 1843, 'On the Jewish Question', in D McLellan (ed), *Karl Marx: Selected Writings*. Oxford: Oxford University Press.

Marx, K, 1844, 'Economic and Philosophical Manuscripts' in D McLellan (ed), *Karl Marx. Selected Writings* 1977, Oxford: Oxford University Press, pp 75–112.

Marx, K, 1849, 'Wage labour and Capital' in D McLellan (ed), *Karl Marx: Selected Writings*, 1977, Oxford: Oxford University Press, pp 248–68.

Marx, K, 1851, 'The Eighteenth Brumaire of Louis Bonaparte', in D McLellan (ed), *Karl Marx. Selected Writings*, 1977, Oxford: Oxford University Press.

Marx, K, 1932, 'The German Ideology' in D McLellan (ed), *Karl Marx. Selected Writings*, Oxford: Oxford University Press, pp 159–91.

Marx, K, 1977, 'Preface to *A Critique of Political Economy*', in D McLellan (ed) *Karl Marx. Selected Writings*, Oxford: Oxford University Press.

McAdams, A, 1997 (ed) *Transitional Justice and the Rule of Law in New Democracies*, Notre Dame: University of Notre Dame Press.

McLeod, I, 2005, *Legal Method*, 4th edn, Basingstoke: Palgrave Macmillan.

Merry, SE, 1988, 'Legal Pluralism', 22 *Law & Soc Rev* 869.

Michelman, F, 1986, 'Foreword: Traces of Self-Government', 100 *Harvard L R* 4.

Michelman, F, 1988, 'Law's Republic', 97 *Yale L.J.* 1493.

Miles, R, 1993, *Racism after 'Race Relations'*, London: Routledge.

Moody, S and Tombs, J, 1982, *Prosecution in the Public Interest*, Edinburgh: Scottish Academic Press.

Mouffe, C, 1999, *The Challenge of Carl Schmitt*, London: Verso.

Muller, J-W, 2003, *A Dangerous Mind: Carl Schmitt in Post-War European Thought*, New Haven: Yale University Press.

Munro, V, and Stychin, C (eds), 2007, *Sexuality and the Law: Feminist Engagements*, Oxford: Routledge-Cavendish.

Mureinik, E, 1988, 'Dworkin and apartheid', in H Corder (ed), *Law in Social Practice in South Africa*, Cape Town: Juta.

Murphy, WT, 1991, 'The Oldest Social Science? The Epistemic Properties of the Common Law Tradition', 54 *Mod LR* 182–215.

Murphy, WT, 1997, *The Oldest Social Science? Configurations of Law and Modernity*, Oxford: Oxford University Press.

Naffine, N. 1990, *Law and the Sexes*, London and Sydney: Allen & Unwin.

Negri, A, 2001, *The Savage Anomaly*, Minneapolis: University of Minnesota Press.

Noon, M, 1993, 'Racial discrimination in speculative application: evidence from the UK's top 100 firms', 3(4) *Human Resource Management Journal* 35–47.

Olsen, F, 1990, 'Feminism and Critical Legal Theory: An American perspective', 18 *International Journal of the Sociology of Law*, 199–215.

Olsen, F, 1995, *Feminist Legal Theory: Foundations and Outlooks*, New York: New York University Press.

Paine, T, 1961, *The Rights of Man*, Garden City: Dolphin Books.

Pashukanis, EB, 1978, *Law and Marxism. A General Theory*, London: Pluto Press.

Pogge, T, 2002, *World Poverty and Human Rights: Cosmopolitan Responsibilities and Reforms*, Cambridge: Polity.

Power, M, 1997, 'From risk society to audit society', 3 *Soziale Systeme* 3–21.

Raz, J, 1979, 'The Rule of Law and its Virtue', in J Raz, *The Authority of Law*, Oxford: Clarendon Press.

Rheinstein, M 1954, 'Introduction', in M Rheinstein (ed), *Max Weber on Law in Economy and Society*, Cambridge MA: Harvard University Press.

Rose, N and Valverde, M, 1998, 'Governed by Law?', 7 *Soc & Leg Stud* 541.

Rosenblum, N, 1994, 'Democratic Character and Community', 1, *The Journal of Political Philosophy*, 67.

Rottleuthner, H, 1989, 'The Limits of the Law: The Myth of a Regulatory Crisis', 17 *Intnl Jnl of Soc of Law* 273–85.

Rumble, WE, 1968, *American Legal Realism*, Ithaca, New York: Cornell University Press.

Sampford, C, 1991, *The Disorder of Law*, Oxford: Blackwell.

Sandel, M (ed), 1984, *Liberalism and Its Critics*, Oxford: Blackwell.

Santos, B de Sousa, 2002, *Toward a New Legal Common Sense*, 2nd edn, London: Butterworths.

Sassen, S, 1996, *Losing Control? Sovereignty in an Age of Globalization*, New York: Columbia University Press, ch 1.

Schmitt, C, 1985a, *Political Theology: Four Chapters on the Concept of Sovereignty* (orig 1922), Cambridge, MA: MIT Press.

Schmitt, C, 1985b, *The Crisis of Parliamentary Democracy*, Cambridge, MA: MIT Press.

Schmitt, C, 1996, *The Concept of the Political*, Chicago: Chicago University Press.

Schmitt, C, 2004, *Legality and Legitimacy*, Durham, NC: Duke University Press.

Schneiderman, D, 2000, 'Investment Rules and the New Constitutionalism', 25 *Law & Social Inquiry* 757.

Shearing, C and Wood, J, 2003, 'Nodal Governance, Democracy, and the New "Denizens" ', 30 *Jnl of Law & Soc* 400.

Sheldon, S, 1997, *Beyond Control: Medical Power, Women and Abortion Law*, London: Pluto Press.

Shklar, J, 1986, *Legalism: Law, Morals, and Political Trials*, Cambridge, MA: Harvard University Press.

Smith, A, 1978, *Lectures on Jurisprudence*, RL Meek, DD Raphael and PG Stein (eds) Oxford: Oxford University Press.

Smith, SC, 1991, 'Beyond "Mega-Theory" and "Multiple Sociology": A Reply to Rottleuthner', 19 *Intnl Jnl of Soc of Law* 321–40.

Social & Legal Studies, 2000, Symposium on Contract Law and Legal Theory 397–447.

South African TRC Report, 1998, 5 vols, Cape Town: Juta Press.

Steele, J, 2004, *Risks and Legal Theory*, Oxford: Hart.

Sunstein, C, 1986, 'Legal Interferences with Naked Preferences', *U Chicago L R* 1129.

Sypnowich, C, 2000, 'Utopia and the Rule of Law, in D Dyzenhaus (ed), *Recrafting the Rule of Law*, Oxford: Hart, 2000.

Tamanaha, BZ, 1993, 'The Folly of the "Social Scientific" Concept of Legal Pluralism', 20 *Jnl of Law & Soc* 192.

Tamanaha, BZ, 2000, 'A Non-Essentialist Version of Legal Pluralism', 27 *Jnl of Law & Soc* 296.

Taylor, C, 1989, 'Cross-Purposes: The Liberal-Communitarian Debate', in N Rosenblum (ed), *Liberalism and the Moral Life*, Cambridge, MA: Harvard University Press, 159–82.

Teitel, R, 1997, 'Transitional Jurisprudence: The Role of Law in Political Transformation', 106 *Yale Law Journal* 2009–80.

Teitel, R, 2000, *Transitional Justice*, New York: Oxford University Press.

Teubner, G, 1987, 'Juridification: Concepts, Aspects, Limits, Solutions', in G Teubner (ed), *Juridification of Social Spheres*, Berlin: de Gruyter.

Teubner, G, 1992, 'Regulatory Law: Chronicle of a Death Foretold', 1 *Soc & Leg Stud* 451–75.

Teubner, G (ed), 1997, *Global Law Without a State*, Gateshead: Athenaeum Press.

Thompson, EP, 1977, *Whigs and Hunters*, Harmondsworth: Penguin.

Thompson, J, 1984, *Studies in the Theory of Ideology*, Cambridge: Polity Press.

Tomkins, A, 2005, *Our Republican Constitution*, Oxford: Hart.

Turner, B, 1996, *For Weber. Essays on the Sociology of Fate*, London: Sage.

Twining, W, 1984, 'Some Scepticism about Scepticisms', 1 *Journal of Law and Society*, 137–71.

Twining, W, 2000, *Globalisation & Legal Theory*, London: Butterworths.

Unger, RM, 1976, *Law and Modern Society*. New York: Free Press.

Unger, RM, 1983, *The Critical Legal Studies Movement*, Cambridge MA: Harvard University Press.

Unger, RM, 1987a, *Social Theory: Its Situation and Its Task*. Vol 1 of *Politics: A Work in Constructive Social Theory*, Cambridge MA: Cambridge UP.

Unger, RM, 1987b, *False Necessity: Anti-Necessitarian Social Theory in the Service of Radical Democracy*. Vol 2 of *Politics: A Work in Constructive Social Theory*. Cambridge MA: Cambridge University Press.

Unger, RM, 1996, 'Legal Analysis as Institutional Imagination', 59 *Modern Law Review* 1.

Vattel, E, 1883, *The Law of Nations or Principles of the Law of Nature Applied to the Conduct and Affairs of Nations and Sovereigns* (ed J Chitty) Philadelphia Pa: T & J W Johnson & Co.

Veitch, S, 2004, 'Legal Right and Political Amnesia', in K Nuotio (ed), *Europe in search of 'meaning and purpose'*, Helsinki: Faculty of Law, University of Helsinki, pp 89–106.

Waldron, J, 1987, *Nonsense upon Stilts*, London and New York: Methuen.

Waldron, J, 1990, *The Law*, London: Routledge.

Walker, N, 2001, 'The EU and the WTO: Constitutionalism in a New Key', in G De Burca and J Scott (eds), *The EU and the WTO: Legal and Constitutional Issues*, Oxford: Hart, p 31.

Walker, N, 2002, 'The Idea of Constitutional Pluralism', 65 *Modern Law Review* 317–53.

Walker, N, 2003, 'Late Sovereignty in the European Union', in N Walker (ed), *Sovereignty in Transition*, Oxford: Hart, p 3.

Walker, N (ed), 2003, *Sovereignty in Transition*, Oxford: Hart.

Watson, I, 2002, 'Buried Alive', 13 *Law & Critique* 253–69.

Weber, M, 1930, *The Protestant Ethic and the Spirit of Capitalism*, London: Allen & Unwin.

Weber, M, 1948a, 'Politics as a Vocation', in HH Gerth and CW Mills (eds), *For Max Weber*, London: Routledge & Kegan Paul.

Weber, M, 1948b, 'Science as a Vocation', in HH Gerth and CW Mills, *For Max Weber*, London: Routledge & Kegan Paul.

Weber, M, 1968, *Economy and Society, An Outline of Interpretive Sociology* (2 vols), Berkeley: University of California Press.

Weiler, J, 1999, *The Constitution of Europe*, Cambridge: Cambridge University Press.

Woodman, GR, 1998, 'Ideological Combat and Social Observation', 42 *Jnl of Leg Pluralism* 21.

Ziller, J, 2003, 'Sovereignty in France', in N Walker.

Zizek, S, 1994, *Mapping Ideology*, London: Verso.

Cases

A (FC) and others v Secretary of State for the Home Dept [2004] UKHL 56.

Daniels & Daniels v R White & Sons [1938] 4 All ER 258.

Grant v Australian Knitting Mills [1936] AC 85.

In re A (Conjoined Twins) 4 All ER 961.

K-HW v Germany, Judgment of the European Court of Human Rights, 22 March 2001 (Application no. 37201/97).

Law v Canada (Minister of Employment and Immigration) [1999] 1 SCR 497.

Mabo v The State of Queensland (No.2) (1992) 175 CLR 1.

Mandla v Dowell Lee (1983) All ER 1062, HL.

R v R (Rape: marital exemption) [1991] 4 All ER 481.

Serco Ltd v Redfearn (2006) EWCA Civ 659.

Stallard v HMA (1989) SCCR 248.

Streletz, Kessler and Krenz v Germany, Judgment of the European Court of Human Rights, 22 March 2001 (Application nos. 34044/96, 35532/97 and 44801/98).

Index

Aboriginal land rights 155–60
accountability: for environmental
	hazards 249–50; in political transitions
	63–8
alternative dispute resolution (ADR)
	209, 211
Althusser, L 233–4
American Legal Realists 99–104, 136
analogy 110–11
anthropological perspectives 208–9
'appeal court jurisprudence' 102–3
Arendt, H 50–1, 64
Aristotle 24, 126–7
Atiyah, PS 40–1
Atkin, Lord 39
Austin, J 12, 14, 15, 16

Bartlett, R 158
Baxi, U 33, 34–5
Beck, U 245–51
Bennett, W and Feldman, M 140–1
Bennion, F 92–3
Bentham, J 12, 29, 95–6, 239
Bernstein, B 141
Bickel, A 47
biopower 237, 239–40
Bland (case) 124–5, 127
Bourdieu, P 223
Brennan, CJ 155–7
Britain *see* United Kingdom (UK)
Browne-Wilkinson, Lord 124, 127
bureaucracy 38, 142, 181, 184, 185–6, 192

capitalism: bipower and development of
	239–40; global *see* globalisation;
	juridification of economic relations
	218–19; liberal mind-set of 252;
	Marxist perspective 21–2, 179–80,
	227–31, 232–3; 'structure-agency map'

210; Weberian perspective 38, 181,
	188–90, 195
charismatic domination 184, 185
citizenship 7, 29, 44–52; citizen–
	government reciprocity 23–4, 26;
	liberal and republican 45–51
civic virtue and common good 49, 51
civil rights 7, 29–32
civil society–state relationship 203–4,
	218
classification problems of legal rules
	107–8, 134
co-ordination achievement of law 25–6
codes, elaborate and restricted speech
	141; codification of law 95–6
coercion 7–8
coherence 110, 115–16
Collins, H 119, 232
colonialism 208–9, 210; Australian
	Aboriginal land rights 155–60
commodification 229–30
common good 49, 51, 125–7
common heritage of humankind 203
'common sense' vs 'legal' construction of
	meaning 139
communitarianism 48–9, 50–1
community: and citizenship 44, 48–9;
	development of 25–6
Conjoined Twins (case) 110–11;
	conflicting rules/principles 105
consequentialism in legal decisions
	109–10
consistency 110, 115
'constitutional patriotism' 44
'constitutional pluralism' 58
constitutional state/constitutionalism 14,
	46–7, 218; beyond the state 57–9;
	paradox of 47–51; separation of
	powers 5–7, 8, 14, 95–6